THE DESTINY OF THE WARRIOR

THE DESTINY OF THE WARRIOR

GEORGES DUMÉZIL

TRANSLATED BY ALF HILTEBEITEL

THE UNIVERSITY OF CHICAGO PRESS
CHICAGO AND LONDON

Originally published as *Heur et malheur du guerrier: Aspects mythiques de la fonction guerrière chez les Indo-Européens*,

International Standard Book Number: 0–226–16970–7
Library of Congress Catalog Card Number: 75–113254

The University of Chicago Press, Chicago 60637
The University of Chicago Press, Ltd., London

Printed in the United States of America

To Stig Wikander

Thirty years after

Der arische Männerbund

CONTENTS

INTRODUCTION

Since 1938, when it was first recognized that the ideological structure of the "three functions"—administration of the sacred, physical force, and abundance and fecundity—had a common Indo-European character, a comparative study of the theological and mythical expressions of each of those functions for the various peoples of the Indo-European family has been undertaken. After thirty years, there is a disequilibrium in the results.

For the first function a simple and fully coherent picture quickly emerged. A well-conserved theological model was furnished by Vedic India, with its Varuṇa and Mitra. Iran provided verification, and Rome furnished yet another parallel tradition in the "history" of her two founders, Romulus and Numa. Scandinavia and Ireland, each with its own particular developments, were then found to confirm this initial perspective. The services and the personages of the two minor sovereigns, along with the two principal aspects and personifications of sovereignty, were also analyzed. These minor sovereigns are to be found among the Indo-Iranians, the Romans, and the Scandinavians: the "manifestations" are diverse, but the underlying meaning is held in common. Though a number of points require closer study, there is apparently little to add to these basic lines. The situation is different for the gods and myths of the other two functions.

One of the more immediately appreciable features of the third function is its breakdown into numerous provinces with indefinite boundaries: fecundity, abundance in men and in goods, nourishment, health, peace, sensual gratification, etc. These are notions which condition one another, which feed into one another by a thousand capillaries, making it impossible to determine a simple order of derivation from one to the others. Another feature of the same function is its close connection with the geographic, topographic, and ethnic bases of each particular society and, further, with the form, the variable components, of each economy. Thus, though the insights gained through the comparative study of the twin gods and heroes—those least engaged in the detail of the *realia*—have indicated a certain number of traits and themes common to several Indo-European peoples, no general structure has yet appeared, and one may doubt whether the future will disclose one.

The second function, force, and primarily, as one might expect, the use of force in combat, presents a somewhat more promising situation for the observer. But in prehistoric times this function did not enjoy complete systematization comparable to that accomplished for the level of sovereignty. Perhaps the theologians and philosophers responsible for the ideology, those who divided sovereignty into its religious and juridical aspects, did not reflect with such care upon activities more removed from their own; or perhaps the realities presented by events thwarted theorization. As a result, comparison here has unveiled less in the way of *structures* than of *aspects*, and even the latter are not entirely coherent. For each of these aspects taken separately, however, the recognition of precise and complex correspondences between India (most often the Indo-Iranians) and Rome or the Germanic world gives clear indications of great antiquity. Three such correspondences constitute the subject of the present book. With a number of excursuses, each of the three parts sets out essentially to obtain the certification or, to put it more colloquially, the label of *Indo-European* for a group of well-known Indian representations of the principal personage of the second level, Indra: the sequence of his most famous exploits; his reputation as "sinner among the gods"; and the elements having to do with his title "Vṛtrahan" and the story of some of his exploits which seem to suggest certain social practices and rituals.

These three essays by no means exhaust what has been said about the warrior function among the Indo-Europeans. They constitute only a personal contribution to this larger investigation. Other "aspects," here only noted or, in the course of the book, merely referred to in passing, are certainly no less important.

First, we have the division of the function between representatives of two types, bearing a relation to each other that is not seen as complementary, like that between Mitra and Varuṇa, but in which, at least, neither figure can be reduced to the other. Such are the types which the Mahābhārata incarnates in the heroes Bhīma and Arjuna, and which the Indo-Iranians, as the scholars from Uppsala recognized so early, saw as being patronized by the gods Vāyu and Indra—the fathers, in fact, of Bhīma and Arjuna in the epic. Heracles and Achilles illustrate these two types among the Greeks. But it is in the Germanic world, with a modification that is its own peculiarity, that this distinction has its greatest bearing: there, the second level has boldly spilled over into the first with the result that the principal sovereign god, the Scandinavian Óðinn, finds himself at the same time one of the gods most preoccupied with war. The contrast between Óðinn, insofar as he presides over battles, and Þórr, the solitary champion, is reminiscent, in certain features, of that between Indra-Arjuna and Vāyu-Bhīma.

Then there is the existence of "warrior societies," effective agencies of conquest. The *mariannu*, chariot fighters who in the second millennium spread terror among the nations of the Near East, are probably the most ancient direct testimony to the existence of such societies, and the *Marút* of Vedic mythology, so often qualified as *máryāḥ*, transpose this type of social organ into the other world. The study of these societies was launched in 1938 and, in its initial foray, greatly advanced by Stig Wikander in his *Der arische Männerbund*, a book which has only begun to receive its due (in the so-called humanities the denial of an advance for twenty-five or thirty years is the usual practice, if not a commendable one); that study has recently been brilliantly continued by Geo Widengren in his book *Der Feudalismus im alten Iran* (1969), especially in chapters 1–4. The Germans of antiquity and of the early Middle Ages knew of such *Männerbünde*; but the double value—sovereign and warrior—assumed by their patron Óðinn, in these societies also, led to a characterization on two levels, thus constituting an original type. Shortly before Wikander's book, in 1935, Otto Höfler dealt with societies of this kind in the first volume—the only one to be published—of his *Kultische Geheimbünde der Germanen*. A variety of articles, some of them short but full of substance, have recently opened up numerous avenues within this domain: connections between the warrior and the king, the mystique of the warrior, etc. Among these are: Andreas Alföldi, "Königsweihe und Männerbund bei den Achämeniden" (*Schweiz. Archiv für Volkskunde* 48 [1951]:11–16); Lucien Gerschel, "Coriolan" (*Hommage à Lucien Febvre* 2 [1953]:33–40); and, in the line of descent from J. W. Hauer's fine works *Der Vrātya* (1927) and *Der Yoga* (1958), Herbert Fischer's "Indogermanischer Kriegeryoga" (*Festschrift Walter Heinrich* [1953]:65–97). French scholars, especially, have concentrated on Greek traditions of the same kind. In particular, Francis Vian, who took up the problem, with special reference to the gigantomachies, at the point to which it was brought by Henri Jeanmaire, has recently presented his discoveries under the title "La fonction guerrière dans la mythologie grecque" in Jean-Pierre Vernant's collective work, *Problèmes de la guerre dans la Grèce ancienne* (1968, pp. 53–60). My personal part in these investigations consists only of an article in *Journal asiatique* (241 [1953]: 1–25), an attempt to demonstrate that in the Zoroastrian reinterpretation of Indo-Iranian mythology the Marut (as they were understood by Wikander) are relieved of their post by the immense horde of the Fravaši.

Then there are the connections between the nature mythology and the social mythology of the second level or, to put it more simply, in the context of India, the double value of Indra and the Marut, at once the models for earthly warriors and the divinities of thunder and storm, the latter with their terrible manifestations and their fortunate consequences. Though it is erroneous to regard Indra's connection with fecundity as his most important feature, as Johann Jakob Meyer did in his learned but confused *Trilogie altindischer Mächte und Feste der Vegetation* (1937; see the assessment by Jan Gonda, "The Indra Festival according to the Atharvavedins," *Journal of the American Oriental Society* 87 [1967]: 413–29), there was, nonetheless, within the god a natural propensity in that direction, just as there was in the Norwegian Þórr, "goodman Þórr," "Þórr the peasant" (the "Hora galles" of the Lapps), and, to a lesser degree, in the thunder god Jupiter of the Roman viticulturists. (Another problem, which can only be formulated in passing since it remains, with diverse solutions, peculiar to a few societies, is the passage of the thunderbolt, or the mythical weapon which corresponds to it, into the hands of a god of the first level—Miθra, Zeus, Jupiter.) In short, Indra is a complex god, one whose main outlines can be properly appreciated in the late Herman Lommel's *Der arische Kriegsgott* (1939), and which has been studied comparatively by Franz-Rolf Schröder in his article "Indra, Thor und Herakles" (*Zeitschrift für deutsche Philologie* 76 [1957]: 1–41). For my part, I have encountered the "nature-society" problem only in one case—a striking one: in the Nart legends of the Ossets where the hero Batraz, who has certainly inherited a part of the mythology of the Scythian war god Ares, includes among his traits, on his passage from birth to death through numerous epiphanies, those of a genie of the storm (*Légendes sur les Nartes* [1930], note 3, pp. 179–89, "Mythes d'orage"; cf. *Mythe et épopée* 1[1968]:570–75).

Then, too, there are the rapports of the warrior function with youth, with the *iuuenes*—at once both a social age group and an organ entrusted with a society's chances for durability or renovation—whose name was shown by Emile Benveniste, in 1937, to have an etymological connection with the notions of "vital force"—Vedic *ā́yu(s)*, Greek *αἰών*—and "eternity"—Latin *aeuom*—(*Bulletin de la Société de Linguistique de Paris* 308:103–12). From the traditions of many Italian towns that proclaim as their founders a band of *iuuenes* led by an animal consecrated to Mars, from such Germanic legends as the origin of the Lombards, the idea emerges that the opposition of age groups figured frequently as a contributing factor to the expansion of the Indo-Europeans. First raised in 1939 in *Mythes et dieux des Germains* (chap. 5, "Conflits d'âges et migrations," pp. 65–78), the question will presently be explored in depth.

It would be easy to prolong this sampling. One could mention, for instance, the connections between the warrior ideology with its social manifestations and the various *realia*, notably the arms, above all the war chariot. But it has served to call attention to the variety and dimension of the problems posed by the second function, and, by the same token, to reduce to their proper place the three "aspects" that are to be dealt with in this book.

The first two essays, with considerable alterations and new notes, reproduce the two parts of a book that appeared in 1956 from Presses Universitaires de France, in the *Bibliothèque de l'Ecole Pratique des Hautes Etudes, Section des Sciences Religieuses*, vol. 68, under the title *Aspects de la fonction guerrière chez les Indo-Européens*. The Wissenschaftliche Buchgesellschaft of Darmstadt published a somewhat modified edition in 1964, rendered into German by Dr. Inge Köck. The third essay revives and rounds out some older publications: sections of two chapters from *Mythes et dieux des Germains* (1939), and several articles from *Revue de l'Histoire des Religions*. This unitary publication of revised studies constitutes part of the general updating in which I have been engaged for the past five years, in an effort to prepare for the inevitable autopsy as proper a cadaver as possible, that is, to deliver to the critic of the near future, in an organized and improved form, the results of the endeavors, of varying success, carried out over the past thirty years. The book thus takes its place in what will be my last series of publications, neither program nor *Vorarbeiten* but a balancing of accounts, alongside *La religion romaine archaïque* (1966; translated as *Archaic Roman Religion* [Chicago, 1970]; here cited as *RRA*), *Mythe et épopée*, volume 1 (1968; here cited as *ME* 1) and volume 2 (in preparation), *Idées romaines* (1969), and two books which will appear later: a definitive *Jupiter Mars Quirinus* and a *Théologie de la souveraineté*.

I have left these three studies in sketchlike form, stressing only what is essential and reducing the references and notes, and the discussions too, to what is strictly necessary: the materials used are in the public domain, and the novelty is only in the way they are brought together or set in order. When he comes to the allusions implied in certain phrases, the informed reader will recognize that everything which is not cited or discussed is not necessarily ignored. Encouraged by some happy experiences, and despite more numerous disappointments, I continue to hope that for each Indo-European province there will be specialists, better equipped than the comparativist but sensitive to the comparative reasoning that has led to the picture submitted to them, who will reconsider the treatment of the portion that concerns them, refining the detail and exploring more fully, uncovering implications which, by giving substance to new comparative inquiries, would make for new Indo-European formulations.

The method will become sufficiently clear from the expositions themselves: it is unnecessary to theorize about it here. I shall content myself with emphasizing an obstinate and settled opinion, which is not a postulate but the conclusion drawn from a great deal of research, and which underlies all my discussion of Indian material: the *R̥g Veda*, the Vedic literature in its entirety, does not yield all the mythology that India inherited from her Indo-Iranian or Indo-European past.

Often what is read in the epics either as established Vedic myths or as myths absent from the *R̥gVeda* is actually a rejuvenated form, of a para-Vedic, pre-Vedic tradition. The hymns, therefore, do not offer the only material that may be utilized in comparisons, nor even, at certain points, is this the best material. This was demonstrated most generally by Wikander, in 1947, in his article on the Pāṇḍava and the mythic background of the *Mahābhārata* (in Swedish, *Religion och Bibel* 6:27–39), which the first part of *Mythe et épopée I* (31–257) merely develops. Up to now few Vedicists seem to know of it. Yet there it is, and the future belongs to whoever takes it into account.

This, moreover, is just a particular case of a larger necessity. In India as elsewhere, one must often abandon one's attempt to determine among the attested versions of a mythical narrative the one form from which all the others, whether contemporary or later, have supposedly derived. Even from the most ancient times variants have existed, each as legitimate as the next. By the same token, narratives about similar but distinct subjects—for example, Indra's various battles—have many times, even before the first documents, resulted in mixed forms, some more stable than others, and not unlike those encountered today by the student of folklore and living oral tradition in general. Philology's claim to such documents is certainly legitimate, but as to the derivations, osmoses, confusions, contradictions, and so on, these call more for the observational and analytic techniques of the folklorist.

I am happy that the University of Chicago Press has decided to make this collection of essays known to American and other English-speaking readers at the same time that it is being published in France; happy also to have met in Alf Hiltebeitel a skillful interpreter whose command of the subject has allowed him to rethink it while translating. I warmly thank the Ecole Pratique des Hautes Etudes (Section des Sciences Religieuses) for permitting me to revise, and to republish outside of its Collection, a work, now out of print, which first appeared under its imprint.

Princeton, Institute for Advanced Study
October 1968

FIRST PART

SERVICES

The Epic of Tullus Hostilius and the Myths of Indra

1

MYTH AND EPIC

"A land that has no more legends," says the poet, "is condemned to die of cold." This may well be true. But a people without myths is already dead. The function of that particular class of legends known as myths is to express dramatically the ideology under which a society lives; not only to hold out to its conscience the values it recognizes and the ideals it pursues from generation to generation, but above all to express its very being and structure, the elements, the connections, the balances, the tensions that constitute it; to justify the rules and traditional practices without which everything within a society would disintegrate.

These myths may be of diverse types. With respect to their origin, some are drawn from authentic events and actions in a more or less stylized fashion, embellished, and set forth as examples to imitate; others are literary fictions incarnating important concepts of the ideology in certain personages and translating the relations between these concepts into the connections between various figures. With respect to their settings and to the cosmic dimensions of the scenes, some are located outside the narrow confines and the few centuries of national experience; they adorn a remote past or future and inaccessible zones where gods, giants, monsters, and demons have their sport; others are content with ordinary men, with familiar places, and with plausible eras. But all these narratives have one and the same vital function.

The comparative investigation of the oldest Indo-European civilizations which has been going on for about thirty years has had to take into account both this functional unity of the myths and this variety of mythic types. In particular, it at once became apparent that the

Romans are not, after all, a people without mythology—as the textbooks, alas, still delight in characterizing them—but rather that, for them, mythology, and in fact a very ancient mythology in large part inherited from Indo-European times, while it has been destroyed at the level of theology, has prospered under the form of history. The test has been applied in several particularly important instances. The narratives and the types of personages, and the very structures of the traditions concerning these personages, which, either totally or in their essential features, were ascribed by the Indians and the Germans to the divine world, have been rediscovered in the Roman setting with the same structure and the same lesson, but ascribed exclusively to men, and to men who bear typical Roman names, belonging to authentic *gentes*. Roman ideology thus offers itself to the observer on two parallel planes which have only rare and narrow points of contact: on one level, a theology, neat and simple in every area of which we have any knowledge, defining abstractly, ordering a hierarchy, and, according to these definitions, setting up groups of powerful gods, but gods without adventures; on the other level, a history of origins tracing the significant adventures of men who, in their character and function, correspond to these gods.

Let us consider the central motif of Indo-European ideology, the conception according to which the world and society can live only through the harmonious collaboration of the three stratified functions of sovereignty, force, and fecundity. In India, this conception is expressed at once in divine and human terms, in a theological ensemble and an epic ensemble; but the gods no less than the heroes are portrayed as having colorful adventures, or at least as performing deeds or interventions which express their essences, their tasks, and their relations.

At the first level of Vedic theology, the two principal sovereign gods, Varuṇa, the all-powerful magician, and Mitra, the contract personified, have created and organized the worlds, with their plan and their overall mechanisms; at the second level, Indra, the physically powerful god, is engaged in a number of magnificent duels, conquests, and victories; at the third level, the twins Nāsatya are the heroes of a whole series of brief but well-defined scenes, which continually bring into relief their qualities of bestowing health, youth, wealth, and happiness. A parallel is found in the epic material from the *Mahābhārata*, which became established only later but which has been shown by Stig Wikander[1] to have prolonged a very ancient and partially pre-Vedic tradition; Pāṇḍu and his five putative sons, by their character and by their actions and adventures, develop the same ideology of the three functions: Pāṇḍu and the eldest of the Pāṇḍava, Yudhiṣṭhira, both of them kings in distinction from the others, incarnate the two aspects—Varuṇian and Mitrian—of sovereignty; the second and third Pāṇḍava, Bhīma and Arjuna, incarnate two aspects—brutal and chivalrous—of the warrior's force which the *Ṛg Veda* brings together in the solitary Indra; the fourth and fifth sons, the twins Nakula and Sahadeva, incarnate several of the qualities of the divine twins: benevolence, humility, readiness to serve, and also skill in the breeding of cattle and horses.

India thus presents a double mythical expression of the trifunctional ideology, both in the adventures of her gods and in those of her heroes. The study of the connections between these two mythologies has only begun, but it is now known that, in part at least, they overlap. It was shown in 1954[2] that one of the Vedic exploits of the warrior god Indra, his duel with the Sun god, has a precise analogue in one of the epic exploits of the warrior hero Arjuna: just as Indra, in the duel, is the victor because he "detaches" or "pushes down" one of the wheels of the solar chariot, so Arjuna, the son of Indra, in the eighth book of the *Mahābhārata*, succeeds against Karṇa, son of the Sun, only because one of the wheels of the latter's chariot sinks itself miraculously into the ground. Five years later, the whole staff of sovereignty was similarly recognized as transposed into the figures of the king Yudhiṣṭhira, his father, and his two uncles.[3]

In the Roman context, another tableau, a documentation of another form, is evolved. Theologically, the three functions are well expressed and patronized, in their hierarchy, by the gods of the pre-Capitoline

1. "Pāṇḍavasagan och Mahābhāratas mytiska förutsättningar," *Religion och Bibel* 6 (1947): 27–39; developed in *Mythe et épopée* 1:53–102. The first volume of *Mythe et épopée*, hereafter cited as *ME* 1, was published in 1968.

2. "Karṇa et les Pāṇḍava," *Orientalia Suecana* 3 (1954) = (*Mélanges H. S. Nyberg*, pp. 60–66; completed (particularly by the theme of the two mothers, common to the Sun and to Karṇa) in *ME* 1:125–44.

3. "La transposition des dieux souverains mineurs en héros dans le Mahābhārata," *Indo-Iranian Journal* 3 (1959):1–16. The investigation, extended to other figures in the poem, resulted in the first part of *ME* 1:31–257.

triad, those of the major flamens. But having observed that Jupiter and his variant Dius Fidius represent the two aspects of sovereignty, "power" and "law," that Mars is the strong warrior god, and that Quirinus expresses and guarantees directly, or serves through his flamen, certain important aspects of the third function (the social mass and vigilant peace; agricultural prosperity), one has exhausted what may be said about these divine figures. Their connection is to be found in their hierarchy, their entire being in their definitions, and these definitions leave no place for any narrative accounts.

In contrast, this dramatic unfolding of character, which is lacking to the gods, forms the very scaffolding of epic, of an epic—accepted as history by Titus Livius and by Plutarch, the former with reticence, the latter with devotion—the history of Rome's first kings. Here we have a sequential history, for Roman mythology has not assembled her "trifunctional heroes," like the *Mahābhārata*, into a group of contemporaries, of brothers hierarchized so that the first alone is king and the others his specialized auxiliaries. As seems to have very soon been the case in the Iranian epic also,[4] Roman tradition has distributed them in time, in a succession of kings each of whom, by his character, his founding actions, his entire life, expresses and adds to the common undertaking one of the functions, or an aspect of one of the functions, necessary to the welfare of the society.

Although the significant character and structure of the first reigns has been analyzed several times in the past thirty years,[5] it is worth reconsidering here, since one of those reigns, that of Tullus, will be the object of our new research.

But let us first observe—and we cannot insist on it too strongly—that the "system" formed by the first kings of Rome is not one of our own findings; the Romans comprehended it, explicated it, admired it as a system, and saw in it the effect of divine benevolence: we have only had to take notice of their own sentiment.[6] Florus (1.8), in his

4. S. Wikander, "Sur le fonds commun indo-iranien des épopées de la Perse et de l'Inde," *La Nouvelle Clio* 7 (1950):310–29.

5. Most recently, *ME* 1:271–74.

6. The passage of the sixth book of the *Aeneid* in which Anchises describes the future founding kings of Rome to Aeneas contains excellent definitions of these functions, each with veritable key words:

"Recapitulation" of the royal history, before characterizing each reign by a phrase, says justly and emphatically that this initial growth of Rome was effected under personages *quodam fatorum industria tam uariis ingenio ut rei publicae ratio et utilitas postulabat.* Before him the Laelius of the *De republica* (2.21) had remarked, basing his authority on Cato: *perspicuom est quanta in singulos reges rerum bonarum et utilium fiat accessio.*

Rome thus concentrated her beginnings, the pre-Etruscan ages, as a progressive formation in several stages, the solicitude of the gods bringing forth each time a king of a new type, founder of new institutions, in tune with the need of the moment. And it has been shown that these stages correspond to the Varuṇian aspect, then to the Mitrian aspect, of the function of sovereignty—creative and terrible power, organizing and benevolent authority—; to the function of martial force; and to certain facets of the complex third function. These kings, then, are: (1) Romulus, the demigod of mysterious birth and childhood, creator of the city, the redoubtable king armed with axes, rods, and bonds; (2) Numa the wise, the religious and totally human founder of cults, priesthood, and laws; (3) Tullus Hostilius, the exclusively warlike leader, offensive, who gives Rome the military instrument of power: and (4) Ancus Marcius, the king under whom there was a large increase in the Roman *plebs*

ROMULUS (vv. 781–82):

En huius, nate, auspiciis *illa incluta Roma*
imperium *terris, animos aequabit Olympo.*

NUMA POMPILIUS (vv. 808–11):

Quis procul ille autem ramis insignis oliuae
sacra *ferens? nosco crinis incanaque menta*
regis Romani, primam qui legibus *urbem*
fundabit. . . .

TULLUS HOSTILIUS (vv. 812–15):

. . . cui deinde subibit
otia qui rumpet patriae residesque mouebit
Tullus in arma *uiros et iam desueta triumphis*
agmina

ANCUS MARCIUS (vv. 815–16):

Quem iusta sequitur iactantior Ancus,
nunc quoque iam nimium gaudens popularibus auris.

Cf. Florus, *Epitome*, 1.8 (presenting a different aspect of Ancus):

Nam quid Romulo ardentius*? tali opus fuit, ut inuaderet regnum. Quid Numa* religiosius? *Ita res poposcit, ut ferox populus* deorum metu *mitigaretur. Quid ille* militiae artifex *Tullus? bellatoribus uiris quam necessarius,* ut acueret ratione uirtutem! *Quid* aedificator *Ancus, ut urbem colonia extenderet, ponte iungeret, muro tueretur. . . .*

and in commercial opulence, and who made war only when compelled for Rome's defense.[7]

This functional interpretation of the founding kings has been generally accepted for the first three: the obviously deliberate antithesis between Romulus and Numa, recalling the two opposite yet necessary aspects of the first function, and the wholly warlike character of Tullus, demand little discussion. It has been otherwise for the fourth king, Ancus Marcius. Despite the anachronisms that have long been recognized in the work attributed to him, one cannot help having the impression that it is with Ancus Marcius that historical authenticity begins to carry some appreciable weight in the traditions; that he represents, in the series of kings, the point at which a purely fictitious history, which is intended merely to explain, is welded to a history retouched, reevaluated, to be sure, but in its inception genuine and recorded. This sort of coming to earth of the speculations that a people or a dynasty makes upon its past is always a delicate point for the critic: Upon what ordinal term, for example, in the series of Ynglingar—those descendants of the god Freyr who little by little become the very real kings of the Swedish Upland, then of southern Norway—must the human mantle first be placed? The matter continues to be debated, and there is considerable divergence of opinion. *Mutatis mutandis*, it is just the same for Ancus, so that one hesitates—and many evince some reluctance—to recognize, even in one part of his "history" or a part of his character, a last fragment of a pseudo history of mythical origin only intended to illustrate the successive appearances of the three functions.[7]

Whatever may be the epic expression of the third function, which always presents complicated and sometimes elusive problems since it is itself multiform, the interpretation of the first two functions and their representatives, the two founders Romulus and Numa and their immediate successor Tullus, is assured. That alone will suffice for the problem we shall now take up.

In a little book, inordinately praised by some, denounced by others as outrageous, which has nevertheless survived more than a quarter-century of self-criticism, the "military function" of king Tullus has

7. The aspects of the third function found in Ancus have been set forth in Dumézil, *Tarpeia* (1947), pp. 176–82 ("Ancus, la guerre, la paix et l'économie"), 182–89 ("Ancus et la plèbe"), 189–93 ("Ancus et la troisième fonction"); cf. *ME* 1:280–81.

been followed in detail, in his character, in his institutions, and in his career. *Horace et les Curiaces* presents him as follows.

The chapter of Florus' *Epitome* which concerns him, and which retains only what is essential (1.3), begins in these terms: "Numa Pompilius was succeeded by Tullus, to whom the kingship was voluntarily offered out of respect for his courage. It was he who founded all military discipline and the art of warfare. So when he had wondrously trained the soldiers [*iuuentus*] of Rome, he ventured to challenge the Albans, an important and for a long time a leading people . . . ."[8] Livy (1.22.20) depicts the king himself as a typical *iuuenis*: "This monarch was not only unlike the last [the pacific Numa], but was actually more warlike [*ferocior*] than Romulus had been. Besides his youth and strength, the glory of his grandfather [the most prestigious of Romulus' companions] was also an incentive to him. So, thinking that the nation was growing decrepit from inaction, he sought excuses everywhere for stirring up war . . . ."[9] Tullus is so much the specialist of war, and more particularly of the military life and of the military formation, that, again according to Livy (1.31.5), even when Rome was afflicted with a pestilence, "no respite from service was allowed by the warlike king who believed, besides, that the young men [*iuuenes*] were healthier in the field than at home . . . ." Finally, his entire funeral eulogy consists in a single phrase: *magna gloria belli regnauit annos duos et triginta.* Four centuries later, offering a bird's-eye view to the history of the world, the Christian Orosius was to reiterate this constant tradition in three words: *Tullus Hostilius, militaris rei institutor . . . .*[10]

On the strength of this functional definition of the third king of Rome, we attempted in 1942, in the book referred to above, to interpret the most celebrated episode in the reign of Tullus—the duel between Horace and the Curiaces—in the light of the comparative study of the myths, legends, and rituals associated, among other Indo-European peoples, with the same function, that of the warrior.[11] It seemed to us that this little drama in three scenes—the duel against the three brothers from which one of the three Roman champions emerges, alone, but victorious; the cruel scene where the warrior, in the intoxication and excess of triumph, kills his sister before the gates of the city for her crime of revealing the feminine weakness of a lover's

8. Translation of Edward Seymour Foster (Loeb Classical Library, 1929).
9. Citations from Livy are from the translation by B. O. Foster, (Loeb Classical Library, 1919).
10. Pp. 79–81.
11. See below, pp. 133–38.

grief; finally the judgment and the expiations which preserve this youthful glory and this youthful force for Rome while effacing its blemish—is but the Roman adaptation, reduced to the usual categories of experience, emptied of its mysterious causality, and colored in accordance with Roman morality, of a series of scenes readily comparable to that in an Ulster legend which constitutes the story of the first combat, the initiatory combat, of the celebrated hero Cúchulainn. Still a child, Cúchulainn makes his way to the frontier of his country, provokes and defeats the three sons of Nechta, constant enemies of the Ulates; then, beyond himself, in a frightful and dangerous state of mystical *furor* born of combat, he returns to the capital where a woman—the queen—tries to calm him by the crudest of sexual propositions. Cúchulainn spurns the offer, but, while he looks aside, the Ulates succeed in seizing him and plunging him in gigantic vats of cold water which literally extinguish him; henceforth, in order to reinvigorate himself when combat demands, and so as not to imperil his own people, he will keep in reserve this gift of *furor* which renders him invincible and which is the precious result of his initiation.[12]

A consideration of the Irish account and the ritual realities which it preserves, placed side by side with the purely literary work of Horace, is the subject of our 1942 study. There we proposed a "model" of evolution to provide an understanding of the passage from one style to the other: once the *furor* which had been the savage ideal and the grand manner of the Italic warriors of prehistory (as it remained that of the warriors of Celtic and Germanic epic)[13] had been depreciated for the sake of legionary discipline, the scenes of the narrative, while retaining their order of succession, were articulated differently, took another point of attack. Passions of the soul took the place of mystical forces; a justified and almost reasonable anger, provoked from without and following the exploit, was substituted for the physical and spontaneous exaltation of the entire being in the course of the exploit; and, above all, the confrontation of aggressive virility with

12. Against a strange interpretation (H. J. Rose) of the legend of the Horaces and the Curiaces, tying this legend in with the places mentioned (Tigillum sororium, Pila Horatia, etc.), and of the adjective *sororius* itself, see in the German edition of this book (1964), pp. 21–22, a polemical note which I will not reproduce here but which is still completely valid.

13. The warrior's *furor* (Irish *ferg*, Hom. Greek μένος, etc.) is the subject of the first chapter of *Horace et les Curiaces* (Paris, 1942), pp. 11–33.

unleashed femininity abandoned the troubled regions of sex and took the form of a moving moral conflict between a homicidal brother and a widowed sister.[14]

It is only in the conclusion of the book (pp. 126–34) that, passing beyond this limited comparison, we mentioned that the exploits of Cúchulainn and Horace are two variants, or rather two neighboring forms of one and the same variant, of a ritual or mythical exploit known from other examples in the literatures of several Indo-European peoples: the combat, fraught with consequences, of a god or hero against an adversary endowed with some form of triplicity. Significantly, the Indo-Iranian tradition knows of other expressions, similar in intent, of the same theme: on the one hand, Indra's duel, or the duel of a hero he is protecting, with a tricephalic being; on the other, Θraētaona's battle with another monster formed from the same mold.[15]

These results are valuable. It remains true that the Irish version, humane and pseudo-historical like the Latin, is the most apt to help explain some important details, especially all that relates, or has related in the probable prehistoric form of the story, to the notion of *furor*. However, less striking at first glance because less colorful, are certain correspondences between the defeat of the Indian Tricephal and that of the Curiaces which illuminate both of these in a more philosophical light, and open perspectives upon the warrior function that are far deeper than those disclosed by the legend of Cúchulainn. Moreover, almost the entire legend of King Tullus Hostilius has, from one stage to the next, found its parallel in the most famous exploits of the god Indra. Thus, between Rome and India, that remarkable and profound identity—first observed at the level of Romulus and Varuṇa, Numa Pompilius and Mitra—will extend itself to the second cosmic and social level, both in the ideology and in its mythical expression.

Let us now go back to the adventure of the young Horace, conqueror of the triple opponent, and confront it with a structured series of Indian materials.

14. See below, p. 135, n. 45.
15. See below, pp. 157–60.

2

THE "HORATII" AND THE "ĀPTYA"

In all the other episodes of his warrior career, the leading role belongs as it must to Tullus, the master warrior, the man who has given his young army its admirable training. Against the Veians, against the Sabines, he will hold sway as he did previously in the definitive settlement of the fate of Alba. He steps aside only once, but at one of the most crucial moments: when it comes to the point of conquering the Latin empire, it is the survivor of the three Horaces who gives it to Rome, and to Tullus her king.

Indeed, Tullus negotiates with the Alban chief for the combat between the two sets of triplets, substituting it for a wholesale battle. It is he who establishes the conditions, accompanies the three Roman combatants and encourages them; and after the victory, it is he who receives the triumphant Horace, helps him to escape the consequences of his homicidal excess, celebrates a triumph, and reaps, with Alba's submission, the political benefit of the victory. But it is not he who fights. *Ferocior Romulo*, he does not, however, enter into a duel with another leader like the one who adorns the legend of Romulus and brings forth the first *spolia opima*.

Dionysius of Halicarnassus would appear to have sensed some difficulty here, for in the interview at which the combat between the Horaces and the Curiaces is worked out he has the Roman king make the following proposition to the Alban:

> For Tullus desired that the fate of the war might be decided by the smallest possible number of combatants, the most distinguished man among the Albans fighting the bravest of the Romans in single combat, and he cheerfully offered himself to fight for his own country, inviting the Alban leader tc

emulate him. He pointed out that those who have assumed the command of armies' combats for sovereignty and power are glorious, not only when they conquer brave men, but also when they are conquered by the brave; and he enumerated all the generals and kings who had risked their lives for their country, regarding it as a reproach to them to have a greater share of the honours than others but a smaller share of the dangers. [3.12.2.][1]

If we do not witness a replica, then, of the duel between Romulus and the king of Caenina, the fault is not that of Tullus, but of his interlocutor:

The Alban, however, while approving of the proposal to commit the fate of the cities to a few champions, would not agree to decide it by single combat. He owned that when commanders of armies were seeking to establish their own power a combat between them for the supremacy was noble and necessary, but when states themselves were contending for the first place he thought the risk of single combat not only hazardous, but even dishonourable, whether they met with good or ill fortune. [3.12.3.]

The controversy and the arguments are from Dionysius, the Greek. But they serve well to underline the feature which brings them forth: in this case and—spanning the royal history and especially the reign of the king who is most typically a warrior—only in this case, an important military advantage is secured for Rome by a combatant other than the king. Beside the king, delegated and encouraged by him, the champion intervenes.

Mutatis mutandis, India presents an analogous situation, merely replacing the relation between king and champion by that between god and hero; for the victory over the triple adversary, over the tricephalic son of Tvaṣṭṛ, does not refer to "history," but to divine mythology. As so often happens, the Ṛg Vedic hymns contradict themselves, sometimes attributing the exploit to Indra alone, sometimes to Indra aided by Trita Āptya, and sometimes appearing to treat the two names as synonymous.[2] But this must be the effect of a divine

1. Citations from *The Roman Antiquities* of Dionysius of Halicarnassus are from the translation by Earnest Cary (Loeb Classical Library, 1939). This and other excerpts from the Loeb Classical Library are reprinted by permission of the publishers, Harvard University Press.

2. When dealing with Trita, Namuci, the sins of Indra, etc., we should not lose sight of the fact that there need not exist a unique, standard tradition, but rather, since Vedic times, numerous variants in keeping with the theme's celebrity and importance. Beyond the indispensable philological analyses of the Vedic references, in verse and in prose, one must also investigate them as ethnographers and folklorists usually do with their materials.

imperialism of which there are other examples, the poet willingly attributing to the divinity, whom he praises or prays to, the entire accomplishment of feats in which, at first, he took only a part. The inverse movement, the dispossession of the god to the advantage of the hero, would at all events be less readily conceived. Variations like this should not depreciate the value of texts like 10.8.8, even if the immediately following strophe restores to Indra the final act itself, the decapitation of the monster.

> Trita Āptya, knowing the paternal weapons and urged on by Indra, combated the three-headed, seven-bridled being, and, killing him, made off with the cattle of the son of Tvaṣṭr̥.

Thus the principal credit for this act, so necessary to the salvation of the gods and the world, falls again to a hero, Trita, only "urged on by Indra," *índreṣitaḥ*. This feature is ancient, Indo-Iranian, as the *Avesta* also attributes the exploit to a man rather than a god: Aži Dahāka of three heads (the Zohak of the epic) is killed by Θraetaona (the Ferīdūn of the epic), whose name is a derivative (with the ever puzzling *ao*) of Θrita, the Iranian form of the Vedic Trita. The only thing which refers us back to the Iranian equivalent of the god Indra Vr̥trahan is that Θraētaona can be assured of victory by partaking of both the power of *vərəθrağna*, the ability to shatter the defense, and of *ama*, the assailant force (*Yašt* 14.40). In other words, as Emile Benveniste and Louis Renou have remarked, the hero "draws from the god Vərəθrağna the offensive force which will hurl down the dragon."[3] But it is he himself, and not the god, who fights.

The Indian and the Iranian names for the heroes who kill the triple adversary are remarkable: Trita, Θraētaona. Since the *R̥g Veda*, *Tritá*—the same word, except for the accent, as the Greek *τρίτος*—has been understood as "third." The Brāhmaṇa made him the third of three brothers, with artificial names, Ekata, Dvita, Trita, "First, Second (cf. *dvitī́ya*, av. *bitya*, old pers. *dūvitīya*), Third," and already *R̥g Veda* 8.47,16 associates him at least with Dvita. For his part, in his

For the extent of the variants concerning Trita and his connection with Indra, after Abel Bergaigne, *La religion védique* 2 (1883): 325–30, and Hermann Güntert, *Der arische Weltkönig und Heiland* (1923), p. 28, see Emile Benveniste and Louis Renou, *Vr̥tra et Vr̥θragna* (1935), p. 106, n. 1. *Vr̥tra et Vr̥θragna* is hereafter cited as *V. et V.*

3. *V. et V.*, p. 193; see below, p. 115.

march against the Tricephal, Ferīdūn is accompanied by his two brothers. In the *ŠāhNāmeh*, the monster's vizier tells his master of their fatal approach in the following terms:

> Three great men with troops have arrived from a foreign land. The one that stands between the other two is the youngest, but he has the stature of a cypress and the visage of a king. Although he is youngest, he is superior in dignity and it is he who stands forth amongst them.[4]

The attempts of several modern critics to justify another etymology for the name Trita (for example, *Trita* as "Kurzname" for **Tri-tavan*, according to Jacob Wackernagel; contra: Jacques Duchesne-Guillemin)[5] have not been convincing, and the majority of scholars hold to the meaning "third." One may recognize here an epic application of a folkloric motif found frequently in the tales of every continent: the youngest of three brothers succeeds where his elders have failed or faltered, or, more generally, he distinguishes himself before them. This interpretation is all the more probable since often, in the stories, the first two brothers, jealous of the last, seek to make him perish, just as Trita, in an *itihāsa* to which there is already a reference in a Vedic hymn, is hurled into a well or abandoned in a well by his two elder brothers,[6] and as Ferīdūn, in the *ŠāhNāmeh*, is forced to outwit his two elder brothers when they try to crush him beneath an enormous rock while on their march toward the Tricephal. One need only add that this feature must have had a special importance for the Indo-Iranian conqueror of the triple adversary, since it gave him his name.

In the Roman version, though his rank is not indicated by his name, it is nevertheless a "third," the third Horace—the sole survivor of the three brothers (Horaces)—who, on his own, kills the "triple adversary," this time interpreted as a group of three brothers.

Let us now confine ourselves to setting forth, without seeking an interpretation, the formula which sustains the Roman intrigue just as it does that of India and Iran: "The third kills the triple."[7]

4. Reuben Levy, tr., *The Epic of Kings* (Chicago: University of Chicago Press, 1967), p. 22.

5. *Indogermanische Forschungen* 54 (1935):205; Manfred Mayrhofer, *Kurzgefasstes etymologisches Wörterbuch des Altindischen* 1 (1956):534–35, s.v. "wohl 'der Dritte.'"

6. See now *ME* 1:199–201.

7. As to the Irish hero Cúchulainn, whose "warrior initiation" is also achieved by combat with a triple adversary (of the Roman type: three brothers, the three sons of

The Indian legend is not content to name the hero "Third," and, consequently, his brothers "Second" and "First." It adjoins to these designations a sort of common family name. The Vedic Trita is *Tritá Āptyá*; the *Brāhmaṇa* refer to Ekata, Dvita, and Trita as "the Āptya" or, more rarely, "the Āpya." This feature is Indo-Iranian as well: the Avestan hero Θraētaona is called Āθwyani, in that he is from the clan or family of the Āθwya. Whatever may be the divergence in the forms, one cannot separate, indeed no critic has separated, Āptya from Āθwya.

The Indians understand Āptya as derived from the theme of *ap*, "water," *ā́paḥ*, "waters." The complex archaic suffix *-tya* serves above all in Vedic Sanskrit to form adjectives and substantives from adverbs (*nítya*, "relative"; *niṣṭya*, "stranger"; *ápatya*, "posterity"; *sánutya*, "distant"; *āvíṣṭya*, "manifest"; *amā́tya*, "belonging to the same house"), a formation that does not apply to our present case. But the argument does not suffice to dismiss an etymology which, on the contrary, is confirmed by ritual acts, surely ancient, in which these personages are mentioned and which are in fact based upon the use and the qualities of water. As to the Avestan Āθwya, which is without direct etymology, it must be understood as the deformation of an Āptya whose sense was no longer perceived.[8] Though we cannot

---

Nechta; see above p. 9–10, and below pp. 133–34), the characteristic of "thirdness" is present in a remarkable form: Cúchulainn's conception, understood as an incarnation of the god Lug, takes place in three stages (Ernst Windisch, *Irische Texte* 1 (1880):138–40, second version). His mother Dechtire gives birth to a boy who dies very soon; then, returning from the funeral ceremony, while drinking, she swallows "a small animal"; a dream reveals it to be identical with the child she has lost, a second form of Lug, but immediately she vomits it forth and again becomes virginal; finally, from her husband she has a third child, or rather a third form of the same, Setanta, who will later take the name Cúchulainn, Dog of Cúlann. Thus we get the expression from the narrative: "And he was the child of the three years," *ocus ba he mac na teoru m-bliadan in sin*. In the case of the Greek hero Heracles, conqueror of the triple adversary (Indian type: Geryon has three heads), "thirdness" is expressed in a different but related way, one which turns to triplicity: his conception occurred not in three years and three attempts, but in one night three times as long as normal (see below, p. 97–98; Diodorus 4.9.2: *τὸν γὰρ Δία μισγόμενον Ἀλκμήνῃ τριπλασίαν τὴν νύκτα ποιῆσαι, καὶ τῷ πλήθει τοῦ πρὸς τὴν παιδοποιίαν ἀναλωθέντος χρόνου προσημῆναι τὴν ὑπερβολὴν τῆς τοῦ γεννηθησομένου ῥώμης*). For Starcatherus, reduced to a third of his original form, see below, chap. 4, n. 4; for Böðvar the third (two elders partially animal, he himself purely human), see pp. 143–44.

8. If one were to adopt the explanation of Jacob Wackernagel (Wackernagel-Debrunner, *Altindische Grammatik* 2, pt. 2 [1959]:700, §513 g, Anm.; cf. Hanns Oertel, *Syntax of Cases* [1926], p. 328, with a table of supposed derivations, making use of a suggestion of Wackernagel), who derives Vedic *Āptya* and Avestan *Āθwya* from an Indo-Iranian **Ātpya*, there would still remain, in the *facts* at our disposal, the definite ritual connection between the

accept the overexclusive and too naturalistic views of Kasten Rönnow on "Trita Āptya als Wassergottheit," his defense (particularly against Hermann Güntert) of the Indian explanation of Āptya is fully as convincing as his critique of the meaning "third," for Trita, is unconvincing.[9] Now, in the Indo-Iranian apportionment of concepts and elements among the three hierarchized functions of sovereignty, force, and fecundity, the waters—fertilizing, nourishing, healing, cleansing—belong as fundamentally as does the earth to the third function. I will recall here only that Haurvatāt̰, the Zoroastrian sublimation of one of the Nāsatya twins, has water for his "associated element," and that in the trifunctional title of the trivalent goddess Arədvī Sūrā Anāhitā, "the Humid, the Strong, the Immaculate," it is Arədvī, "the Humid," which gives the differential note for the "third function."[10]

In the Iranian tradition, where the connection between the name and the waters is forgotten and **Āptya* is corrupted into *Āθwya*, the relationship of Θraētaona, and of the Āθwya, to the third function is nonetheless conserved. One tradition, which we will treat again in fuller detail, tells how the *x*ᵛ*arənah*, "the Glory," of Yima abandoned him three times or in three stages, each *x*ᵛ*arənah*[11] or each third then incarnating itself in a different personage. According to *Yašt* 19.34–38, these personages are Miθra, "Θraētaona of the clan (*vīs*) of the Āθwya, who killed the Tricephal," and the hero Kərəsāspa.

Āptya and the water, which would have favored the transformation of the name into an apparent derivation from *ắp*-, "water(s)." But the hypothetical word **Ātpya* has a strange form, without significance; Manfred Mayrhofer, (*Kurzgefasstes etymologisches Wörterbuch* I [1956], s.v.), says rightly: "Wahrscheinlich ist *āptya* von *apaḥ* beinflusst, wenn nicht direkt (trotz manchen Schwierigkeiten in Iran) als *āp-tyá* von diesem hergeleitet. . . . Gegen Trennung von *ắp*- (die Wackernagel bei Oertel 328 gefordert hatte) vgl. mit richtigen Gründen Lommels *Festschr. Schulring* 31 Anm. 2 (auch zu aw. *āθwya*)."

9. Kasten Rönnow, *Trita Āptya, eine vedische Gottheit* I = (Uppsala Universitets Årsskrift, 1927), pt. 5, pp. xix–xx.

10. See *Tarpeia*, pp. 58–59; *ME* 1:104–5.

11. Marijan Molé, in *La légende de Zoroastre selon les textes Pehlevis* (1967), p. 157 (referring to H. W. Bailey, *Zoroastrian Problems in the Ninth Century Books* [1943]), writes: "There is no doubt that the translation of *x*ᵛ*arənah* by "glory" should be dropped; but if the term is derived from the root *ar*- "to obtain," its meaning is not simply "fortune." What we are really dealing with here is the "lot" attributed to each man in order to make him able to fulfill his task. This meaning, at the same time broader and more precise than that postulated by Mr. Bailey, takes into account all the uses of the term, notably its near equivalence to *xvēškārīh*"; and Molé then refers to his 1963 book *Culte, mythe et cosmologie dans l'Iran ancien*, p. 434. With this in mind, we can consider "glory" as a *verbum technicum*.

Darmesteter[12] has set forth the grounds for recognizing representatives here of the first (Miθra), of the third (Θraētaona), and of the second (Kərəsāspa) functions. The ascription is quite clear for Miθra and for Kərəsāspa. For Θraētaona, Darmesteter was disturbed by the hero's well-established title of conqueror of the Tricephal—mentioned in this very passage—a feat which would seem more likely to classify him within the warrior function, under the same heading as Kərəsāspa but with different nuances, than within the third function. The learned commentator argued, however, that "the family of the Āθwya seems to have been above all a family of agriculturalists, for the great number of its members bore names composed from the name of the ox."[13] His insight was a sound one. Another variant of the tripartition of the Glory of Yima, more homogeneous and in many respects more satisfactory, derived from a lost portion of the *Avestan* corpus, has been conserved in the *Dēnkart*[14]; this time, it is the text itself which declares the trifunctional interpretation. Here then, from the translation which Marijan Molé so kindly communicated to me, is the destiny of the third of the Glory which pertains to the third function:

> It [the "transmission of the word"] returned, in another epoch, from the share allotted by the distribution of Yam's "Glory" to the religious function [*dēn pēšak*] of agriculture, to Frētōn of the family of Āswyān] the Pehlevi name for " Θraētaona of the clan of the Āθwya"], when the latter was found in the womb of his mother, and thereby he became victorious. [§25]

And, after mentioning the victory over the Tricephal (§26), the text continues:

> By agriculture, the third religious function, he taught men the medicine of the body which makes it possible to diagnose the plague and chase away sickness. [§27]

Later we will have a better understanding of this mobilization of the third function, by the second, into the zone of combat—the association with the warrior god of a hero who is equally martial but named in accordance with a concept from the zone of fertility

12. *Le Zend Avesta* 2 (1892):624–26, and nn. 50–56.

13. Ibid., n. 55.

14. 7.1.20–36; Edward W. West, *Pahlavi Texts* 5 = *Sacred Books of the East* 47 (1897): 9–15.

and still maintaining a connection with this latter zone. For the moment, the fact of this mobilization is significant in itself, for it is found again in the Roman legend.

While Livy tells us that historians were in disagreement over the question of who—the Horaces or the Curiaces—had been the champions of Rome, he himself conforms to the side unanimously preferred by our sources: Rome was represented by the Hŏratii, and saved by the third Hŏratius. Now, this name is derived, by the complex suffix *-tius*, from Hŏra, the very name of the goddess who is paired, as "spouse," with Quirinus. In other words, Hŏra is the name of the feminine entity who is simply intended to express the essence, or one of the essences, of Quirinus, just as Nerio expresses one of the essences of Mars—and Quirinus, as we know, figures in the ancient triad as the canonical god of the third function. We will soon see that the religious service of the *gens Horatia* in Roman society corresponds to an important mythical and liturgical service of the Indian Āptya, a service of purification which, as such, belongs to the third function.

The murder of the Tricephal, son of Tvaṣṭṛ, has in every period of Indian tradition been viewed as an ambiguous act: justified, necessary either because of certain unspecified dangers threatening the gods or because of considerable and clearly specified injuries; but at the same time contrary to a moral rule presented in some cases as a violation of the Tricephal's rank within the society of superhuman beings, in others as an infraction of the kinship which unites him to the murderer.

The Brāhmaṇa and the epic literature hold above all the crime of brahmanicide, one of the gravest of all crimes: the Tricephal was a brahman. And more than just a brahman; he was, despite his demonic affinities, the chaplain of the gods. It is in fact in this very role, and through its offices, that he betrays them: "Publicly," says *Taittirīya-Saṃhitā* (2.5.1), "it is to the gods that he allocated the benefit of the sacrifice, but, secretly, he allocated it to the demons"; and liturgically only the secret allocation counts.[15]

As Tvaṣṭṛ's son, however, he had another connection with the gods, which lessens the strangeness of the preceding account: this

15. See "Deux traits du monstre Tricéphale indo-iranien," *Revue de l'histoire des religions* 120 (1939):7–11, and now Molé, pp. 8–10 (text), pp. 9–11 (trans.).

chaplain of the gods was their nephew, their "sister's son," *svasriya.* He was one of those beings whom a double kinship relates to both of the parties—the asura and the deva, the demons and the gods—who dispute over sacrifice and the world.

The *ṚgVeda* does not articulate the terms with such precision. But the theology of the hymns admits readily of an alliance between Tvaṣṭṛ and the gods, and the result is the same: the murder of Tvaṣṭṛ's son by Trita at Indra's instigation, or by Indra himself, is perpetrated in violation of the very bonds which should have prevented it. These are the terms in which *ṚgVeda* (2.11.19) addresses itself to Indra:

[Unto us] who desire [optative] to win by vanquishing all enemies, the dasyu, with your help, with the arya,—unto us [you delivered of old into our hands] the son of Tvaṣṭṛ Viśvarūpa,—you delivered unto Trita [i.e., unto one of us, to a man like us] [the son] of the being bound by friendship.[16]

This last word, *sākhyá*, an adjective of appurtenance derived from *sakhyá*, "friendship," probably concerns Tvaṣṭṛ, who is related to the gods through marriage, yet still their rival. Moreover, the translation "friendship" is inadequate, but it is difficult to establish with precision the variety of social relationship which the word *sákhi*—probably from the same root as the Latin *socius*—signifies.

The Roman legend, as one can see, admits of a parallel feature. In Livy, the Horaces and the Curiaces are described as future brothers-in-law, one of the Albans being betrothed to the sister of the Romans. But Dionysius of Halicarnassus, and there is no reason to think that this is his own invention, adds consanguinity to this bond: the three Horaces and the three Curiaces are first cousins, their two mothers being sisters, daughters of the Alban Sicinius. For their Roman adversaries, the Curiaces are ambiguous beings, representing and sustaining the power hostile to Rome, yet united to them personally, on the feminine side, by the closest bonds of kinship.

16. One could also translate the second half of the strophe by giving a different sense to the dative which opens verse 3 and to the one which ends verse 4: "It is *for* us, for our benefit, that you have delivered Viśvarūpa, the son of Tvaṣṭṛ, [the son] of the being bound [to you] by friendship, over *to* Trita." The other construction and the other meaning proposed for *sākhyásya* (. . . "to Trita, [member] of the friendship-group") are improbable; *sākhyásya*, in line 4, is more readily connected with the genitive included in the patronymic *tvāṣṭrám* and, thus detached, isolated for effect, it suggests the idea: "*even though* he was the son of a being bound to you by friendship."

In Indian mythology this natural and social situation results in the gravest consequences. The *R̥g Veda,* a book of eulogies and invocations, does not, indeed could not, emphasize this troublesome side of the necessary exploit accomplished or patronized by Indra: how could the allusion (in 2.11.19) to the *sakhyá* between the murderer and his victim be fraught with reproach when the author of the hymn mentions Trita's exploit only to ask Indra for more help of the same kind? Nonetheless, all the later literature is in agreement on one point: Indra's victory, or that of Indra and Trita, produces a stain.

The Roman legend, as recounted in the third book of Dionysius, elegantly avoids this consequence. The subtle text deserves appreciation, despite its verbosity. When the Alban dictator Mettius Fuffetius tells Tullus that divine providence has prepared these two groups of triplet cousins—equal in beauty, force, and courage—to serve the two cities as champions, the Roman king responds that the idea is good; but he makes an objection on principle: it would not conform to divine law, *ὅσιον*, for cousins, fed on the same milk, to take up arms against each other. And if their respective chiefs should compel them to execute these sacrilegious murders, *μιαιφονεῖν*, the stain produced by the shedding of familial blood, *τὸ ἐμφύλιον ἄγος*, *τὸ συγγενὲς μίασμα*, would fall to those responsible. Mettius Fuffetius has foreseen the difficulty: to prevent any stain upon the chiefs and the cities, it is necessary and sufficient that the combatants fight voluntarily. And so, with this in mind, he has already consulted the Curiaces, who have accepted with enthusiasm (15.3–4). In turn, Tullus addresses himself to the Horaces, leaving their choice entirely free. They put the question to their father, who again leaves it entirely up to them. Then the eldest of the three brothers makes this reflection: "As for the bond of kinship with our cousins, we shall not be the first to break it, but since it has already been broken by fate, we shall acquiesce therein. For if the Curiatii esteem kinship less than honour, the Horatii also will not value the ties of blood more highly than valour" (17.4–5). Thus, in the last analysis, the sole bearers of the *ἐμφύλιον ἄγος* are the Curiaces. Not only do Rome and her king avoid stain by not compelling their champions, but so do the champions themselves by establishing juridically that the bond has already been broken in the choice taken by their partners. Yet this does not prevent the host of spectators, less expert at sophisms, from blaming the chiefs (18.3), at the moment when the champions come forth, for "great heartlessness, in that, when it was possible to decide the battle with other champions, they had limited the combat on behalf of the cities to men of kindred blood and compelled the pollution of fratricide (εἰς ἐμφύλιον αἷμα καὶ συγγενικὸν ἄγος)."

We are well aware of the revenge which the familial blood will take in the course of the story. The young, victorious Horace will kill his sister, herself as guilty of ambiguous behavior as the Indian Tricephal—Roman in race and name, Alban at heart, in words and tears: μισάδελφε καὶ ἀναξία τῶν προγόνων (21.6), the "executioner" will say to her, piercing her with his sword. This episode is without parallel in the Indian plot. Moreover, it brings an element into play that is foreign to the action of Trita: anger or indignation. As we suggested above, such a disposition is itself a psychological and probably specifically Roman transposition of the *furor*—both physical and supernatural—which, in Indo-European times, was engendered by combat in the warrior elite, a power experienced and put to use by Indra and his Marut companions in numerous circumstances, although not in the one under discussion. The conflict between the brother and the sister, the loving woman and the triumphant warrior, the provocation of the one and the excessive violence of the other are the end result of a different "theme of the second function," added to the one—juridico-religious in nature—that we are now analyzing, and this secondary theme has attached to itself the notion of stain, which was inherent in the first: the young Horace is brought to trial (Dionysius 22.3) "on the ground that because of his slaying of his sister he was not free of the guilt of shedding a kinsman's blood," ὡς οὐ καθαρὸν αἵματος ἐμφυλίου διὰ τὸν τῆς ἀδελφῆς φόνον.

The stain demands expiation, purification. And it is probably here that the functional correspondence of Trita and the Āptya on the one hand, and of Horace and his *gens* on the other, appears in its most suggestive form. Beyond the particular episode of the murder of the Tricephal or of the Alban triplets, and no longer mythically, but ritually—for India, in the ordinary liturgy of the sacrifice, and for Rome, in an annual ceremony—the Āptya and the Horatii are lastingly and repeatedly charged—in the former for the advantage of the sacrificers, in the latter for the Roman state—with the role of cleansing the stain caused inevitably, and renewed increasingly, by the blood of Indian sacrifices (and, analogically, by other causes), and by the blood of Roman battles.

We know the conclusion of the story of young Horace: at first condemned to death for the familial murder which, if left unpunished, would contaminate the city and, on this account, deserves the heavy designation *perduellio*, the young hero sees his sentence finally commuted to a purification. Says Livy:

> And so, that the flagrant murder might yet be cleansed away, by some kind of expiatory rite, *aliquo piaculo*, the father was commanded to make atonement for his son at the public cost, *pecunia publica*. He therefore offered certain piacular sacrifices, which were then handed down in the *gens Horatia*, and, erecting a beam across the street, to typify a yoke, he made his son pass under it, with covered head. It remains to this day, being restored from time to time at the state's expense, and is known as "the Sister's Beam," *sororium tigillum*. [1.26.12–13]

We shall never know the details of these expiations which the *gens Horatia* conserved, probably until its extinction. Dionysius says only that these were the expiations which customarily cleansed involuntary homicides, *οἷς νόμος τοὺς ἀκουσίους φόνους ἁγνίζεσθαι καθαρμοῖς*. It is the Roman state which has taken them over, in the light of history, by maintaining the beam and offering a sacrifice to it once a year. Every October first, in fact, a public sacrifice was celebrated at the *tigillum sororium* near the altars of Janus Curiatius and Juno Sororia. The ancients approximated Horace's passage beneath the Beam to the passage under the yoke which freed captives of war after their capitulation; and I myself observed, in 1942, that the rite calls to mind certain well-known modes of desacralization, of transfer from one world to another, of return from the supernatural or the exceptional to the ordinary and the human. On the other hand, the date of October first is remarkable: just as the *feriae Martis* of March first opens the month of the *Ecurria*, of the Salian festivals, of the *tubilustrium*, and, in practice, the month in which the armies set out on campaign, the Horatian ceremony of October first opens the second military month of the year, that of the *October equos*, of the *armilustrium*, the month of the armies' return. From these short but precious ritual indications the idea emerges that the legend of Horace—victorious, furious, criminal, and purified—served as myth at the annual ceremony which marked the end of the military season, in which the warriors of primitive Rome passed over from the domain of Mars unleashed to that of "Mars qui praeest paci," thus to Quirinus, thereby desacralizing themselves, and also cleansing themselves for their acts of violence in battle which, if not "involuntary," were at least necessary. Presumably the *gens Horatia*—whose name derives from the wife-and-essence of Quirinus—was the depository for the efficacious secret of this cleansing.

The liturgists of India, who are here our only guides, have differed in their application of the privilege of purifying, which Trita and his brothers, the Āptya, possessed. What interested this class of authors was not war but sacrifice, the casuistry of sacrificial techniques which, like those of war, require that there be destructions, acts of violence, necessary murders. At the end of the last century, Maurice Bloomfield devoted to "Trita, the Scapegoat of the Gods," a penetrating article[17] which Kasten Rönnow[18] has deservedly appreciated and reinforced, and which today, in our perspective, acquires its full value. Trita and the Āptya are purifiers, in charge of expiations, in a double sense: once, in the distant past of the Great Time, in the myth of the murder of the Tricephal; and still today, in the ever repeated sacrifices.

The two forms, the mythical introducing and justifying of the liturgical, both preceded by a "birth" of the Āptya, are found rejoined in the following text from *ŚatapathaBrāhmaṇa*:

1. Fourfold, namely, was Agni [fire] at first. Now that Agni whom they at first chose for the office of Hotr̥ priest passed away. He also whom they chose the second time passed away. He also whom they chose the third time passed away. Thereupon the one who still constitutes the fire in our own time concealed himself from fear. He entered into the waters. The gods, having discovered him, dragged him out of the waters. He spat upon the waters, saying, "Bespitten are ye who are an unsafe place of refuge, from whom they take me away against my will!" Thence sprung the Āptya deities, Trita, Dvita, and Ekata.

2. They roamed about with Indra, even as nowadays a Brahman follows

17. *American Journal of Philology* 17 (1896):430–37.

18. *Trita Āptya*, pp. 25–36.

in the train of a king. When he slew [*jaghāna*] Viśvarūpa, the three-headed son of Tvaṣṭṛ, they also knew of his going to be killed; and straightway Trita slew him [*jaghāna* again = became the murderer, by mystic transference of the guilt]. Indra, assuredly, was free from that [sin], for he was a god.

3. And the people thereupon said: "Let those be guilty of the sin who knew about his going to be killed!" "How?" they asked. "The sacrifice shall wipe it off you [shall transfer it to] them!" they said. Hence the sacrifice thereby wipes off upon them [the guilt or impurity incurred in the preparation of the offering], when they pour out for them the water with which the dish has been rinsed, and that in which he [the adhvaryu] has washed his fingers.

4. And the Āptyas then said: "Let us make this pass on beyond us!" "On whom?" they asked. "On him who shall make an offering without a dakṣiṇā [gift to the officiating priests]!" they said. Hence one must not make an offering without a dakṣiṇā; for the sacrifice wipes [the guilt] off upon the Āptyas, and the Āptyas wipe it off upon him who makes an offering without a dakṣiṇā.

5. ... That [rinsing water] he pours out [for each Āptya] separately: thus he avoids a quarrel among them. He makes it hot [previously]: thus it becomes boiled [drinkable] for them. He pours it out with the formula, "For Trita thee!" "For Dvita thee!" "For Ekata thee!" [1.2.3][19]

This sacerdotal text, in which Trita's role as murderer in the Tricephal episode has evidently been transformed into a sort of sin by intent, or rather by prescience, does afford a glimpse of a more ancient form—alluded to at the level of the hymns—in which Trita, by actually killing the Tricephal himself on Indra's behalf and with his encouragement, contracted the blood stain and was obliged to discharge it, to transfer it. As to this transfer, to which two hymns in the *AtharvaVeda* (6.112 and 113) make precise allusions, other brāhmaṇic texts present it as an operation in multiple stages, only the first of which involves the Āptya. Such is the case in *Maitrāyaṇī-Saṃhitā* 4.1.9. Furthermore, there is a specification in this text as to the nature of the "sacrificial stain" which the Āptya wipe away: it is the bloodshed, "the bloody [*krūra*] part or aspect" of the sacrifice. This detail should bring us closer to the original mythical form, since the decontaminating vocation of the Āptya first manifests itself on the occasion of a murder, the spilling of the blood of the Tricephal.

19. Citations from *ŚatapathaBrāhmaṇa* are from the translation by Julius Eggeling, *Sacred Books of the East*, vols. 12, 26, 41, 43, and 44 (1882–1900).

The gods did not find a person upon whom they might be able to wipe off from themselves the bloody part of the sacrifice [that is, any one upon whom they might transfer their guilt]. Then Agni spoke: "I will create for you him upon whom ye shall wipe off from yourselves the bloody part of the sacrifice." He threw a coal upon the waters; from that Ekata was born. [He threw] a second one [*dvitīyam*]; from that Dvita [was born]. [He threw] a third one [*tṛtīyam*]; from that Trita [was born]. . . . the gods came wiping themselves upon [Ekata, Dvita, Trita]; they [in turn] wiped themselves on one who was overtaken by the rising sun [i.e., one over whom the sun rises while he is asleep]; this one [wiped himself] upon one who was overtaken [asleep] by the setting sun; he upon one afflicted with brown teeth; he upon one with diseased nails; he upon one who had married a younger sister before the older one was married; he upon one whose younger brother had married before himself; he upon one who had married before his older brother; he upon one who had slain a man; he upon one who had committed an abortion. Beyond him who has committed an abortion the sin does not pass.[20]

Thus the Āptya are less the "scapegoats" of the sacrificing gods and the priests who imitate them than technicians of purification, in effect, at once both passive and active, who burden themselves with the sacrificial stain only, in turn, to "wipe it off" from themselves, to transfer it, through a few or through many intermediaries, onto such criminals as are unworthy of pity and utterly lost.

Beginning, it seems, from the myth of the Tricephal and the ritual usage which corresponds to it, the competence of the Āptya as technicians of purification soon involved them in other matters: different kinds of stains and even other human perils such as sins, bad omens, illnesses. *Ṛg Veda* 7.47 implores the gods to remove onto Trita Āptya "that which, overtly or secretly, has been wrongly done," *duṣkṛtám* (strophe 13), then asks the Dawn to bear away bad dreams, *duṣvápnyam* (strophes 14–18), toward Trita Āptya. The extant Avesta knows Θrita—the exact onomastic equivalent of Trita—(*Vidēvdāt* 10.1–4) only as the first of men who, thanks to hundreds, thousands, and myriads of medicinal herbs given him by Ahura Mazdā, repulsed

20. Translated by Maurice Bloomfield (see n. 4 above), p. 430. Concerning the parallel text of *Taitt.Brāhm.* 3.2.8.9–12, see Paul-Emile Dumont, *Journal of the American Oriental Society* 76 (1956):187–88. In the epic, "the partition of the stain" of Indra (Trita being eliminated) is depicted in diverse ways; see Edward Washburn Hopkins, *Epic Mythology* (1915), pp. 130–32. We find it also applied to the "terrible warrior" Batraz, who has conserved certain traits of the Scythian Ares (*ME* 1:570–75, and below, pp. 137–38), in the Nart epic of the northern Caucasus. See my *Légendes sur les Nartes* (1930), p. 73 (variant f).

illness, death, the varieties of fever, contagion, and all the calamities created by Anra Mainyu to counter the welfare of men. And then one recalls that,[21] according to *Dēnkart* 6.1.27, Θraētaona (Frētōn), once provided with the third of the Glory of Yima pertaining to the agricultural estate, not only conquered the Tricephal, but "taught men the medicine for the body which permits one to diagnose the plague and to drive off disease."[22]

It will probably be of some value to set in a double table, at the risk of some impoverishment and hardening of the materials, both the logical sequence of the moments in the drama, and the points of agreement and divergence between the Indian and the Roman versions of the plot (see table 1).

Some huge questions emerge when one reads such a table: What is the significance of the agreements and the divergences? What is the meaning itself, the "lesson" of the structure set in evidence? Let

21. See above, p. 18.

22. There is probably a survival or Θrita in the Srīt of several Pahlavi texts, "the seventh of seven brothers," a warrior and the servant of the legendary king Kayus (av. *Kavi Usan*, ved. *Kavi Uśanā*). Kayus commands him to go and kill the marvelous ox which, at every dispute, justly indicates the true frontier between Iran and Turan and thus keeps the king from making illegitimate annexations. The ox lectures the king's emissary severely, announcing to him that in the future, Zaratušt, "the most eager of all beings for justice," will make his wicked deed known. Srīt hesitates and returns to the king, making him confirm the order, which the king does. Then he kills the ox. But his soul is immediately filled with grief, and he presents himself again before the king, this time asking the king to kill him for his misdeed. "[Why] should I kill you, when it is not you who decided it?" "If you will not kill me, then I will kill you," responds Srīt. "Do not kill me, for I am the sovereign of the world [*dēhpat i gēhān*]." Srīt's pleas continue until the king tells him: "Go to such a place; there is a sorceress there in the form of a dog; she will kill you." Srīt goes to the place indicated, strikes the sorceress, who immediately divides herself in two. And so it goes until, when there are a thousand of her, "they" kill Srīt and tear him apart (*Zātspram* 12.8–25 [9–26 in the edition of Behramgore T. Anklesaria, Bombay, 1964]; translated by Marijan Molé, *La légende de Zoroastre selon les textes Pehlevis* [1957], pp. 166–67; cf. *Dēnkart* 7.2.62–66, and Molé, pp. 24–25 [text], pp. 25–27 [trans.]). Here one will recognize the "scapegoat" who kills following an order, like Trita in the Tricephal myth; and, again, as Trita does for Indra, Srīt takes the king's sin upon himself, expiating him by taking his place (but without the power to transfer the sin: it is not even said that it passes on to the sorceresses). What he expiates is the murder of the ox, just as, in the rite, Trita (with his brothers) expiates the cruel, bloody aspect of every animal sacrifice. The deed itself is simply more serious in Iranian than in Indian mythology, since the murder of the ox, even sacrificially, is condemned by Zoroastrianism. Moreover, the ox which is killed by Srīt is actually a veritable *iudex*: he "shows the right." Finally, Srīt is still presented as the youngest of a group of brothers, but because the etymology of his name, transcribed from the Avestan, was no longer apparent in Pahlavi, the number has been changed, "three" being replaced by "seven," a sacred number frequently used in Mesopotamia and Iran: he is said to be "the seventh of seven."

TABLE 1

India	Rome
1. (a) In the great rivalry between the gods and the demons, the life or the power of the gods being menaced by the Tricephal, (b) who is the "son of the friend" (*RV*) or the first cousin (*Br*) of the gods and, moreover, a brahman and the chaplain of the gods (*Br*),	1. (a) To settle the rivalry *de imperio* between the Romans and the Albans, the Horatii triplets fight against the Curiatii triplets, (b) who are their first cousins (D. Hal), or at least their future brothers-in-law (Livy, D. Hal).
(c) Trita, the "third" of the three Āptya brothers, urged on by Indra (*RV*), or Indra aided by Trita (*RV*), or else Indra alone (*RV*, *Br*), (d) kills the Tricephal and saves the gods.	(c) The lone survivor of the three brothers, the third Horatius, acting as Tullus' champion, (d) kills the Curiatii triplets and gives the empire to Rome,
2. (a) This murder, in that it is the murder of a kinsman or of a brahman, involves a stain; (b) Indra discharges it from himself onto Trita, onto the Āptya (*Br*), who ritually liquidate the stain (*Br*).	2. (a) without incurring a stain, thanks to a dialectical artifice which annuls the duties of kinship (D. Hal). (a′) But in the proud furor of victory, the third Horatius kills his sister, the desolate fiancée of one of the Curiatii; this murder of one's own kin involves crime and stain; (b) Tullus organizes the procedure which circumvents the legal punishment for the crime and sees to it that the ritual liquidation of the stain is assured by the Horatii themselves.
3. Ever since, the Āptya receive upon themselves and ritually liquidate the stain which every sacrifice entails (*Br*), due to the spilt blood, and, by extension, they absolve and liquidate other stains or mystical threats (*RV*, *AV*, *Br*).	3. Ever since, each year, at the end of the military season, at the expense of the state, the Horatii renew the ceremony of purification (probably for the benefit of all combatants, the Roman "spillers of blood").

us postpone these questions, for it is possible to establish a second table which, by analogy, will make the questions more precise and orient us toward their solution.

3

METTIUS FUFFETIUS AND NAMUCI

The features common to the Indian and to the Roman forms of the murder of the triple adversary, discussed in the previous chapter, invite an extension of the confrontation of the warrior king Tullus with the warrior god Indra to other incidents of their careers. But these careers are neither of the same scale nor of the same richness. Whereas Indra is the hero and the victor of a number of combats, Tullus, after the war settled by the duel of the Horaces and the Curiaces, has no further tasks than the definitive, highly picturesque liquidation of Alba, and a Sabine war, drab and with no incidents of note. But by a chance which is perhaps not a chance at all, rather an indication that the path we are following is reliable, the liquidation of Alba lends itself to a structural analysis of the same type as the preceding and to a comparison with another of Indra's exploits, the second, it would seem, in importance and notoriety—the liquidation of Namuci.

It is now seventy-five years since Maurice Bloomfield[1] underscored the fact that the *R̥gVeda* contains unquestionable allusions to two significant features of traditions known to the *Brāhmaṇa*. On the one hand, it tells us that Indra "severed the head of Namuci with the foam" (*RV* 7.14.13 = *Vājasan.Saṃh.* 19.71); on the other, that Sarasvatī and the Aśvin aided Indra when he drank, to the point of nausea, of the evil alcoholic beverage known as *súrā* (*RV* 10.131.4–5 = *V.S.* 10.33–34; 20.76–77). These indications—on the basis of which it is more than imprudent to reconstruct, as Karl F. Geldner has done,

1. Maurice Bloomfield, "Contributions to the Interpretation of the Veda, pt. 1, The Story of Indra and Namuci," *Journal of the American Oriental Society*, 15 (1893):143–63.

a complete version—suffice at least to show that at the time of the redaction of the hymns the myth of the murder of Namuci was well known; it was no doubt appreciably close to its traditional, more or less constant form, attested from the *Brāhmaṇa* on, which we shall now proceed to analyze.

Namuci, as early as the *R̥gVeda*, is qualified as a demon (*ásura, āsurá*; *dā́sa*; *māyín*) and named in some groups of demons. However, Bloomfield notes: "As clearly as this evidence places Namuci in the position of a natural enemy of Indra, ultimately to be slain by him, there is on the other hand conclusive proof that for some reason or other a friendly agreement, in the nature of an alliance, truce, or compact, existed between the two prior to the final falling out."[2] In his commentary on *VājasaneyiSaṃhitā* 10.34, Mahīdhara, for example, says that the asura Namuci was *indrasya sakhā*, "the socius of Indra," and in *Mahābhārata* 9.42.30[3] Indra, having in the previous śloka formed a friendship, a social bond, with him (*tenendraḥ sakhyam akarot*), calls him *asuraśreṣṭha sakhe*, "the best of the asura, my *socius*." Their accord is based upon an agreement: Indra and Namuci, as many texts say, *sam adadhātām*, "have made an agreement" (*sam dhā-*: cf. Greek *συντίθεσθαι εἰρήνην, φιλίαν*; *συνθήκη*). For example, *MaitrāyaṇīSaṃhitā* 4.3.4 says that at first the two had fought, or rather that Indra had tried to trap Namuci without succeeding, and that Namuci had proposed: *sakhāyā asāva*, "let us both be *socii*!" In response to this, Indra promised: "I will not kill you [*nā'haṃ haniṣyāmi*]!" And he added: "I am going to agree to an agreement with you [*saṃdhām te saṃdadhai*]; that I will kill you neither by day nor by night, with neither the dry nor the wet [*yathā tvā na divā hanāni na naktaṃ na śuṣkena nārdreṇa*]!" Such is the short form, and probably the primitive one, of the pledge. It has soon expanded: in *ŚatapathaBrāhmaṇa* 12.7.3.1, for instance, Indra relates that he is bound by oath (*śepāno'smi*) to kill Namuci neither by day nor by night, neither with staff nor with bow, neither with palm nor with fist, neither with the dry nor with the wet. As to the circumstances which precede the pact, these are variable: either, as we shall see, there was a struggle, and it is Namuci, the stronger, who makes the

2. Ibid., pp. 146–47.

3. The *Mahābhārata* is cited according to the Poona edition, but other variants of the text have sometimes been preferred.

proposition; or else, in the epic, it is Indra, finding himself inferior, who takes the initiative. In either case, the two personages are henceforth bound to their agreement.

One day Namuci abuses the trust which has resulted from this agreement—an incident already alluded to in *R̥gVeda* 10.131.4–5. Taking advantage of the state of inferiority which has been forced upon Indra by Tvaṣṭr̥, who was enraged by the murder of his son the Tricephal, it seems that Namuci puts the finishing touch to Indra with the help of the evil liquor *sūra*, stripping him of all his advantages: force, virility, soma, nourishment (*ŚatapathaBrāhmaṇa* 12.7.1.10–11).

In distress, Indra addresses himself to the canonical divinities of the third function—the function of health, fecundity, and abundance —that is, he calls upon the twin Aśvin and the goddess Sarasvatī; *R̥gVeda* 10.131.4–5 alludes to this also. These divinities intervene in two capacities: first the Aśvin, who are the healers, and Sarasvatī, the true "remedy," care for Indra and restore his force, after which they demand a recompense (this being the origin of the sacrifice of three animals known as the *Sautrāmaṇī*[4]); second, informed by Indra of the agreement which protects Namuci, the same divinities, playing the role that the *kluge Rätsellöser* plays in many folktales, teach him how not to uphold it while all the time fully upholding it: he can assail Namuci at dawn, which is neither day nor night, and with foam, which is neither dry nor wet. Or else it is they who fashion the weapon of foam, as in *ŚatapathaBrāhmaṇa* 12.7.3.3: "The Aśvin and Sarasvatī then poured out foam of water [to serve] as a thunderbolt, saying, 'It is neither dry nor moist.'"

Provided with this strange weapon, "at the departure of night, but before the rising of the sun" (*Śat.Brāhm.*, ibid.), Indra kills Namuci without warning, "while walking with his *socius*," the *Mahābhārata* will say. The agreement is thus eluded, not violated. And, in order to underline sufficiently that it has been upheld, the act of murder is noted with preferential treatment, as early as the *R̥gVeda*, by the use of unusual verbs, proper to this adventure: "to churn" (*manth*-: *RV* 5.30.8; 6.20.6), "to cause to turn" (causative of *vr̥t*-: 5.30.7; with

4. See Dumézil, *Tarpeia*, pp. 123–24, and *La religion romaine archaïque* (1966; to be published in translation by the University of Chicago Press; hereafter cited as *RRA*), pp. 238–41.

the preverb *ud*: 8.14.13). It is difficult to specify the nature of this churning, or spinning, but, as Bloomfield remarks with humor: "Why not? The act of taking off a head with the foam of the waters is correspondingly unusual. The root *manth* means 'rub, churn'; the conception that the head was churned off in a mass of foam offers quite as natural a picture as any other means of taking off a head with foam."[5]

Indra is thus disencumbered of his perfidious enemy. Has he acted well? The exacting consciences of his faithful worshipers, the priests, have taken up this question and resolved it with a severe turn, one which may evoke surprise. Again Bloomfield remarks judiciously: "A Western reader of this story would not easily repress the feeling that the artful device of the gods in slaying Namuci 'with the foam of the waters' was a permissible evasion of the compact, inasmuch as Namuci had not played Indra fair. Some of the *Brāhmaṇa* and the *Mahābhārata* take the occasion to moralize, to accuse Indra of deceiving a friend."[6] In fact, it has become a commonplace in the literature for the blame to fall upon the god. In *TaittirīyaBrāhmaṇa* 1.7.8, the severed head of Namuci expresses the current opinion itself when, pursuing the murderer, it cries out: "*Mitradruh*, liar, betrayer of friendship!" In the epic, it is none other than the odious Duryodhana who, in order to persuade his father to lay a trap, under the pretext of friendship, for the virtuous Pāṇḍava brothers, supports his argument by referring to Indra's treatment of Namuci and brazenly affirms that it aroused universal approbation (*Mahābhārata* 2.50.20). But Duryodhana is not an authority on matters of morality.

Such are the three moments of what one can hardly call a victory; in any case, it is a victory quite different from that over the Tricephal. The narrative is built entirely around the notion of *saṃdhā*, "agreement." It displays a diplomatic casuistry in accord with the best models of all times, distinguishing the letter from the spirit. And it is exhibited in a short drama: Indra, at first the victim of a definite disloyalty, rather than denounce the pact, holds to it instead, the better to surprise his partner, who suspects nothing, and to execute him.

5. Bloomfield, p. 157.
6. Ibid., p. 160.

The same casuistry of the pact underpins the second episode in the career of Tullus Hostilius, after the story of Horace and the Curiaces. The "liquidation" of the dictator of Alba and of Alba itself are now at stake. The narrative, outlined below, is built entirely around a sort of depravation of *fides* and of *foedus*, and displays dramatically a theory of legitimate duplicity.

The Alban dictator, Mettius Fuffetius, is himself the one who has planned, by an agreement drawn up with Tullus, the duel between the Horaces and the Curiaces, and has accepted its consequences. After the defeat of the Alban champions, in conformity with the agreement, he placed himself at the command of the Roman king, who confirmed him in his rank and ordered him to hold himself ready, saying that he would require his services in case war broke out against Veii (Livy 1.26.1).

From this moment on, Mettius Fuffetius changes character. Livy (1.27.1–2; cf. Dionysus 3.23.3) shows him seeking to regain the popularity he has lost among his own countrymen for having left the destiny of the state in the hands of only three men. His *recta consilia* having proved unsuccessful, he turns to *praua*. He desires *in pace bellum*, a confused state of affairs, particularly detestable to the land of the *fetiales*, the land which distinguished so carefully between Mars and Quirinus. And so he adopts a political attitude in which he keeps up the appearance of a *socius* while planning treason, *suis per speciem societatis proditionem reseruat*. From behind the scenes, he induces the Veians and the Fidenates to go to war against Rome, while he himself joins ranks with the Roman army, appearing as a loyal ally. On the battlefield, where he occupies the right flank, facing the Fidenates, what will he do? He betrays without betraying, thinking, as one might say, "just so nobody sees." He withdraws to high ground and observes the course of events, placing Tullus and the Romans in mortal danger while biding his time so as to throw in his lot with the victor (Livy, ibid., 5–6: *Albano non plus animi erat quam fidei. Nec manere ergo nec transire aperte ausus, sensim ad montes succedit. Inde ubi satis subisse sese ratus est, erigit totam aciem, fluctuansque animo, ut tereret tempus, ordines explicat: consilium erat, qua fortuna rem daret, ea inclinare uires*).

Tullus, however, saves the day by his presence of mind, first of all by ordering his cavalry to raise their spears to conceal the Alban maneuver from the foot soldiers, thus avoiding any demoralizing effect, and, in addition, by loudly shouting, so as to alarm the enemy, that Mettius has acted by his command in order to carry out an outflanking maneuver. But he also addresses himself to the gods: he vows to establish a new college of Salian priests, these of Quirinus, and to build temples to Pavor and Pallor (Livy 1.27.7; the authenticity of Pavor and Pallor is rightly suspected). Now Dionysus of Halicarnassus, apparently for reasons of literary balance, has transferred this vow to a later war, one which would otherwise be lacking in all color, just as it is in Livy. But Dionysius is more explicit and more satisfactory with respect to the names of the gods (3.32.4; cf. 2.70.1–2): here Tullus promises to establish the *Salii Agonales*, that is, the *Salii* of Quirinus, in opposition to those of Mars allegedly founded under Numa,[7] and to establish public festivals to Saturn and to Ops: thus, in each case, concerning himself with divinities who clearly patronize the various aspects of the third function.[8] And so Tullus and the Romans are saved.

In the face of the Roman victory, thinking that Tullus has not noticed his betrayal, Mettius makes his troops descend (Livy 1.28.1). According to Dionysius (3.26.1), he makes himself truly detestable at the end of the battle by doubling his zeal in destroying the vanquished Fidenates. In either case, Tullus pretends to be taken in, congratulates the Alban, and speaks to him with friendship (*gratulatur, alloquitur benigne*). It is his turn to play the part of the *fides*: he brings the two allied armies together into one camp, ostensibly to perform the lustral sacrifices of the morrow. At dawn, *ubi illuxit*, he convokes them to a *contio*; moved by curiosity, without defiance and unarmed, the Albans come up to the front ranks to hear him; meanwhile, the armed Roman troops, whose centurions have received previous orders, surround them (Livy 1.28.2–3). In Dionysius (3.27.3), the stage settings for the *fides* are more clearly delineated: Tullus invites the Alban dictator and his leading officers to come before him, as if he is about to honor them. Then he rises to speak.

It is at this point that vengeance takes its toll. Tullus denounces

7. See the important article of Lucien Gerschel, "Saliens de Mars et Saliens de Quirinus," *Revue de l'histoire des religions* 138 (1950):145–51.

8. See "Les cultes de la *regia*, les trois fonctions et la triade Juppiter Mars Quirinus," *Latomus* 13 (1954):129–39; *RRA*, pp. 177–79.

Mettius' treason and has him seized; then he says to him: "If you were capable of learning, yourself, to keep *fides* and abide by treaties, you should have lived that I might teach you this; as it is, since your disposition is incurable, you shall yet by your punishment teach the human race to hold sacred the obligations you have violated. Accordingly, just as a little while ago your heart was divided [*ancipitem*] between the states of Fidenae and Rome, so now you shall give up your body to be torn two ways" (Livy 1.28.9). Mettius then dies by a truly dreadful torture, one which conforms symbolically to his conduct: his body is torn apart by two teams of horses pulling in opposite directions (Livy, ibid. 10). Then the Roman army demolishes the city of Alba.

Tullus and Rome are thus rid of a perfidious enemy. But has Tullus acted well? As to the principle behind the act, the Roman annalist answers without hesitation: there is only one traitor in the affair, and that is the Alban; the ruse by which Tullus has had him neutralized, seized, and punished, is legitimate. Rome can only congratulate herself for having had so ingenious a leader, and Mettius is only shameless when, on being delivered to the executioner, he becomes indignant, cries out loudly, and invokes the pact which he himself has annulled by violating it (Dionysus 3.30.5: τὰς συνθήκας ἀνακαλούμενον, ἃς αὐτὸς ἐξελέγχθη παρασπονδῶν). Whatever blame Tullus incurs is relegated to a single detail, which is no more than incidental: Tullus has sinned, but right at the end, by an excess of cruelty, in the odious form of punishment he inflicted on Mettius. Livy writes: "All eyes were turned away from so dreadful a sight. Such was the first and last punishment among the Romans of a kind that disregards the laws of humanity. In other cases we may boast that with no nation have milder punishments found favor" (ibid., 11).

As to the meaning of the *exemplum* presented in this piece of epic, we see, from beginning to end, that the two leaders have rivaled each other in duplicity and in playing deceitfully with *fides*: the diplomatic duplicity of Mettius, bringing about *in pace bellum*, associating these opposites in a different manner but just as sadly as they have been associated in our own day in certain episodes of the "cold war"; the military duplicity of the same Mettius, who withdrew from his post without passing over to the enemy, *nec manere nec transire aperte ausus, fluctuans animo*; in response, the duplicity in protocol and matters of ceremony on the part of Tullus, lavishing the marks of honor and friendship upon the one who has secretly betrayed him, the one whom he is about to surprise and crush; and finally the material and symbolic "duplicity" of a torture which tears the body in two in imitation of the soul.

How necessary is it to delineate the close parallelism in both structure and meaning between this episode and the myth of Namuci, between the variations upon *fides* or *συνθήκη* and the Indian variations upon *saṃdhā*?

One point must again be emphasized: there is a sin on both sides; but between the *Brāhmaṇa* and the Roman accounts, the same distinc-

TABLE 2

India	Rome
1. After the initial hostilities, Indra and Namuci make an agreement. They will be *sakhāyaḥ*, friends. On this occasion, Indra lays himself under the particular obligation to kill Namuci "neither by day nor by night, neither with the dry nor with the wet."	1. After the initial hostilities, in conformity with a previous agreement, Tullus and Mettius are *socii*. Tullus confirms Mettius as leader of the Albans and the latter receives the particular order to aid Tullus in an upcoming battle.
2. (a) Thanks to the trusting familiarity born of this agreement, by surprise, under cover of drunkenness, Namuci strips Indra of all his forces.	2. (a) Thanks to this agreement, catching Tullus by surprise in the midst of battle, Mettius breaks his trust, stripping him of half his military forces and placing him in mortal danger.
(b) Indra addresses himself to the canonical gods of the third function, the goddess Sarasvatī and the twin Aśvin, who restore his force to him,	(b) Tullus addresses himself to the canonical divinities of the third function, Quirinus [Ops and Saturn], who apparently give him the means to restore the situation and achieve victory.
(c) and tell him the means to surprise or to kill Namuci with the help of the agreement and without violating it ("foam," "dawn"); and he acts accordingly.	3. (a) Acting as if he respects the agreement and does not suspect the preceding treachery, Tullus surprises Mettius unarmed, and has him killed.
3. By a bizarre technique, depending upon ambiguities, employed only this once, and adapted to the instrument which allows Indra to get around the agreement (churning, turning the head in the foam), Namuci is decapitated.	(b) By a horrible technique, employed only once in Roman history, which transfers onto the body the duplicity with which he has abused the agreement, Mettius is dragged apart, divided in two.

tion can be perceived that has been perceived earlier in connection with the murder of the triple adversary: in India, we recall, it is the murder itself that causes the stains of Indra and of Trita, whereas it leaves Horace and Tullus innocent: the additional murder of Horace's sister is the act that leaves the young hero stained with sin.

Here it is just the same: the sin of Indra, recognized and deplored by ancient Indian authors, lies in the very ruse by which Indra gets around the agreement, in the very act of getting around it. These authors are less sensitive, as we have seen Bloomfield remark, to the fact that Namuci was the first to act treacherously than they are to the fact that Indra has made a commitment which has meaning only if it amounts to an unconditional and total renunciation of violence.

The sin of Tullus, recognized and deplored by Livy, lies elsewhere: Tullus was justified, even morally, in punishing a traitor and in meeting duplicity with duplicity. His offense began only with his cruelty when he inflicted an excessive, inhuman punishment on the guilty party.

Thus, in the Roman version it is not in the essential, in the center of the episode, that the fault emerges, but in a supplementary, peripheral, ideologically superfluous detail. If one believes, as I do, that the Indian accounts are more reliable on this point, simpler and stronger in tenor, one will admit that in the Roman version there was a shift of the points on which the blame was fixed. Perhaps, no less for the conqueror of the Curiaces than for the murderer of Mettius, this retouching resulted from the national, even nationalist, character assumed by the epic: Rome could not consider two murders committed in her own most obvious interest as sins, for these would have soiled Rome herself; it was necessary that the exploit of Horace and the ruse of Tullus, to the degree that these two personages saved and represented Rome, should be depicted as entirely "good" deeds. The notion of "sin" which tradition had probably attached to the prototypes, to the pre-Roman forms of these two acts, was not thereby lost in the shuffle; it was only transferred to points at which neither Horace nor Tullus implicated Rome, where the one gave way to his pride and anger, where the other gave vent to his cruel nature, transforming a necessary execution into a revolting torture.

In the history of the reign of Tullus, there is not only a succession, but a causal bond, between the episode of the Curiaces and that of Mettius: the Curiace triplets and, through them, Alba, are defeated by the third Horace, and this leads directly to the exchange of fraudulent uses of the *fides* by Mettius and Tullus, ending in the ruin of Mettius and, through him, of Alba. The connection between the two episodes is that Mettius seeks revenge for the defeat of the Curiaces. Has Indian tradition a counterpart to this interrelated body of material?

Where interrelation is concerned, the testimony of the Vedic hymns will always be evasive. The *R̥gVeda* is not, indeed cannot be, narrative. Assuming that traditions—the so-called *itihāsa*, the "fifth Veda"—are known, the authors of the poems who give praise to Indra sometimes make multiple references to the most diverse parts of this tradition, sometimes exalt one particular point, but they do not trouble themselves to present an episode in full, or to establish, between their allusions to several episodes, a logical or chronological nexus; they do not even confine themselves to a single variant, as we have seen in the case of Trita, or balk at contradictions in the same hymn: what does it matter, when all the versions of these grand events work together for the glory, the "increasing," of the god? One must not expect a document of a special type to provide information it cannot give.

Despite their later date, the *Brāhmaṇa* and the epics are in this respect the better texts. To be sure, the setting, the detail, and the spirit of these adventures may have been brought up to date, but, when it comes to considering the dogmatic or dramatic representations, the authors are attentive to the coherence, to the causal connections in an episode, and sometimes to those between several episodes. Certain "links" are repeated with too great a consistency from variant to variant, no matter how appreciably different these may be, for them not to rely on an authentic tradition. Thus, whereas the natural pointillism of the hymns does not openly reveal these "links," it does not on that account authorize a denial of their existence. Is such a "link," then, to be found in the body of material that we are dealing with here?

The Brāhmaṇic tradition has not established a regular connection between the Tricephal and Namuci episodes: each is often recited on its own. Nevertheless, certain texts do declare a logical sequence: in the *ŚatapathaBrāmaṇa* account cited above (12.7.1–9 and 10–13),[9] if Namuci can strip his "friend" Indra of his powers, it is because Indra has previously been enfeebled by Tvaṣṭṛ, the Tricephal's father, who sought to avenge his son. In a number of epic and purāṇic versions of the second episode, Indra's victim sometimes keeps the name Namuci, sometimes receives that of Vṛtra.[10] In the latter case, the conflict is very frequently presented as a logical consequence, even more direct, of the Tricephal's defeat: enraged at the murder of his son, Tvaṣṭṛ engenders or magically creates Vṛtra, a very powerful being, to avenge him, and it is with Vṛtra that Indra concludes the pact, the same pact as with Namuci, often enriched with new, colorful clauses which he gets around in the same manner. We will soon rediscover this correlation in an even greater structure. Is it possible that, under one form or another, the most ancient Indian mythology had already established a temporal and causal succession between these two enormously consequential acts of Indra, and that the two lessons complemented each other there as they did in the deeds of the warrior king of Rome?

9. See *Tarpeia*, pp. 123–24.
10. See already Léon Feer, "Vritra et Namoutchi dans le Mahābhārata," *Revue de l'histoire des religions* 14 (1886):291–307.

4

THE WARRIOR FUNCTION AND ITS RELATIONS TO THE OTHER TWO FUNCTIONS

A great number and variety of questions arise from a reading of the "parallel lives" of Indra and Tullus and the tables that summarize them. Here only the principal ones need detain us.

For one thing, no great emphasis can be placed on the interrelationships of *fact* and *fiction* in this fragment of the Roman legend of origins: few authors, it seems, are inclined to seek a historic basis for the Alban war or, more generally, even for the reign of Tullus. Even interpreters whose methods and views differ considerably from those expressed here have remarked how improbable it is that the "Romans" of the Palatine huts, so close to their beginnings, would have been in a situation to take the lead in the politics of Latium, to provoke, to humiliate, and to supersede the old metropolis. Is it to be assumed that these traditions rest upon posterior events, simply set back several generations, transposed to the legendary reign of Tullus? Perhaps, but this is only an unverifiable hypothesis and in any case tells us little. The material furnished by this historical basis, if indeed the latter existed, would have been so thoroughly rethought and cast along the lines of the traditional ideology of the second function, itself constitutionally bound up with the figure of Tullus, that it would interest us as no more than dramatic expression of this ideology. This structure itself, then, such as it is, must be interpreted before all else.[1]

The complementary meaning of the two episodes, in Roman as in Indian tradition, appears most clearly and most simply when the personages of the second function are viewed from the perspective

1. See *ME* 1:9–10, 261–62, 281–82, 432.

of their relationships to the leading concepts and personages of the first and the third function.

In the murder of the Tricephal and the murder of Namuci, the post-Vedic Indian literature—the hymns purposely do not fully reveal the views of their authors—acclaims two neccessary acts and denounces two stains: after the second, Indra is *mitradruh*, "betrayer of friendship," after the first, he is *brahmahan*, charged with "brahmanicide," and at the same time murderer of a kinsman or some variety of "socius." We see at once that these various themes all involve assaults upon the "Mitra half" of sovereignty: the brahman and the chaplain are people of Mitra, who is himself the prototype of the priest alongside of Varuṇa, the cosmic king; equally, the social ties—kinship by blood or by marriage, treaties and friendships, all the key notions of the two narratives—also fall under the jurisdiction of Mitra or his assistant, Aryaman.

Even though they are fully relegated to peripheral points in the two accounts, the faults committed by the young Horace in the first and by king Tullus in the second belong to the same ideological province: Horace, though no longer guilty for spilling the blood of his cousins, becomes so by spilling the blood of a still closer relation; Tullus, though no longer guilty for having responded to the treason of Mettius with treason of his own, becomes so for having inflicted an excessive and terrible punishment upon him, that is, for having abused *justice* and offended *humanity*, two fundamental "Mitrian" values or, in the Roman context, "Pompilian" ones. As we know, the bond between the just and good Numa Pompilius and the terrible and capricious Romulus forms a close parallel, on the plane of legend, to the Vedic bond between the gods Mitra and Varuṇa.

In the background of the second Roman account, there is, besides, a sin that is more general and more serious, one the Roman historians have been careful not to dwell upon, but which has occasionally troubled some consciences, the same that were deeply disturbed also by the sack of Corinth: *Roma interim crescit Albae ruinis*. Rome, under the reign of Tullus, and Tullus, accounting for Rome, destroyed Alba, the mother of Rome. To be sure, when Dionysius has Mettius justify to his officers the treason which he is about to commit, the discourse abounds in Greek rhetoric and Greek conceptions: that is how we must take it when he says, for example, that Rome was the first to violate more than an agreement, more than oaths—namely, the fundamentals of the "universal law of both Greeks and Barbarians," which urges that fathers shall rule over their children and mother-cities over their colonies (3.23.19). But there is no doubt that, since before the time when the canon of royal history was established, probably between 350 and 270, and perhaps because of a tenuous but firm memory of a historic reality, the Romans sought their ancestry in Alba, and took care both in politics and in religion to present themselves in the Latin confederation as the natural heirs of the Albans. The annalist's reassuring, almost noble-minded account relieved the scruples but did not alter the fact. From the heights of his tribunal, Livy's Tullus can thus proclaim:

> "May prosperity, favor, and fortune be with the Roman people and myself, and with you, Men of Alba! I purpose to bring all the Alban people over to Rome, to grant citizenship to their commons, to enroll the nobles in the senate, to make one city and one state. As formerly from one people the Alban nation was divided into two, so let us be reunited into one." [1.28.7]

Nevertheless, when the unifying troops arrive in condemned Alba, what meets them is a *tacita maestitia*. It is not by chance that the royal legend has conferred this mission—so painful and, one may add, somewhat *impia*—upon Tullus. The anachronism justifies itself ideologically: such an enterprise could have been attributed neither to Ancus Martius, the king of defensive wars, not to the pious and peaceful Numa; and would it not also have run counter to the spirit of Romulus, who, before departing for his Palatine adventure, had restored his grandfather to the Alban throne? Indeed, the pure warrior, the almost irreligious Tullus, was the only one qualified for such a task.

Symmetrical to this opposition of a god or hero of the second function to the Mitra- (or Dius Fidius-) half of the function of sovereignty is an opposition, well attested by other myths, to its Varuṇa- (or Jupiter-) half. Certain hymns of the *R̥g Veda*—from which the historicists have drawn imprudent conclusions as to the respective ages of Indra and Varuṇa, whereas the hymns only put the antithesis between the functions in dramatic form and push it to extremes—

show Indra either defying the magical sovereign, or inviting him in a superior tone to place himself under Indra's laws, in the manner that an Eddic poem in dialogue, the *Hárbarðsljóð*, from which chronological consequences have also been drawn with no more justification, presents a flood of defiances and ironies exchanged between the magical sovereign Óðinn and the brutal Nordic divine champion Þórr. Perhaps it is a tradition of the same kind that led the Zoroastrian reformers to make Indra into the archdemon opposed to the archangel Aša Vahišta, "the Best Order," that is, to the moral sublimation of *Varuna. In Roman mythology, the end of Tullus' career conserves a trace of this antagonism in the terrible revenge that the great master of magic, Jupiter, exacts upon the warrior king who has flouted him for so long:

Not long after this Rome was afflicted with a pestilence. This caused a reluctance to bear arms, yet no respite from service was allowed by the warlike king, who believed, besides, that the *iuuenes* were healthier in the field than in the home, until he himself contracted a lingering illness. Then that haughty spirit was so broken, with the breaking of his health, that he who had hitherto thought nothing less worthy of a king than to devote his mind to sacred rites, suddenly became a prey to all sorts of superstitions great and small, and even filled the minds of the people with religious scruples. Men were now agreed in wishing to recall the conditions which had obtained under King Numa, believing that the only remedy left for their ailing bodies was to procure peace and forgiveness from the gods. The king himself, so tradition tells, in turning over the commentaries of Numa discovered there certain occult sacrifices performed in honour of Jupiter Elicius, and devoted himself in secret to those rites; but the ceremony was improperly undertaken or performed, and not only was no divine manifestation vouchsafed, but in consequence of the wrath of Jupiter, who was provoked by his faulty observance, he was struck by a thunderbolt and consumed in the flames of his house. [Livy 1.31.5–8]

In the theater of the myths, such are the relations of the canonical representatives of the warrior function to those of sovereignty: disregard or defiance. Since the service of the myths is to define sharply, by magnification, the distinctive features of the ideological concepts and of the figures of the theology, the antagonisms between some of these concepts or functions must, when it comes to myth, naturally be translated into the terms of clashes, indeed of war, in the same way as the likenesses and logical affinities between some others become alliances or family ties. But let us not suppose that these spirited definitions exhaust the understanding that the faithful had of their gods. They do not even account for what is essential.

While the myths have rudely taught that Indra for example, is "altogether other" than Mitra and Varuṇa and that contracts and laws are not his proper concern, practical piety and ritual strategy hasten to return things to their place, that is, to make these divinities, happily so diverse, collaborate for the best interests of the world, of society, and of the individual. The eloquent verses of *R̥g Veda* 10.89 cast a reassuring light on the disquieting Indra of the Tricephal and Namuci myths:

8. You, Indra, who cleverly make the debts[2] be paid, are a clever requiter; as the sword (upon) the limbs, so do you cut asunder the falsehoods (of whoever) violates, as people violate the alliance of friendship, the laws of Mitra and Varuṇa.

9. Against the wicked ones who violate Mitra, and the agreements, and Varuṇa, against these foes, o male Indra, bull-like, fire-colored, sharpen a strong murder!

12. . . . Like the stone hurled from the sky, strike with your most fiery rage the betrayer of friendship!

To be *drógharnitra* already counted as one of the greatest sins of the Indo-Iranians, and, in the Avesta, the *Miθro.druǰ* is both he who lies to Miθra and he who breaks contracts. Here we find the object of Indra's vengeful acts justly designated. We are far from the myth where it is Indra himself whom the severed head of Namuci can stigmatize with the name *mitradruh*.

The preceding reflections have set the stage for understanding the inverse relationship which necessitates that Indra and Tullus, in their respective difficulties, have recourse to the auxiliary services of the third function.

The reader will remember the essential significance of the Āptya and the Horatii: heroes who for the sake of the god or the king undertake the act which involves or occasions a stain, and who then, passively or actively, have the task of cleansing and continuing to cleanse, throughout all history, all such stains as are like their own. Thus the

2. Or "faults": *r̥ṇá* has both meanings; see Louis Renou, *Etudes védiques et pāṇinéennes* 16 (1967):123.

Āptya bear the qualities of water in their name, their Iranian counterparts the Āθwya are the representatives of rural prosperity, and the *gens Horatia* draws its name from Hora, the partner of the canonical god of the third function, Quirinus.

Similarly, in the second episode, at the moment of distress, when the one has lost his own physical forces and the other half of his military forces, Indra and Tullus, seeking to restore the situation, turn one to Sarasvatī and the Aśvin, the other to Quirinus (and, if we reinstate in the Alban war the vow that Dionysius of Halicarnassus transferred to the Sabine war, then also to Ops and Saturn), that is, once again, to the canonical gods of the third function. In a situation that resembles Tullus' plight in many features, Romulus, according to legend, had made his appeal to Jupiter.

The essential features of this relationship between the second and the third functions have been indicated in my 1947 essay devoted to the Roman sacrifice of the *suouetaurilia* (a boar, a ram, and a bull offered to Mars) and the parallel Vedic sacrifice of the *sautrāmaṇī* (a goat offered to the Aśvin, a ram to Sarasvatī, a bull to Indra)—a sacrifice for which the adventure with Namuci serves as the etiological myth.[3] In the broader perspective that we have now attained, we can orient these remarks more precisely and summarize them in a few words: in the same circumstances in which he violates the rules of the first function and ignores its gods, the god or king of the second function mobilizes into his service the gods of the third function or some heroes born within it. And it is through these purifiers, healers, and givers of substance that he either hopes to escape, and, in effect, does escape from the grievous consequences of his useful but blameworthy deeds, or to recover the forces he had lost because of a false ally's duplicity. In other words, in these ambiguous situations the third function—itself paying no great attention to the first—is put, or puts itself, at the disposal of the second, in accordance with its rank and nature.

3. See *Tarpeia*, pp. 154–58; *RRA*, pp. 238–41.

5

THE INDO-EUROPEAN HERITAGE

Now that we have depicted the parallel ideological settings for the legend of Tullus and a segment of the mythology of Indra, we are faced with a more difficult problem: What import should be attributed to the correspondences, to what extent is a common Indo-European heritage to be presumed?

It is difficult to believe that, in the functionally homologous personages of Indra and Tullus, chance conjoined two complex episodes which, here and there, present one direction and so many common elements. In contrast, all is explained quite readily if we admit that the Indians and the Romans—once again, as in the parallels between the conceptions of the sovereign gods Varuṇa and Mitra and the founding kings Romulus and Numa—conserved one and the same ideological datum, the Indians setting it in scenes of the Great Time, as fragments of the cosmic, supramundane history, the Romans in episodes of Roman time, as events of the national annals.

Note that we are dealing with one and the same "ideological datum" and not with "mythical datum." Indeed, it is through the ideology, and through the *lesson* that we have been able to draw from the various scenes, that the correspondences appear rigorous and striking, and not through the details of the narratives, which are very different on each side. Mettius has certainly never been a demon like Namuci; neither have the Curiaces been a tricephalic monster! What the Indian and Roman thinkers have maintained in clearcut form, are:

(1) the idea of a necessary victory, a victory in single combat in which, inspired by the grand master of the warrior function (either king or god) and for his sake, "a third hero triumphs over a triple adversary"—with stain implicit in the exploit, and with a purification

of the "third" and of the society which he represents, so that he finds himself to be the specialist, the agent, and the instrument of this purification, a sort of scapegoat after having been a champion;

(2) the idea of a victory brought off not by combat but by a surprise which follows upon a betrayal, betrayal and surprise succeeding one another under the pretext and within the context of a solemn agreement of friendship, with the result that the surprise act of revenge includes a disquieting note.

This is the doctrine, moral and political, the piece of second-function ideology, which the Indo-European stewards of the collective memory and thought—probably priests of some sort—and their Vedic and Latin heirs continued to understand and depict in dramatic scenes. The personages, the places, the interests, and the ornaments of these scenes might renew themselves, and the literary levels as well, sometimes epic or history, sometimes phantasmagoria. The motivation remains the same. And it is the sum of such motivations, well articulated, that everywhere constitutes the moral conscience of a people.

Here we have a situation fully comparable to one that we have outlined several times in connection with the Roman and Scandinavian forms in which the pair One-Eyed and One-Handed has come down to us.[1] In the scene where Horatius the Cyclops alone holds the Etruscan army at bay and saves Rome, in the twin scene where the other savior of Rome, Mucius, becomes the Left-Handed as a result of burning his right hand before the Etruscan king as a gesture which guarantees a false affirmation, the narrative is entirely different from the scenes of the Scandinavian epic in which Óðinn the One-Eyed god, paralyzes the combatants, and the mythical scene in which the god Týr loses his right hand in the mouth of the Fenris wolf, as security for a false affirmation, in order to save the gods. And yet the motivations for these two groups of actions are the same. The connection between the diptych of actions or intentions and the diptych of mutilations are also the same in the two cases: the single eye fascinates and paralyzes the adversary; the right hand deliberately sacrificed to guarantee an affirmation leads the adversary to believe what is said, and it is on this that the salvation

1. Dumézil, *Mitra-Varuṇa*, chap. 9; *ME* 1:424–28.

of the society depends. How can such a concurrence, so complex and rich in meaning, be taken as fortuitous, when it has not been noted in any instance outside the Indo-European world, and, more particularly, when it does no more than depict a particular form of the general diptych in which the Indo-Europeans distributed the modalities of the first function, magic and law? It is far more likely that we have here, conserved by the two "bands" after the dispersion, the result of the reflection of the Indo-European thinkers on a question that their tripartite ideology might naturally have raised: With what means, signs, advantages, and risks do the magician and the jurist operate when they have to take the place of the warrior, whom exceptional circumstances, in particular, most dreadful enemies, have rendered inadequate?

Cases of this kind have begun to multiply. So, before entering into debate, let the critic avail himself of two more comparative analyses of the same type: a comparison of the war between the Æsir and the Vanir with the battle between Romulus and Titus Tatius, the definitive form of which is to be found in *L'héritage indo-européen à Rome* (pp. 126–42);[2] and a comparison of the production and the liquidation of the Indian Mada with the production and liquidation of the Scandinavian Kvasir, as proposed in *Loki* (pp. 97–106; pp. 62–74 in the German edition). The confrontation of these very different studies[3] will afford a better understanding of the principles and procedures involved.

Reflections such as these are sometimes objected to on the grounds that it is not permissible to treat myths in this way, to extract "schemas" from them which are supposed to epitomize their substance but which, all too easily, only distort them. Let us be careful to distinguish between principle and practice. In particular cases, the analyst may very well deceive himself by regarding secondary traits as characteristic, and retaining them, while neglecting traits that are truly primary. He will have to reconsider every case in which this abuse has been diagnosed with serious arguments. But as to the opportunity, the necessity, of extracting the motivation and, accordingly, the meaning, the raison d'être, of a myth, there can be no yielding. For a believing society, as we said at the outset, a myth or

2. The essentials of this text are reproduced in *RRA*, pp. 78–84.
3. Cf. "Le puits de Nechtan," *Celtica* 6 (1963): 50–61 (Indo-Iranian–Irish correspondence.)

an entire mythology is not a gratuitous product of fancy, but the repository of traditional wisdom; myths perform the same service —but surely more amply and on more levels—for adults of successive generations, as Aesop's fables, with all that derives from them, performed for the educators of the young throughout the occident; and, as with these fables, so we must grasp the lesson contained in the myths, that very lesson which coincides with the development of the plot, with the "schema" itself. It is now simply a matter of tact, of rigorousness, probity, and submission with regard to the subject; and one may hope, with progressive studies and more and more numerous applications of the principle, that the control over previous results imposed by every advance will progressively lessen the danger of error and subjectivity.

The two "schemas" extracted here are thus submitted to fair-minded examination. If investigations and discussion confirm their validity, scholars will have to concede that the complexity of these "schemas," and the fact that they are linked together in order to illustrate the careers of two figures who occupy, in Roman "history" and in Indian mythology, the same rank in the same functional structure, make it unlikely that they are independent inventions, and suggest that to explain them in terms of the Indo-European ideological heritage remains the most satisfactory solution.

SECOND PART

FATALITIES

The Three Sins of the Warrior

1

SOLITUDE AND LIBERTY

The oldest document in Indian theology to have come down to us —the list of gods under whose guarantee an Aryan king of Mitanni from the fourteenth century B.C. gave his word, enumerates the canonical patrons of the three functions.[1] First of all, closely associated by the grammatical expression of a compound dual, are Mitra and Varuṇa, the two sovereigns; then comes the warrior god Ind(a)ra; then the twins, the Nāsatya. Between the two pairs, Indra is alone.

When the religion of Zoroaster, in abolishing Indo-Iranian polytheism, sought to preserve and moralize the analysis of the cosmic and social forces which had sustained its ancestral theology, it substituted a hierarchic list of Entities for the list of patron gods of the three functions.[2] The following scheme was thus produced: at the fore, nearest to God, were two closely allied Entities, Vohu Manah and Aša, sublimations of *Mitra and *Varuna; next came an Entity whose name, Xšaθra, evokes the Indian *kṣatriya* who had Indra for their special god; and, at the third level with Ārmaiti, "The Pious Thought," patroness of the Earth (who replaced some Indo-Iranian goddess), were the two nearly inseparable Entities, Haurvatāt̰ and Amərətāt̰, patrons of Waters and Plants, transpositions of the twin *Nāsatya. Between the pair of sovereign Entities and the group "Ārmaiti + pair" of the third level, the substitute for Indra remains alone.

Does this mean that the warrior god of the Vedic and pre-Vedic Indians was a stranger to the game of associations, undisposed to the pattern of pairing? Certainly not. In fact, a juster understanding,

1. See Dumézil, *Naissance d'Archanges* (1945), chap. 1; *ME* 1 (1968):147–49.
2. *Naissance d'Archanges*, chaps. 2–5; *ME* 1:105–6.

richer in nuance, of his basic position can be attained by observing his partnership in the pairs into which he enters easily. For it is upon this idea of the pair that the Indo-Europeans probably, and the Vedic Indians certainly, constructed their mythology of the three functions, as well as several other provinces of the mythology. On the whole, at each of the functional levels, even at those whose essence was oriented either toward unity or toward multiplicity, the pair appeared as soon as the theological presentation took on some dimension. But the values and the formulas of composition are distinct in each case.

On the level of the first function, the results of the cumulative research carried out in *Mitra-Varuṇa* (1940; 2d ed. 1948), *Le troisième souverain* (1949), and *Les dieux des Indo-Européens* (1952: chap. 2, "Les dieux souverains") offer a detailed picture, valid for most of the Indo-European field, of how this divine realm was populated. To confine ourselves to the Vedic domain, where sovereignty is the responsibility of the Āditya, the formula of the pair is here fundamental. First in rank in the realm of sovereignty are two gods, Mitra and Varuṇa, whose connection is so close that they are often named in a compound duel, with the sense "the two, Mitra and Varuṇa." Both gods have beside them lieutenants, two minor Āditya[3] (Aryaman and Bhaga beside Mitra, Dakṣa and Aṃśa beside Varuṇa), who reconstitute pairs among themselves (Aryaman-Dakṣa, Bhaga-Aṃśa) according to the same formula as the principal pair. And the mechanism is so well established that, as the mythology of the Āditya developed in extent at the same time that it reduced in comprehension and importance, the gods were always added to their number in pairs so that a passage from the *Mahābhārata* could describe them as "the supreme kings invoked by pairs of names."

3. The second chapter of *Les dieux des Indo-Européens* began the study of these minor divinities of the sovereign function; it has been corrected, with regard to the Scandinavian materials, in the third chapter of *Les dieux des Germains* (1959); now see *ME* 1:149–51. These successive sketches will be coordinated and updated in a forthcoming book on the Indo-European theology of sovereignty (University of Chicago Press). Also examined in that work will be the recently developed views of several Indologists and Iranicists, notably Heinrich Lüders (Varuṇa, *ṛtá*); Paul Thieme (the Āditya, *arí*, *arya*); Bernfried Schlerath (the Vedic god-kings); Ilya Gershevitch (the Aməša Spənta, Mitra-Miθra). In the meantime, see the various discussions in: *Journal asiatique* 246 (1958):67–84 (Thieme); 247 (1959):171–73 (Thieme, Gershevitch); 249 (1961):427–30 (Schlerath); *Bulletin de l'Académie Royale de Belgique*, Classe des lettres, 5ᵉ série, 47 (1961):265–98 (Thieme).

The meaning of this tenacious structure is clear. Sovereignty aligns itself on two planes, at once antithetical and complementary, necessary to each other and consequently without hostility, with no mythology of conflict. Every specification on one plane calls forth a homologous specification on the other; and, between them, they exhaust the whole domain of the function. These planes, defined above all by the comportment of Mitra and Varuṇa, are those of juridical sovereignty, near to man, luminous, reassuring, etc., and magical sovereignty, far from man, dark, terrible, etc. On almost every matter each god has his word to say, his moment to act, but their tasks do not overlap. On the matter of contracts, for instance, Mitra—whose own name bears the notion—seems to help men to conclude and honor them, while Varuṇa, the "Binder," oversees and snares whoever infringes upon them. Their collaboration is so intimate and so constant, not in spite of the opposition between the two gods, but rather because of this opposition, that, most often, this theme of collaboration is what the hymns continually emphasize, whereas only rarely do they express the need to define the characters of Mitra and Varuṇa separately. Sometimes, however, a differentiation is found, and in the ritual books the number of such distinctions increases; but always in the sense we have outlined.[4] To complete

4. Most recently, and provisionally, the articulation of the natures of the two gods has been summarized in *ME* 1:147–49; the two aspects of sovereignty are distinguished as follows:

A. As to *domains*: in the cosmos, Mitra interests himself more in what is close to man, Varuṇa in the immensity of the universe as a whole. The *ṚgVeda*, with a clear differential intent, already connects Varuṇa with the sky, Mitra with the earth (4.3.5), or again Varuṇa with the sky, Mitra with the *vṛjána*, the human sacrificial enclosures (9.77.5). Going even farther, the *Brāhmaṇa* say (e.g. *Śat.Br.* 12.9.2.12) that Mitra is "this world here," Varuṇa "the other world." Likewise, very soon, well before Sāyaṇa's commentaries on the hymns (e.g., on *RV* 1.14.1.9, etc.), Mitra patronizes the day, Varuṇa the night (*Taitt.Br.* 1.7.10.1; *Taitt.Saṃh.* 6.4.8, etc.)—and Abel Bergaigne has noticed probable allusions to this doctrine in the *ṚgVeda* (cf. also Louis Renou, *Etudes védiques et pāṇinéennes* 15 (1966):7 and 24 ad *RV* 1.115.5 and 5.81.4).

B. As to *modes of action*: Mitra is properly, in the etymology of his name, "the contract" (Antoine Meillet, 1907), and serves to bind, to facilitate, alliances and treaties between men; Varuṇa is the great magician, having at his disposal, first, more than any other being at the sovereign level, the power of *māyā́*, the magic power to create forms, whether temporary or lasting, and, second, the "knots" with which he can "seize" the guilty with a sudden and irresistible hold.

C. As to *characters*: if both are connected with the *ṛtá*—the moral, ritual, social and cosmic order—and demand that it be respected, Mitra is "friendly" (that is one of the meanings that his name has taken), benevolent, reassuring, progressive; Varuṇa is violent, alarming, sudden. While the *ṚgVeda* is filled with hymns and strophes telling of man's fear and

this brief sketch, which has been documented and developed in the three books cited above, a few more remarks will suffice: (1) In the pairs of sovereigns, and above all in the principal one, the two members are of equal rank, neither Mitra nor Varuṇa being superior to his partner; (2) the two gods are equally good, and the antithesis "benevolent-terrible" never degenerates into an opposition of good and evil; (3) Despite the fundamental dichotomy and the pairs which express it, a tendency toward unity can be sensed. This last is not true only, as noted, where the hymns mention Mitra and Varuṇa together and associate them in an undifferentiated service, but also, to judge by a statistical enumeration of the invocations, where the hymns refer to Varuṇa as "the" sovereign par excellence, he who embraces

---

trembling before Varuṇa the judge, the single hymn addressed to Mitra alone (3.59) expresses nothing but confidence in a god who is as well disposed as he is powerful. The *ŚatapathaBrāhmaṇa*, which often speaks of Varuṇa's knots and shows him seizing creatures with violence (5.4.5.12), says that Mitra, in contrast, "injures no one, nor does anyone injure him" (5.3.2.7). There are numerous applications of this theologem: to Mitra belongs what is well sacrificed, to Varuṇa what is badly sacrificed (*Śat.Br.* 4.5.1.6; *Taitt.Br.* 1.6.5,5; Sylvain Lévi, *La doctrine du sacrifice dans les Brāhmaṇas* [1898; reprinted 1967], p. 154); to Mitra "that which is broken off by itself," to Varuṇa "that which is hewn by the axe" (*Śat.Br.* 5.3.2.5); to Mitra "what is cooked by hot steam," to Varuṇa what is roasted, "seized" by the fire (ibid. 5.3.2.8); to Mitra the milk, to Varuṇa the intoxicating soma (*Śat.Br.* 4.1.4.8); etc. This violent energy of the one and this calmness of the other are even expressed by coupled equivalences in which Varuṇa consistently corresponds to the beginning or to the fullness of a process, Mitra to the end. Thus Varuṇa is the waxing moon, Mitra the waning moon (*Śat.Br.* 2.4.4.18); Varuṇa is the fire which already blazes ("to seize creatures"), Mitra is the fire after it has begun to go out (*Śat.Br.* 2.3.2.10 and 12); etc.

D. Finally, in relation to functions other than their own, Mitra has more affinity, in his mode of action, with pastoral prosperity and peace (third function), Varuṇa with Indra (*Indra vai Varuṇaḥ*, *GopathaBr.* 2.1.22) and with the violence that conquers (second function); and, even among the provinces of sovereignty, Mitra, as Ananda Coomaraswamy says with an intended anachronism, is rather "the spiritual power" and Varuṇa "the temporal power"—the *bráhman* and the *kṣatrá* respectively (*Śat.Br.* 4.1.4.2 and 3; cf. 2.5.2.34, etc.).

From the fact that this antinomy of the two great sovereigns is expressed with increasing frequency and vitality in the ritual books and commentaries, some have sought to deduce that it has developed, or even taken form, after the period of the composition of the hymns. One need not even look to other Indo-European theologies, however, to verify that this antinomy and the double aspect of sovereignty which it expresses are anterior to the Vedic epoch. After the hymns, Varuṇa and Mitra, and the Āditya in general, are gods in retreat, gods without future. It would certainly be astonishing if such an important trait had been added to their theology during this retreat, or even if such a trait had continued to develop. It is far more probable, as Abel Bergaigne has suggested, that the poets of the hymns, who did not compose a systematic catechism but lyrical works oriented toward action, would have put the accent on the profound unity of sovereignty rather than on its subdivisions. Cf. Hermann Güntert, *Der arische Weltkönig und Heiland* (1923), pp. 123–24.

within himself the whole function; or again, where they subordinate the variations within the function to a "great Asura,"—a figure of uncertain value, who is perhaps simply Varuṇa, perhaps a pale replica of the supreme divine figure who, in Iran, took the form which we recognize as Ahura Mazdā.

The patronage of the third level—a very rich and complex one—the Indo-Iranians, as the Indo-Europeans had already done, most readily entrusted to a pair of gods, who, moreover, were twins. Fundamental no less than on the first level, the pair here presents another meaning. The terms are no longer antithetical or complementary, but identical and equivalent, at least with regard to essentials. By examining them closely, as Stig Wikander has done,[5] we shall see that one of the two Nāsatya or Aśvin is concerned with bovines and the other with horses, just as, in the Zoroastrian transposition, with their homologues[6]—the inseparable Entities Haurvatāt̰-Amərətāt̰—one is concerned with the waters, the other with plants. Several allusions also indicate a deeper difference, making one twin the son of the heaven and the other the son of a man, in the manner of the Greek Dioscures.[7] But such distinctions remain unmarked in the services they render, in the character of their benefits, or in the prayers by which they are addressed: they always act together and do the same things. Their duality, then, results not from a differentiation but from a doubling, and it is constantly by their collective name, in dual form, not by any individual names, that they are called upon: they are "the two Nāsatya," "the two Aśvin." Identical in nature and activity, they are naturally equal in rank and equally good. Finally, their character as twins may itself refer to the nature of the functional level which they represent, for this level implies, among other things, abundance and fecundity, qualities for which, according to many peoples, twins are both the symbol and the measure. Let us add that, unlike Mitra and Varuṇa who together exhaust the content of their function, the twins—beneficent, generous, healers—are far from expressing theirs in its totality: actually, behind this

5. "Nakula et Sahadeva," *Orientalia Suecana* 7 (1957):66–96; *ME* 1:73–89.

6. The demonstration, begun in the fifth chapter of *Naissance d'Archanges* in 1945, has been completed by Father Jean de Menasce, "Une légende indo-iranienne dans l'angélologie judéo-musulmane: à propos de Hārūt et Mārūt," *Etudes asiatiques* 1 (1947):10–18.

7. Cf. *La saga de Hadingus* (1953; to be published in English translation by the University of Chicago Press), appendix 1, "Le noyé et le pendu," pp. 135–59; *ME* 1:76–81, 87–89.

facade of the "pair," the true numerical index of the third function is that of multiplicity, an indefinite multiplicity. The function itself contains numerous aspects (abundance, health, fecundity, peaceful life, the social totality); further, many of these aspects divide themselves into numerous separate manifestations (abundance, for example, will concern men, animals, plants, gold, etc.; it will consist of sons, wealth, food, drink, etc.); and, finally, the function integrates details into itself from the landscape and the material base of the society's life (water will be from a certain river, a certain lake; each cultivated terrain, every type of tillage will bring forth its own special patron, etc.). Also, very often (and this is the type of arrangement which is found beneath the surface in the case of the Zoroastrian Entities), the pair of twins is accompanied at least by a goddess, who recalls the feminine, maternal aspect of the function.

At the second level, with Indra, the formula is again different. Pairs in which this god forms the first member are not lacking; there is a profusion of them. But whereas Varuṇa is found in the compound dual only with Mitra and with Indra, and whereas the Nāsatya never associate themselves in one compound word with any divinity other than Indra, the *R̥gVeda* includes, beside the forms *Índrāváruṇā* and *Indranāsatyā*, the compounds *Indrāgnī́*, *Índravāyū́*, *Índrāsómā*, *Índrābŕ̥haspátī*, *Indrābrahmaṇaspatī*, *Índrāviṣṇū*, *Índrāpūṣáṇā*, *Indrāparvatā*, and *Indrāmarutaḥ*. Truly, no other god is so partial to companionship, and these various liaisons are most valuable for a knowledge of Indra and for an exploration of his particular sphere of activity.[8] But the superabundance of associations and the instability of the second term reveal that the form is not fundamental.

Indeed, most often, Indra decides and acts alone. When he is not alone, when the Marut for example, or Viṣṇu, accompany him, it is nearly always he who performs the central feat. His one or more companions go along to praise him, to sing him incantations, to "increase" and "strengthen" him, to make way for him, or, at most, to give him momentary aid; they do not constitute together a balanced pair, on equal terms, like those we have discussed above. In the frequent association of Indra with the Marut, Indra is the captain, the Marut are the troop. Other associations, such as *Índrā-*

8. See "Viṣṇu et les Marut à travers la réforme zoroastrienne," *Journal asiatique* 242 (1953):1–25; *ME* 1:233–37.

váruṇā and *Indrānasatyā*, express a rapport, an interfunctional affinity, the first between the terrible, magical aspect of sovereignty and the service of the warrior, the second between personages of different but equal service and aid to human individuals. Still another, *Indrāgní*, has several values following various contexts, Agni himself signifying many things. But the essential fact remains that, if Indra can have so many liaisons, none of these results necessarily from his defined role. There are also negative indications. One of the most remarkable is the absence of any articulated relationship between Indra and Rudra, who, in certain respects, is also a god of the second level but with characteristics other than those of Indra and with profound and mysterious delvings into the first and the third levels. Thus, the divisions within the second level do not form a structure like those within the first.

The only exception would be the liaison indicated by the compound *Índravāyú*. The first part of this book discussed in some detail how, in the Indian epic, as in the Scandinavian and the Greek, the function of the warrior is realized in two types of heroes, which the names Heracles and Achilles characterize quite adequately. The works of several scholars from Uppsala—Henrik S. Nyberg, Geo Widengren, Stig Wikander—have made it appear probable that this distinction, in pre-Vedic times, was extended to the world of the gods, where it was expressed in the persons of Vāyu and Indra. In Vedic theology, however, Vāyu would seem to have been dispossessed of this ancient role, and if he is closely associated there with Indra, it is rather in his other function, that of "initial god,"[9] by which he performs a service for Indra in the domain of time analogous to the service Viṣṇu renders in the domain of space.[10] Under such circumstances, the compound *Índravāyú* does not suffice to prove that, in a pre-Vedic epoch when each god still patronized a different martial behavior, Indra and Vāyu were then neatly associated as warriors in a diptych comparable to the one formed by Mitra and Varuṇa at the level above them. The diptych would in itself be a very improbable combination, since the heroes of the Vāyu type, like Heracles and Bhīma, are more readily independent than are, say, Achilles and Arjuna, heroes in the mold of Indra.

9. *ME* 1:47–48.
10. Ibid., pp. 210–11, 234–37.

Finally there is another type of pair, that of unequals, so unequal, in fact, that one can barely speak of a pair. Such is the relationship which sometimes brings the combatant god together with one of his human protégés or employees, together, that is, with a hero. Generally Indra arouses the hero, gives him the material or moral means of victory; but sometimes they collaborate: such is the case of the hero Trita.[11] Probably this is a very ancient representation. In any case, it is reminiscent of the god Þórr's association with an inferior personage in several myths,[12] as well as in the designs on certain Lappish drums, an association which the Danish mythographer Axel Olrik has considered in his celebrated article "The Thunder-God and His Valet."[13] But this unbalanced form of the pair is no more stable, no more essential to the god than that which brings Indra into a connection with Viṣṇu or with the Marut.

It would be interesting to explore the formulas for the constitution of the pair in other zones of the mythology, particularly with respect to the "initial god," in whom the pair often takes the form of a double being, *bifrons*, and above all embraces not the complementary but the incompatible, and where ultimately, as with the twin Mainyu of Zoroastrianism (probably formed from the double *Vāyu of Indo-Iranian polytheism), the opposition at times takes on a moral value, one of the two terms being "good," the other "bad." But our interest lies elsewhere. It suffices for us to have established that, even within the formula of the pair, Indra is not bound by any profound necessity to his partner of the moment. The list of the gods of Mitanni, brief as it is, reveals what is essential: Indra by nature is alone.

The vocabulary of the *R̥gVeda* gives a striking expression of this theologem: the word *éka*, "one," including every meaning of this word ("alone in the face of many"; "alone among . . ."; "alone, without aid"; "unique, eminent"), is used, as applied to divinities, seventy-five times in the hymnal. Of these, sixty-three concern Indra, a total to which the two compounds *ekavīrá*, "unique hero" (10.103.1) and *ekarā́j*, "unique king" (8.37.3)—both of which are hapax legomena which qualify him—must be added.[14]

11. See above, pt. 1, chap. 2 at n. 2.
12. See below, pp. 158–59.
13. "Tordenguden og hans dreng," *Danske Studier* 2 (1905):129–46.
14. Cf. Bernfried Schlerath, *Das Königtum im Rig- und Atharvaveda* (1960), pp. 28, 32, 49.

He wishes not to be associated with five, with ten, he does not ally himself to whoever does not press the soma, even though he be opulent. He sooner defeats him, just so, or kills him, rumbling, while to the pious he gives a share in the cattle herd.

The very strong, who stays the wheels in combat, hostile against whoever does not press the soma, increasing whoever presses it, Indra, subduer of all, terrible, the arya, draws on the *dāsá* at his will. [*RV* 5.34.5–6]

Yathāvaśám, "according to his own will." Independent even in the alliances which he seems to make, Indra is moreover the master of his own designs. He is no more limited in the choice of his goals than in the choice of his companions. He is alone and he is free. Witness the celebrated strophes of *R̥g Veda* 6.47.15–18, which, in a few splendid images, call to mind the *Magnificat*, and in which the capricious changes of favor are put on the same plan as his power of metamorphosis, a trait that is essential to the warrior function.

... As one sets one foot and then another before him, so he makes the second to be first by his powers.

It is said that the hero conquers sometimes one strong [man], sometimes another, and exalts sometimes the one, sometimes the other ...

He ceases his friendship for the former and, in turn, he goes with the others ...

He has conformed sometimes to one form, sometimes to another: such is his form, to contemplate him. By his magic, Indra goes in many forms, for ten hundred bay steeds are yoked to him.

The instability and the gratuity of the warrior god's favor are repeatedly recalled to the more faithful by the god's own special element, battle. *Mars caecus*, say the Romans. Free Indra, think the Indians more devoutly. When two parties, both of them arya, confront one another, they invoke him equally and place in him the same hope; and freely, he chooses:

When it would be necessary that the generous Indra should favor two peoples, rich in boons, who fight each other with their entire warrior bands for the stake of beautiful cows,[15] he, the terrible one, joins with the one, and, with the rumbling warriors, he drives forth the cattle [of the other] out [from the pen]. [*RV* 5.34.8]

Indra and the warriors in general, and notably Indra's troop, the Marut, are free, or more precisely, "auto-nomous." *R̥g Veda* 3.45.5

15. Geldner; despite Sāyaṇa, the probable meaning of *sáṃ yád ... ávet*.

proclaims this by tripling the expression and underlining it with a comparative:

> You, Indra, are independent [*svayúḥ*], king by yourself [*svarā́j*] . . . , more glorious by yourself [than any other] [*svávyaśastaraḥ*].[16] Increased in strength, O widely praised, be for us the most attentive.

Indra and the Marut, in the *R̥g Veda*, draw to themselves the greater part of the epithets formed by joining the prefix *sva-*, "auto-,"[17] with an abstract noun: of the 4 examples of *svákṣatra*, "who has power by himself," 2 go to Indra, 1 to the Marut; of 12 of *svátavas*, "strong by himself," 2 go to Indra, 6 to the Marut; of 7 of *svábhānu*, "luminous by himself," 5 go to the Marut; of 3 of *svápati*, "his own master," 2 go to Indra, etc. And the contexts are significant; for example (one among many):

> Autonomous [*svákṣatram*], audacious is your spirit, slaying at a single stroke, O Indra, is your male force. [5.35.4]

or again:

> Strong by himself [*svátavān*] like a mountain, born of old for victory, the heroic, the vigorous Indra [pierces the demon Vala] . . . . [4.20.6]

One of the most interesting terms of this stock of compound words[18] is the substantive *svadhā́*, "quality, nature, own will."[19] The

16. Geldner: "Indra, du bist dein eigener selbständiger Herr, . . . gar selbstherrlich."

17. In most cases there is no reason to seek in *sva-* a variant of *su-*, "good," rather than the reflexive.

18. Naturally, Indra is the exemplary *svarā́j*, "king by himself": the word is applied to him 10 times in the *R̥g Veda* of the 16 uses in the singular (other applications: once probably to one of Indra's protégés, once probably to the king at the time of consecration; once to Parjanya, who is by nature associated with Indra in the making of rain; once probably to the newly dead on his way to partaking of the joys of the beyond; once only to Varuṇa, under the name "Āditya"; a sixteenth example is unclear; in the plural, the word qualifies the Marut once, the mythical horses once, the Āditya once under the name *rā́jānaḥ*, "kings"). The corresponding abstract substantive *svarā́jya* is applied to Indra, in a refrain, in two hymns (16 times in 1.80.1–16; 3 times in 1.84.10–12) and once again to Indra (other applications: once to Savitr̥, the "impeller" god; once to Mitra-Varuṇa; another text is probably corrupted). Finally, and most important, there is one text in which *svarā́j* appears beside *samrā́j*, "universal king," in a distinction which has the value of a theological definition: Indra is *svarā́j*, Varuṇa is *samrā́j*. On this subject, see my discussion of method (*Journal asiatique* 249 [1961]:430) with Bernfried Schlerath (*Das Königtum im Rig- und Atharvaveda* [1960], pp. 132–33).

19. On this word, see Emile Benveniste, *Origines de la formation des noms en indo-européen* 1 (1935):199; Louis Renou, "Etudes védiques," *Journal asiatique* 243 (1955):434, n. 1 ("élan autonome"), *Etudes védiques et pāṇinéennes* 16 (1967):11 ("le seul sens avéré pour *s.* dans le

term appears with its precise meaning about sixty times in the *Ṛg Veda*, applied rarely to men, sometimes to certain notions such as enigmas or the funerary ritual, but above all to such gods as the Dawn, the Sun, Apāṃ Napāt, Agni. Considered in its connection with the gods of the first two functions, it presents an eloquent statistic: never does it concern, either collectively or individually, the sovereign gods; in contrast, twenty-one times, a third of the total number of usages, it concerns Indra or the Marut. Several examples will set the tone:

> By your strength, you surpass the extremities of heaven, Indra, the terrestrial space does not hold you, you are increased by your *svadhā́*. . . . [8.88.5]

Again to Indra:

> If my liquor rejoices you, if you take pleasure in my praise, come from afar, according to your *svadhā́*. [8.32.6]

To the Marut:

> On your shoulders, O Marut, buckles are fixed, on your chests are plates of gold. . . . They (= the Marut) glitter like the lightning through the rain, with weapons, appropriate to their *svadhā́*. [7.56.13]

Nature and individual comportment, and probably also, as in the last example, comportment as a "class." The effects of the collective *svadhā́* of the Marut, like the effects of Indra's *svadhā́*, are not entirely unforseeable: their acts are those of warriors.[20] And let us not forget, over and above the words related to *svadhā́*, in which the Greek and Germanic languages recognize the meaning "habit," "custom," that there is also the Latin derivative *sodālis*, designating the member of a small autonomous group, one included within the society but sometimes opposed to it: fraternity, corporation, political cabal, secret or illicit association, band of revelers.

This signal from the Latin vocabulary directs us to the threshold of an immense problem. The autonomy of which the warriors are so proud, which the poets acknowledge with such emphasis in the

RV est *autonomie*"); Philippe Colinet's rendering in his "Etude sur le sens du mot *svadhā́* dans le Rig Veda," *Mélanges Sylvain Lévi* (1911), p. 172 ("maniere habituelle, propre, habitude, coutume") is insufficient.

20. In certain forms of Iranian dualism, the concept *x*ᵛ*at-dōšakih*, "own will," is characteristic of the part of the second function which belongs to the bad creation: Robert C. Zaehner, *Zurvan* (1955), pp. 374–81 (extracts Z 11 and Z 12 from the *Dēnkart*).

combative gods when they invoke them, is weighted with temptations and risks for the one who possesses it, and is disturbing as well for the social order and the order of the cosmos. *Svadhā́* does not adjust itself to the social community any more than *sodalitas* does. At least once, speaking of men, the *R̥gVeda* has made clear this dangerous, injurious side of the concept. A group of strophes in 7.104 hurl a curse against the liar. At strophe 9 (cf. *AV* 8.4.9), we read:

> Those who falsify the right declaration by their ways [*évaiḥ*], or those who turn the good to bad by their *svadhā́*, may Soma give them over to the serpent or consign them to the lap of destruction.

But the hymns never envisage the *svadhā́* of the warrior gods, or of any god, in such a light: prayers, eulogies, they admit no dark spots in their portrayals. But there are shadows. They are found in the mythology, richer than any other, on the warrior level—a mythology to which the hymns make only lyrical allusions but which the discursive and logical expositions of the *Brāhmaṇa* and the epics inform us completely. The antiquity of these myths, moreover, is guaranteed by the parallelism which is to be observed between the themes of several such myths and the traditions of other Indo-European peoples. By examining one of these thematic settings, inherited from the common Indo-European prehistory, we shall now follow the warrior god of India, the model champion of Scandinavia, and the most illustrious hero of Greek legend, with all their faults and their misfortunes, right to the logical limit of this awesome freedom.

2

INDRA THE SINNER

In the *Brāhmaṇa* and the Epics, Indra is a sinner. He is not, however, so designated in the *R̥g Veda*. Hanns Oertel's efforts (1898)[1] to discover, in some passages from the hymns, a trace of censure, an allusion to what is later to be denounced as criminal or shocking, have come up with nothing convincing.

When *R̥g Veda* 6.47.16–17 shows Indra sometimes inclined to help one person and sometimes another, abandoning his initial friends to take new sides, we need only refer to the context in order to understand that what the poet senses here is simply a manifestation, which he registers with neither blame nor complaint, of the *independence*, the necessary and wholesome *autonomy*, of the warrior god.[2] It is mere artifice to see here, as does Oertel, the breaking of the word which we encountered, on the level of the Brāhmaṇa, in the story of Namuci.

When *R̥g Veda* 6.46.3 calls Indra *sahasramuṣka*, "of a thousand testicles," this epithet surely alludes to the supervirility which every people readily attributes to its human and divine warriors: the songs of soldiers, century after century, continue to draw together the diverse offices of the male, just as the Avestan Vərəθraγna, the god called upon for victory—in part homologous to Indra Vr̥trahan—is also invoked to obtain *ərəzōiš xā̊*, *fontes testiculorum*. But here there is no reason to look, as Sāyaṇa does, for a precise reference to the sexual sins, the adulteries, of Indra which the epic literature will expose with such relish.

As to 5.34.4, the verse probably does not say what Oertel and many

1. *"Indrasya kilbiṣāṇi," Journal of the American Oriental Society* 19:118–25.
2. See above, pp. 61–62.

others have tried to make it say. The symmetry induces one to translate the *kílbiṣāt* of the last verse as an objective ablative, referring not to a fault of Indra, to which there will be no echo in the remainder of the hymn, but to the fault of a man with whom Indra, despite this fault, enters into a relationship. Accordingly, the meaning gains in both force and beauty:

From the one, whose father or mother or brother he, the strong one, has killed, from that one he does not remove himself; making an arrangement, he seeks even his offerings. From the fault he does not remove himself, he, the giver of boons.[3]

"From the fault" means "from the guilty party." The intention of this verse as of the entire strophe is to remind us that Indra, in contrast, for example, to Varuṇa, keeps no tight accounts, acknowledges no blind paths of justice. He is not held back in his relations with men at that point where the two sovereigns must check themselves perforce. This strong god, who upon occasion kills (that is his mission), is ready to become reconciled with the sons or brothers of his victims; and he does not automatically excommunicate the sinner.

There remains, in the hymn of Indra's painful "births" (4.18), the famous verse in which it is said that he killed his father (str. 12, v. 4). This would be grave indeed, if only we knew what was involved. But this dreadful crime has caused very little commotion, which seems strange when one thinks of the zeal of the Brāhmaṇa and epics in spreading the worst and least of rumors about Indra. Moreover, in the strophe where it is mentioned, the crime is presented under such conditions that it comes out incoherent, nonsensical. One is strongly tempted to adjust the person of the verb: by changing a single letter, one will fall back on a theme of story and novel that is recognizable and clear, that of the future hero—such as Batraz of the Ossets—persecuted at his birth in every way and, in particular, left an orphan. The poet, full of commiseration, asks the unfortunate infant:

3. Karl F. Geldner's version: "Der Mächtige geht dem nicht aus dem Wege, dessen Vater, dessen Mutter, dessen Bruder er erschlagen hat. Er fordert sogar noch Geschenke von ihm, wenn er Vergleich macht. Er scheut vor keinem Unrecht zurück, der Verschenker des Gutes."

Who has made your mother a widow?
Who wished to kill you, lying still or moving?
Which god was compassionate with you . . .[4]

and then adds, in the fourth verse, against every expectation:

. . . when you seized your father by the feet and caused him to perish?

The strangeness of this last question is more than obvious: by what right can this child who has committed the worst of murders expect the pity of the gods? A paternal persecution, a sequence of the same type as that of the Ouranides, has been supposed, but that is gratuitous. The question initially posed in the first verse suggests rather that the persecutor "who has made your mother a widow" is unrelated to the family and that the father has been the victim of the same enemy or enemies as the mother and child. The strangeness disappears if, in the fourth verse, it is "someone" who killed his father, as, in the second verse, "someone" wished to kill Indra himself. We need only read *ákṣinan* (3d. plur.), "they [the enemies] caused to perish," or *ákṣināt* (3d. sing.), "he [the persecutor designated by the "who" of verses 1 and 2] caused to perish" in place of *ákṣinā̄ḥ*, "you caused to perish." Whatever scruples one may have about tampering with the Vedic textual tradition, one must sometimes resign oneself to doing so.[5]

Thus, in the *R̥g Veda*, Indra has no criminal record. But let us not rush to proclaim him innocent, or to conclude that the fuss made about his sins must come from later times. Though Oertel does not succeed in his quest, he does at least, from the first page, wisely perceive its reduced importance.

If the Vedic hymns offer but little material of this kind, this fact is simply due to the character of these poems. They are invocations and songs of praise—*nahī́*

4. Geldner: "Welcher Gott fand Gnade vor dir . . . ." This interpretation of *te* appears to contradict the attitude of the gods toward Indra as indicated in the second verse of the preceding strophe, well rendered by Geldner (the words of the infant Indra's mother): "Mein Sohn, jene Götter lassen dich im Stich." Moreover, everywhere else in the *R̥g Veda*, the gods are givers, not beneficiaries of *mārdīká*, "pity, favor, grace" (root *mr̥d-* "to pardon, to spare, to be favorable").

5. One could object to these considerations on the grounds that, on the contrary, we should keep *ákṣināḥ*, since it is the *lectio difficilior*. If one chooses this alternative, the fact remains that no other passage in the hymnal mentions the parricide of Indra, and the enormous crime appears in none of the lists of Indra's sins recorded in Vedic prose literature.

nv ásya mahimā́nam indriyáṁ svàr gr̥ṇánta ānaśúh (*RV* 8.3.13)—in which allusions of this sort would be manifestly out of place. An argumentum ex silentio would therefore here be patently wrong.

That is entirely true. The Vedic poets could hardly give a bad role to the very god they considered most useful, of such usefulness as is attested quite adequately by statistics alone. Courageously, as good servants, they would rather have assumed his more questionable responsibilities along with him. One example of this attitude has been shown in the earlier part of this book. In all later literature, the murder of the Tricephal entails a stain. The monster is at once both a brahman, chaplain of the gods, from a tradition that is probably post-Vedic, and the gods' first cousin, a feature that is certainly archaic. Now we have seen how the *R̥gVeda* mentions only a single time, and with a light touch only, with a single word, those social relations between the murderer and the murdered that make the slaying juridically questionable. Indra, according to 2.11.19, has delivered into Trita's hands the son of Tvaṣṭr̥, the son of "the one united [with him] by bonds of friendship," *sākhyásya*. One seeks in vain, if one examines the context, for any trace of blame: it is for our sake, for us men, *asmábhyam*—in the person of Trita—that Indra has performed this delivery, and if the poet recalls it, it is to ask the god to continue the good work, as the inverted syntax of the phrase does indicate: "May we be able to triumph, to conquer all enemies, the barbarians, with your aid, with the arya [that is, probably, with you, the god of the arya], us unto whom you have formerly delivered . . . , etc." When one makes one's addresses to the divine striker, one cannot dictate the manner in which he strikes.

Having explained the *R̥gVeda*'s silence, and by the same token eliminated the objection which one might draw from it as to the antiquity of the representation of Indra's sins, one can only share Oertel's observation on the extent and importance which come to be attached to the theologem of Indra the Sinner, and even to the systematization of his sins, when we come to the *Brāhmaṇa* and the ritual treatises. Indeed, the authors have arranged his faults in lists which, with slight variations, can be found in the texts of various schools, and which allude to adventures which we know of only in part. Oertel cites *AitareyaBrāhmaṇa* 7.28:

When the gods shunned Indra, saying: "He hath intrigued against Viśvarūpa, Tvaṣṭṛ's son [that is, the Tricephal]; he hath slain Vṛtra; he hath given the Yatis to the sālāvṛka-wolves; he hath killed the Arurmaghas; he hath interrupted Bṛhaspati," then was Indra excluded from the soma-draught.

In *KauśitakīUpaniṣad* 3.1, it is Indra himself who classifies his misconduct:

I killed the three-headed son of Tvaṣṭṛ; I gave the Arunmukhas, the Yatis to the sālāvṛka-wolves; transgressing many a covenant [*bahvīḥ saṃdhā atikramya*], I smote in heaven the Prahlādīyas, in the atmosphere the Paulomas, on earth the Kālakāñjas.

To these Oertel added a long passage (2.134) from *JaminīyaBrāhmaṇa*, that precious text from which he then published many extracts and made a special study:

The creatures condemned Indra, saying: "He hath killed the three-headed son of Tvaṣṭṛ, he hath given the Yatis to the sālāvṛka-wolves, he hath killed the Arurmukhas, he hath interrupted Bṛhaspati, transgressing the covenant he had covenanted [*saṃdhāṃ saṃhitām atītya*] he cut off the head of the asura Namuci." From these sins against the gods [*etebhyo devakilbiṣebhyaḥ*] he walked away into the forest not descending [?] to the gods. He said to the gods: "Perform a sacrifice for me." "No," they said, "these agreements thou hast transgressed, thou hast committed those sins against the gods. We will not perform a sacrifice for thee." Now Agni might have been called his best friend; so among the gods he spoke to Agni: "Sacrifice for me." "Yes," he said, "but I desire some one among the gods with whom I may sacrifice for thee." He did not find any among the gods with whom he might sacrifice for him. He said: "I cannot find any one among the gods with whom I might sacrifice for thee." "Then do thou alone sacrifice for me." "Yes." Agni by himself succeeded. He performed this *agniṣṭut*. With that he sacrificed for him. With it he at once burned away all his [Indra's] evil. As a serpent would get rid of its skin, as one would pull the blade of the reed-grass out of the sheath, even so he got rid of all his evil.

This text is interesting in many respects, especially because it says in its own way that only fire could cleanse, could atone for this career in which sins were mingled with services. Here we have an optimistic version of what is also the lesson, with different nuances, of the pyre of Heracles, the burning of the impious Tullus by the bolt of Jupiter, and, in Iranian tradition, the moving dialogue with the god Fire, by which Zoroaster, in the other world, obtains pardon for Kərəsāspa,[6] the Iranian Hercules.

Even more than the *Brāhmaṇa*, the epic will also obligingly take note of the sins of the god Indra. But a particular type of sin comes to take on increased importance: the sexual sin, adultery, and especially adultery committed by seduction, surprise, or deception with the wife of a brahman. The prototype for this regrettable sin is surely the god's adventure with Ahalyā. Of this the *Brāhmaṇa* have little to say, but here again the *argumentum ex silentio* cannot be trusted; as early as 1887, Albrecht Weber remarked that in certain important ritual formulas, those by which the soma sacrifice is announced on a fixed day to the gods (*subrahmaṇyā*) and which, in particular, refer to Indra by a series of vocatives that allude to his qualities or his adventures, the following salutation is to be found: *Ahalyāyai jāra, Kauśika brāhmaṇa, Gautama bruvāṇa*, "spouse for Ahalyā, brahman Kauśika, named Gautama." It is thus certain that in the definitely early period when this ritual was fixed, the story of Ahalyā was known: wife of the brahman Kauśika Gautama, she was approached by Indra, as Alcmene was by Zeus when the god passed himself off as her husband. If the *Brāhmaṇa* do not incorporate this into the canonical list of the god's sins, one reason, at least, can be found. As sacerdotal literature, in contrast to epic, it would probably seek to avoid drawing attention to a type of conduct declared sinful yet glorified by an august divine example, which could easily establish an awkward precedent for the powerful of this world. It seems that one of the concerns of the brahman caste from its very beginnings as a caste, as can be seen from *R̥gVeda* 10.109, has been to protect its women from the schemes of princes and warriors.

Even if we did not have the evidence provided by the *subrahmaṇyā* formulas, we could scarcely doubt the antiquity of this type of excess: the warrior everywhere takes liberties with the codes by which the *seniores* seek to discipline the ardor of young men, everywhere lays claim to "unwritten rights" to other men's wives, to maidenly

6. Henrik S. Nyberg, "La légende de Kərəsāspa," *Oriental Studies in Honor of Cursetji Erachji Pavry* (1933), pp. 336–43; in the first text published (*Dēnkart* 9, analysis of *Sūtkar Nask*, 14), Kərəsāspa repents of "having killed men without number"; but his principal sin, for which Ōhrmazd reproaches him and the god Fire demands the punishment of hell, is having "struck the fire."

virtue. Stig Wikander, in the first two chapters of his *Der arische Männerbund* (1938), established that even in Indo-Iranian times this sexual note clung to the conception of the *márya*, "young man of the second function," and that it counted for a great deal in the condemnation thrust upon the *márya* by the Zoroastrian reform (Avestan *mairya*, Pehlevi *mērak*).[7] In other parts of the Indo-European world, on the level of legend, let us recall the rape of the Vestal Ilia by Mars, of Lucretia by the soldier Tarquin, the scandals which fill the histories of the Scandinavian *berserkir*, the *contubernales* of King Frotho (Saxo Grammaticus 5.1.11),[8] and the innumerable bastards sired by Heracles.

7. After numerous discussions, often misdirected, this interpretation of *márya*, like the general thesis of the book, has gained credence: Manfred Mayrhofer, *Kurzgef. etym. Wörterbuch des Altindischen* s.v., 2 (1957):596–97. Louis Renou, who in *Etudes védiques et pāṇinéennes* 4 (1958):49 justly defined *márya* "terme mi-érotique mi-guerrier" (for *RV* 8.54.13), was less inspired when he deleted the second element in ibid., 10 (1962):64 (for *RV* 1.64.2).

8. See below, pt. 3, chap. 4 at n. 9.

3

THE SINS AND LOSSES OF INDRA

Let us now turn our attention to a relatively recent text, in which the theory of Indra's sins appears in a remarkable form: book 5 of the *MārkaṇḍeyaPurāṇa.*

At the beginning of this Purāṇa, Jaimini, a disciple of Vyāsa, seeks out Mārkaṇḍeya to get him to resolve some difficulties concerning the *Mahābhārata*. The sage refers him to certain birds, as famous for their intelligence as for their sacredness, and so it is that, in the fourth section, we learn of the four points which trouble Jaimini about the great epic: What led Janārdana, or Viṣṇu, to assume human form? How did Kṛṣṇā, or Draupadī, become the common wife of the five Pāṇḍava brothers, the principal heroes of the poem? How was Baladeva, or the third Rāma, the brother of Kṛṣṇa, expiated for the murder of a brahman? How could the sons of Draupadī all die before being married? By the end of the fourth section we are enlightened as to the incarnations of Viṣṇu, and the fifth takes up the truly delicate problem of the polyandric marriage of Draupadī.[1]

I have already alluded to Stig Wikander's memorable article published in 1947, "The Legend of the Pāṇḍara and the Mythical Basis of the Mahābhārata," and its important findings.[2] These five brothers, engendered successively by the functional gods in the wombs of the two wives of Pāṇḍu, have an ordered relationship of their own, forming a hierarchized functional team. In numerous epic passages their respective modes of behavior, whether they are acting alone or together, offer an excellent definition of the three

1. This text has been treated differently, from the viewpoint of Draupadī, and in connection with *Mbh* 1.189.1–40 (= Calcutta 197.7275–7318), in *ME* 1:103–24.

2. See above, pt. 1, chap. 1, n. 1.

functions which are at the base of the Vedic, Indo-Iranian, and Indo-European ideology. Thus, in total independence of the system of *varṇa* or strict social classes (brahmans, kṣatriya, vaiśya)—which is an essentially Indian development, a hardening of the social structure around the principle of the three functions—and with traits that are almost more Iranian, in any case more Indo-Iranian, than Vedic (for example, the role of Vāyu within the warrior function, which is very nearly effaced in the *Veda*), vast sections of the *Mahābhārata* present themselves as a series of variations on the theme of the three functions and as a projection on the human plane, in heroic adventures, of the ideology which gave life to that grouping of gods which is like an axis for the Indo-Iranian pantheon: the sovereigns Mitra-Varuṇa, the warriors Vāyu and Indra, and the beneficent twin Nāsatya.

Yudhiṣṭhira, the eldest, is the son of Dharma, "Law, Order," a rejuvenation of the concept of Mitra. Of the five, he alone is king, a thoroughly just and virtuous king.

Next come two warriors of very different natures: Bhīma, son of Vāyu, "the wind," is a brutal and not very intelligent Hercules, one who acts readily on his own, armed with a simple mace, but above all sustained by his colossal force; Arjuna, Indra's son, is the warrior-knight, leader of the army, master of the bow and of all classic weapons.

The group is completed by a pair of twins, Nakula and Sahadeva, sons of the twin Nāsatya; beautiful, amiable, servitors devoted to their brothers, they are also, as a characteristic episode demonstrates, specialists in the care of cattle and horses.

We have only begun to take stock, for the interpretation of the *Mahābhārata*, for the history of Indian thought, for the detailed analysis of the Indo-Iranian ideology, and even, by contrast or by analogy, for the study of the Persian Book of Kings, of the consequences of this discovery, which, now that it has been made, looks easy and obvious, but which no one had made before Wikander.[3] As to the shocking nature, from the *arya* standpoint, of the figure of Draupadī, the common wife of the five brothers, Wikander immediately succeeded in proposing the first simple and satisfactory explanation. In Indo-Iranian mythology, to judge from the Vedic and Avestan

3. This is the subject of the first part of *ME* 1:31–257.

materials that have been conserved, the team of the functional gods is completed by a single goddess, who ideologically is not confined to any of the three functions, but is situated, and operates, within them all. Her nature is thus synthetic, as is probably signified by the curious triple name which the *Avesta* gives such a goddess: "The Humid (third function), the Strong (second), the Pure (first)," Arədvī Sūrā Anāhitā.[4] The Indian epic has expressed this fundamental idea dramatically, on the human plane, by matching the trifunctional team of the five Pāṇḍava with a single woman, their common wife.

It is this archaic theory of the three functions, expressed in the group of Pāṇḍava, which we are now about to see the *Mārkaṇḍeya-Purāṇa* connect and adjust to the theory of the sins and punishments of Indra, presenting the latter at the same stroke in a systematic and trifunctional form. Here follows the literal version of the text, hardly poetic but tightly constructed, which I have divided into its natural sections, indicating the numbers of the twenty-four distichs.

I. (A) *The First Sin*

1. Once, when he had killed the son of Tvaṣṭṛ [that is, the Tricephal], oh brahman, the majesty [*tejaḥ*] of Indra, overpowered by this brahmanicide, underwent a considerable diminution;

2. It entered the god Dharma, this majesty of Śakra [= Indra], because of this fault; and Śakra found himself deprived of majesty [*nistejāḥ*], when his majesty went over into Dharma.

(B) *The Second Sin*

3. Then Tvaṣṭṛ, lord of creatures, learning that his son had been killed, tore out one of the chignons he wore as an ascetic, and said:

4. "Let the three worlds with their divinities today see my force! Let him see it, the brahmanicide of evil thoughts, the punisher of the demon Pāka [= Indra],

5. by whom my son, devoted to his duty, has been killed!" Thus having spoken, eyes red with anger, he placed his chignon on the fire as an offering.

6. Out of that Vṛtra, the great asura, came forth, amidst garlands of flames, with great stature and enormous teeth, comparable to a mass of ground collyrium.

7. Enemy of Indra, of immeasurable essence, fortified by the energy [or majesty: again *tejaḥ*] of Tvaṣṭṛ, he grew each day the length of a bowshot, he, the being with the great force.

4. See above, pp. 16–17.

8. Seeing that Vṛtra, this great demon, was destined to kill him, Śakra, wishing for peace, sick with fear [*bhayāturaḥ*], sent the seven sages to him,

9. who, between him and Indra, made friendship [*sakhyam*] and agreements [*samayān*], they, the sages of pious soul, devoted to the welfare of all beings.

10. When, in violation of the agreement [*samayasthitim ullaṅghya*], Vṛtra had been killed by Śakra, then, overwhelmed by the murder [he had committed], his physical force [*balam*] declined.

11. This physical force, having escaped from Indra's body, entered Māruta [another name for the Wind, Vāyu] who penetrates all, invisible, the supreme divinity of physical force [*balasya . . . adhidaivatam*].

(c) *The Third Sin*

12. And when Śakra, having assumed the appearance [*rūpam*] of Gautama, had violated Ahalyā, then he, the Indra of the gods, was despoiled of his beauty [same word as for "form, appearance": *rūpam*]:

13. The gracefulness of all his limbs, which charmed so many souls, abandoned the tarnished Indra of the gods and entered the two Nāsatya.

II. *The World's Distress*

14. Having learned that the king of the gods was abandoned by his justice and his majesty [*dharmeṇa tejasā tyaktam*], deprived of physical force [*bala-hīnam*], and without beauty [*arūpinam*], the sons of Diti [demons] undertook to conquer him.

15. Desirous of conquering the Indra of the gods, the Daitya, extremely strong, oh great muni, took birth in the families of kings of immeasurable vigor.

16. Some time thereafter the Earth, oppressed by its burden, went to the summit of mount Meru, where the denizens of heaven have their abode.

17. Crushed by so much burden, she told them the origin of her suffering, caused by the Daitya, Danu's sons:

18. "These asura with vast strength, whom you had overthrown, have all come to be born in the world of men, in the houses of kings;

19. their armies are numerous and, oppressed by their weight, I am sinking down. See now, you thirty [= the gods], that I find relief."

III. *Birth of the Heroes*

20. Then, with portions of their energy [*tejaḥ*], the gods descended from the sky to the earth, for the service of creatures and to lift the burden from the earth.

(A) 21. The male [Dharma] himself set free the majesty [again *tejaḥ*] which had come to him from the body of Indra, and in Kuntī (the queen, Pāṇḍu's wife) he engendered the King, Yudhiṣṭhira of great majesty [*mahātejaḥ*].

(B,B′) 22. The Wind then set free the physical force [*balam*], and Bhīma was born; and from the half [the remainder] of the vigor [*vīryam*] of Śakra, Pārthi Dhanañjaya (or Arjuna) was born.

(C) 23. The pair of twins [*yamajau*] [Nakula and Sahadeva, engendered by the Nāsatya] came into the world in [the womb of] Mādrī [second wife of Pāṇḍu], endowed with Śakra's beauty [*rūpam*], adorned with great luster;

(D) 23. [In continuation] Thus the blessed Śatakratu [or Indra] descended [and incarnated himself, *avatīrṇaḥ*] in five parts,

24. and his most fortunate wife Kṛṣṇā [or Draupadī] was born from the Fire: [consequently] she became the wife of Śakra alone, and of no other.

Whoever the author and whatever the epoch when it was established, this complex account is admirably trifunctional.

The functional values of the five Pāṇḍava, recognized by Wikander, are covered here not only by the names of their divine fathers, but by abstract substantives which fittingly characterize the essence of each function: *tejas*, a somewhat vague term, taken even here with diverse connotations, but one which always indicates, in opposition to the force of the body, a power of the soul, correlates with the god and the hero of the first function, Dharma and Yudhiṣṭhira. Two varieties of physical force, *bala* and *vīrya*, the first certainly more athletic and brutal, are attributed to the two gods and the two heroes of the second function, Vāyu and Indra himself, Bhīma and Arjuna. And beauty, *rūpa*, comes from the pair of divine Nāsatya to adorn the human twins, Nakula and Sahadeva.

But these various elements, these powers whose harmonious incarnation produces the team of the Pāṇḍava, are only transmitted to the sons from the gods, their fathers. On their part, the gods have received them from a sort of three-staged disintegration of Indra, resulting from three sins. The substratum of the three functions can be discerned just as clearly in these three sins as in the three losses that follow them:

1. The loss of *tejas*, spiritual force or majesty, is provoked by a sacrilege and by an outrage against the social structure at its most exalted level: a *brahmanicide*.

2. The loss of *bala*, physical force, is provoked by a sin which, while remaining a breach of contract, is also considered *cowardly*, since the conclusion of the pact was provoked by fear before a superior force.

3. The loss of *rūpa*, beauty of form, is provoked by an *adultery*

committed with the help of the shameful fraud of changing into another's form.

Brahmanicide, fear bringing about a dishonorable act, and adultery: the three sins, like their punishments, are situated respectively in the domains of the religious order, the warrior ideal, and well-regulated fecundity.

Given the literary genre in which it appears, one is inclined to see in this systematization of the faults of Indra a late arrangement, made by an intelligent author, of the older, less-organized traditions concerning Indra's sins. This is possible. But it must be acknowledged that if it was conceived in a period when Aryan India no longer meditated on the *functions* as such and knew only the guidelines of the three *social classes*, the arrangement still presents, on the third level, a conception that arises from the Indo-Iranian or Indo-European third function, and not from the third social class of India. By no Indian thinker was beauty thought of as characteristic of the class of breeders and agriculturists, the vaiśya, and, for that matter, neither was sensuality and the sins it entailed. In classical India, such men were defined solely by their planting and stockraising activities. In contrast, in Indo-European times, and still in the Vedic period (the Aśvin were "masters of beauty"), the third function, along with opulence and fecundity, included other attributes, beauty and sensuality among them, with their own conditions and consequences.[5] These latter were not lost by the Scandinavian gods Freyr and Freyja; nor does the functional goddess Aphrodite neglect them in the well-known legend in which, as the competitor of Hera, giver of sovereignty, and of Athena, giver of victory, she offers Paris nothing less than "the most beautiful woman."[6] So in the Pāṇḍava legend, beauty, just as much as competence in matters of breeding and an aptitude for service, is the characteristic of the twins, a trait which, like the identity and importance accorded to the god Vāyu, roots

5. In a scene, surely archaic, from the ritual of the *aśvamedha*, the Vedic horse sacrifice, the cause-and-effect connection between beauty and fecundity is set forth clearly: *Śat.Brāhm.* 13.1.9.6; cf. *ME* 1:59 (and, for opulence and sensual gratification, p. 491 and p. 560, n. 2).

6. "Les trois fonctions dans quelques traditions grecques," *Eventail de l'histoire vivante = Mélanges Lucien Febvre* 2 (1953), pp. 25–32; now see *ME* 1:580–86 and the parallel cases, pp. 586–601, and on a question of method, "L'idéologie tripartie, MM. W. Pötscher and M. van der Bruwaene," *Latomus* 20 (1961):524–29.

this legend directly in the Indo-Iranian and Indo-European ideology. We must therefore suppose, at the very least, that the author of this late arrangement had exceeded the ideology of his contemporaries and reconstituted the rich "third function" of former times.

His treatment of the second sin, the violation of the pact concluded with Vṛtra (substituted here, as often in the epic, for Namuci), is no less archaic. It lends authority to one element that the ancient forms of the episode could not eliminate, since it is fundamental to them, but which they could scarcely proclaim: though Indra had concluded the initial agreement and this dubious friendship with the demon, instead of treating him at the outset as the warrior god must treat every demon, it was because he did not feel himself equal to the task, because he was afraid. All that follows is merely the result of this defect in the essential vocation of the warrior, in his force and his pure bravery. The author of our text makes this element explicit: at the very beginning of the scene, he says (distichs 8–9): "Seeing that Vṛtra, this great demon, was destined to kill him, Indra, wishing for peace, sick with fear, sent the seven sages to him, who, between him and Indra, made friendship and agreements . . . ." And Indra's punishment is exacted in the loss of this physical force, *bala*, in which, for once, he did not dare put his trust.

These archaic, even fossil-like treatments of the third and second level are better explained if we assume that the theme of the three sins that the warrior commits within the framework of the three functions already existed before the author of the Purāṇa applied it to Indra.[7]

As for the idea that guides this whole development, it too is ancient: the warrior, by his actual weaknesses, loses his virtual powers, and, from these lost powers, new beings are born. In the story of Namuci, inasmuch as it is the myth that justifies the *sautrāmaṇī*, the *Śatapatha-Brāhmaṇa* presents an analogous disintegration, though it is only in the animal, vegetable, and mineral realms that the lost powers are productive, and not in terms of gods or men.[8]

In the *Avesta* a very similar theme can be found, but there it is applied not to a god or hero homologous to Indra—Vərəθragna or

7. See the passage from the first book of the Mahābhārata, cited above, chap. 7, n. 1.
8. See *Tarpeia*, p. 123.

Kərəsāspa, for example—but to the complex, total, trifunctional personage of Yima, the most illustrious of the "first kings." Immediately after presenting Yima in his majesty and power, *Yašt* 19—the "*Yašt* of the Earth," actually almost entirely dedicated to the sovereign power, the *x*ᵛ*arənah*, a sign which may assume diverse forms, which appears on the prince designated by God, accompanies him in his actions, and leaves him when he has become unworthy—warns us, at the end of verse 33, that this good fortune will last only until Yima should begin to give himself over "to the deceitful, false world." Yima, indeed, sins gravely. One could even expect to see him commit three sins, since the *x*ᵛ*arənah* leaves him three times or, if we translate literally, since three *x*ᵛ*arənah* leave him in succession. This is not the case. There is never more than one sin: in the *Avesta*, it is the lie, the greatest sin of Mazdaism; in later texts, it is pride and revolt against God, or even the usurpation of divine titles, all sins against the rules and proprieties of the *first* function.[9] The consequences of the sins, however, are set in a triple structure; and this structure, in the two known variants, is as clearly trifunctional as that of the incarnations of Indra's lost powers.

According to *Yašt* 19.34–38, the first of the three *x*ᵛ*arənah* of Yima comes to reside in Miθra, "the lord-of-land of all lands, which Ahura Mazdāh has made, of all the *yazata* of the world of spirits, the most suited for the *x*ᵛ*arənah*"; the second in Θraētaona, "son of the clan of the Āθwya," who killed the Tricephal; the third in "Kərəsāspa of heroic soul," "the strongest of strong men," the Iranian Hercules, whose labors, here as so often, are obligingly enumerated. It is clear, as Darmesteter recognized, that Miθra and Kərəsāspa represent the first and second functions respectively. The attribution of the third—agricultural prosperity—to Θraētaona raised a difficulty which Darmesteter began to alleviate, and which, in the first part of the present book, has been completely eliminated.[10] In any case, no such difficulty can be pointed to in the explicit affirmation of the second variant, from *Dēnkart* 7.1.25–32–36, which says that one third of Yam's *x*ᵛ*arr* (the Pehlevi form of Avestan *x*ᵛ*arənah*), related to agriculture, passed into Frētōn (Θraētaona), who immediately eliminated plague and

9. In the third part of *ME* 2, I shall examine, going beyond the parallel described here, the record concerning the "sin of the sovereign," different from the "sins of the warrior."

10. See above, pp. 17–19.

sickness by medical treatment; one-third, relating to the warrior estate, passed into Karšāsp (Kərəsāspa); and one-third—that of the "sovereign function," although this time the word itself is not declared—passed into Ōšnar (Aošnara), who is presented in these terms (§§36–37; from the translation by Marijan Molé):

In the same epoch it [= the "transmission of the word"] returned, thanks to the Glory [x^v*arr*] of Yam, to Ōšnar who was very wise, when he was in the womb of his mother. Speaking from his mother's womb, he taught her several wonders. At his birth, he struck the Evil Spirit and refuted the propositions [*frāsnān*] of *mar* Fračya, worshipper of the *dēv*.

He became minister for Kayus and administered the seven continents under his dominion. He discovered [and] taught the art of ordering speech and several other sciences useful to men; and the non-Arya were defeated in debate. He lavished the wisest counsels in the lands of the arya.

It can be seen that the three functions are presented clearly, regularly, and in ascending order: the agricultural function and the warrior function are properly depicted and the first function is abundantly described, joining the faculty of intelligence with the science of administrative technique on the highest level, and also with certain more precise features of this class of "scribes," who often attempted to create an advantageous place for themselves on the social ladder. The test of intelligence in which the demon-debater is conquered by Ōšnar takes its place beside the Vedic practices attested, among the priests, by the important contests of enigmas, to which Louis Renou has recently drawn attention, and the ordeal by questions, in the *Mahābhārata*, to which Dharma, himself invisible, submits the Pāṇḍava, and to which, naturally, only his own son, "the Pāṇḍava of the first function," can respond.[11]

The plan and object of this legend accord well with the plan and object of the fifth book of the *MārkaṇḍeyaPurāṇa*. In both cases an eminent figure, a ṛṣi or a god, commits certain sins—one here, three there—which deprive him in three stages of the three factors of his eminence. And these factors are defined by the three fundamental functions: Yima loses three x^v*arənah*, or the three parts ofhis x^v*arənah*, one related to the sacred and the intelligence, one to the warrior force, and one to agriculture and health; Indra, for his part, first

11. *ME* 1:62.

loses majesty or spiritual force, then physical force, and then beauty, as a consequence of his three sins—against the sacred, against bravery, and against the conjugal bond. But these factors of eminence are not lost: the three *x*^{v}*arənah*, lost by Yima, inspire three heroes; and the three advantages lost by Indra pass over into the functional gods who correspond to them, whereby, each in its turn, these advantages are enabled to engender the team of functional heroes in whom Indra finally, in fragmented form, is revived.

4

THE THREE SINS OF STARCATHERUS

Scandinavian epic is rich in heroes. And the most illustrious betray a family likeness: all are beautiful, brilliant, young, sociable, beloved, of princely birth and eager for power, devoted to their homeland whether it be large or small. Sigurðr, Helgi, Haraldr; and the rest are certainly not interchangeable, but knowledge of one is knowledge of them all. There is nothing surprising about this, and the designation given them by modern criticism provides an adequate explanation: they belong to the common type of the "Odinic hero." Over against them, set apart, is Starkaðr, the Starcatherus of books 6–8 of the *Gesta Danorum*. Monstrous at birth, descended from giants, disfigured by horrible wounds, old before his time and of prolonged old age, surly, brutal, errant, solitary, with neither love nor indulgence for the weakness of love, hardened by suffering, austere and frugal, with no other ambition than to fight at the service of frequently changing masters, for whom—barring accidents—he professes a grumbling devotion based on a solidly conservative conviction: such is the strange figure, intriguing rather than appealing, for whom Saxo Grammaticus hardly conceals his predilection.

If one considers these heroic types in diptych, one cannot help thinking of the Greek Achilles and Heracles, of the Arjuna and Bhīma of the *Mahābhārata*. Here, in epic form, we can probably see that duality of the warrior type, mentioned several times above (pp. 58–59, 73), which the skillful Iranicists of Uppsala perceived in the most oriental of the Indo-Europeans—even though the *Ṛg Veda* had already altered it and unified it to Indra's advantage—and which, just before the dawn of recorded history, must have taken the form of the double patronage of Vāyu and Indra. The giant Bhīma, the chivalrous captain Arjuna, one the son of Vāyu, the other of Indra, prolong the ancient distinction, thus showing themselves to be more archaic than their divine fathers are in the Vedic hymns.

Starkaðr has inspired numerous studies by the greatest names of Germanic philology and Scandinavian literary history, representatives of every school; Johann Ludwig Uhland (1836); Karl Müllenhoff (1883); Sophus Bugge (1889); Gustav Neckel (1908); Andreas Heusler (1911); Axel Olrik, that exciting writer who devoted to "Starkad den Gamle" more than half of the second volume of his enthusiastic *Danmarks Heltedigtning* (1910); Paul Hermann, the erudite commentator on Saxo (1922); and, in the reedition of *Grundriss der germanischen Philologie*, the historian of Nordic epic, Hermann Schneider (1933).[1]

But here, as in the case of Hadingus, it appears that, though many critical efforts have clarified numerous details, they have somewhat obscured the essential. Without exception, they all take their departure from implicit, very dubious postulates. Among the most dubious are such notions as: so great a body of material must have been composed from various fragments; originally there must have been several distinct Starkaðr, a hero and a giant. Then there has been an effort to define cultural layers. According to their content and tone, in the greater or lesser role, for example, played by religion, austerity, the ideal warrior, or, on the other hand, by wealth, dexterity, or debauchery, one can, it is argued, detect the position of the episodes in a chronological sequence, and attribute their redaction to different centuries and different strata of civilization.

It is of course probable a priori that, as with Heracles, the epic of Starkaðr was enriched over the centuries by numerous additional episodes, local legends too, more or less analogous to the contents it already had; but it is improbable that these additions would have

1. During the printing of the first French version of this book (October 1955) Jan de Vries published an important study, "Die Starkadsage," in the *Germanisch-Romanische Monatsschrift* 36 (N.F. 5):281–97. I then added an appendix to my book, a "Discussion sur Starkaðr," which underlined our numerous points of agreement and also our disagreement on several rather important points. Reviewing my book in the *Beiträge zur Geschichte der deutschen Sprache und Literatur* 78 (1957):468–71, Jan de Vries himself settled a good deal and sided with my interpretation on the most important question (Starkaðr's second sin). Therefore I eliminated this appendix when the German edition was prepared (1964). In the first part of *ME* 2 (see below, n. 11) I shall again have the pleasure of bowing to the opinion of my late colleague and friend on another aspect of Starkaðr (his relations to Óðinn).

disturbed the overall plan, itself too simple and too significant to be passed off as secondary.

Again, Saxo's lengthy account, the only one that follows Starcatherus from birth to death, is certainly far removed from the few sagas that include only one or two of the great scenes from his life, without allusion to the others. But this is not a sufficient reason to consider the reunion of all these great scenes in Saxo as the result of an artificial compilation. This fragmentary evidence could just as well result from extracts, distorted through separation from more complete traditions. Indeed, certain signs indicate just that.

And again, Saxo himself certainly presents discordances in tone and spirit between various episodes in the hero's career. But are we sure that the only adequate explanation here must lie in a literary chronology? Is it not conceivable that the plan might have imposed—constitutionally, at the very outset—a certain diversity, and that it is simply a matter of understanding this diversity?

As generally happens when there is no objective criterion available to buttress decisions, there has been infinite debate over these probabilities. But just such a criterion is furnished by the results of our previous studies. The simple and significant plan of the epic of Starcatherus, alluded to twice just above, is clearly modeled on the Indo-European and ancient Germanic structure of the three functions (religious sovereignty, martial force, wealth), each of the three parts of the whole requiring the two others, and each contributing a necessarily new coloring to the whole. Starcatherus is a magnificent hero, ever holding true to his rough, pure definition of character. But on three occasions his actions have a different cast: he commits three successive sins, each connected with one of the three functions. First, in the service of a Norwegian king, he helps the god Othinus to stage a human sacrifice in which his own master will be killed; then, in the service of a Swedish king, he shamefully flees from the battlefield after the death of his master; and, in the service of a Danish king, he vilely assassinates his master for one hundred and twenty pounds of gold. Here follows Oliver Elton's enduring translation[2] of the passages from Saxo which contain these essential formulations, but first the account of his strange birth.

2. Oliver Elton, trans., *The First Nine Books of the Danish History of Saxo Grammaticus*, The Folklore Society, vol. 33 (London, 1894).

(A) *Origin and Character of Starcatherus* [6.5.1–2][3]

1. At the same time one Starcatherus, the son of Storwerkus, escaped alone, either by force or fortune, from a wreck in which his friends perished, and was received by Frotho as his guest for his incredible excellence both of mind and body. And, after being for some little time his comrade, he was dressed in a better and more comely fashion every day, and was at last given a noble vessel, and bidden to ply the calling of a rover, with the charge of guarding the sea. For nature had gifted him with a body of superhuman excellence; and his greatness of spirit equalled it, so that folk thought him behind no man in valour. So far did his glory spread, that the renown of his name and deeds continues famous even yet. He shone out among our own countrymen by his glorious roll of exploits, and he had also won a most splendid record among all the provinces of the Swedes and Saxons.

2. Tradition says that he was born originally in the country which borders Sweden on the east, where barbarous hordes of Esthonians and other nations now dwell far and wide. But a fabulous yet common rumour has invented tales about his birth which are contrary to reason and flatly incredible. For some relate that he was sprung from giants, and betrayed his monstrous birth by an extraordinary number of hands, four of which, engendered by the superfluity of his nature, they declare that the god Thor tore off, shattering the framework of the sinews, and wrenching from his whole body the monstrous bunches of fingers; so that he had but two left, and that his body, which had before swollen to the size of a giant's, and, by reason of its shapeless crowd of limbs looked gigantic, was thenceforth chastened to a better appearance, and kept within the bounds of human shortness.[4]

There follows (§§3–5) an interesting digression, a dissertation on the difference between the gods Othinus and Thor, and the inadequacy of their *interpretationes* as Mercurius and Jupiter. Then the account is resumed.

(B) *The Gift of Three Lives and the First Sin* [6.5.6–7]

6. Ancient tradition says that Starcatherus, whom I mentioned above, offered the first-fruits of his deeds to the favour of the gods by slaying Wicarus,

3. The division into chapters and paragraphs and the orthography of the proper names are those of the edition of Jørgen Olrik and Hans Ræder, 1931.

4. The birth and the surgery are perhaps clarified by the considerations made above, chap. 2 at n. 7. If Starcatherus does not fight an adversary marked by a form of triplicity (a feat reserved for the god Þórr, see below, p. 159), he is no less the typical hero. Like Trita, like Horace, like Cúchulainn, he himself bears the mark of the "third" in a certain form. Just as Cúchulainn is third in relation to himself, having succeeded in being born only after two vain attempts, so Starcatherus, as to his arms, finds himself only a third of what he was initially.

the king of the Norwegians [*in Wicari Noruagiensium regis iugulo deorum fauori facinorum suorum principia dedicasse*]. The affair, according to the version of some people, happened as follows: Othinus once wished to slay Wicarus by a grievous death; but, loth to do the deed openly, he graced Starcatherus, who was already remarkable for his extraordinary size, not only with bravery, but also with skill in the composing of spells, that he might the more readily use his services to accomplish the destruction of the king. For that was how he hoped that Sarcatherus would show himself grateful for the honour he paid him. For the same reason he also endowed him with three spans of mortal life, with the condition that he commit in them as many abominable deeds. So Othinus resolved that Starcatherus' days should be prolonged by the following crime [*quem etiam ob hoc ternis aetatis humanae curriculis donauit, ut in his totidem exsecrabilium operum auctor euaderet. Adeo illi consequente flagitio uitae tempora proroganda constituit*].

7. Starcatherus presently went to Wicarus and dwelt awhile in his company, hiding treachery under homage. At last he went with him sea-roving. And in a certain place they were troubled with prolonged and bitter storms; and when the winds checked their voyage so much that they had to lie still most of the year, they thought that the gods must be appeased with human blood. When the lots were cast into the urn it so fell that the king was required for death as a victim. Then Starcatherus made a noose of withies and bound the king in it; saying that for a brief instant he should pay the mere semblance of a penalty. But the tightness of the knot acted according to its nature, and cut off his last breath as he hung. And while he was still quivering Starcatherus rent away with his steel the remnant of his life; thus disclosing his treachery when he ought to have brought aid. I do not think that I need examine the version which relates that the pliant withies, hardened with the sudden grip, acted like a noose of iron.

After committing this first crime, Starcatherus associates with a Danish viking, and travels, at first with him and then alone, through vast territories: Russia, Biarmia, Ruthenia, Sweden, Ireland, Slavia, Russia again, Byzantium, Poland, and Saxony; and then he comes to the Danish king Frotho (§§8–19). Everywhere he performs remarkable deeds, setting an example of martial virtue and expressing emphatically, as occasion offers, his respect for the majesty of kings (§16). The end of book 6 (6–9) is filled with the heroic services and the rough lessons that he gives to the children of the deceased king Frotho, especially to the weak young Ingellus, whom he is able to transform into a sovereign worthy of the name. In book 7, where little is said of him, he is found in the service of the Swedish king Regnaldus who has fallen into conflict with the Dane Sywaldus.

(c) *The Second Sin* [7.5]

After this a battle was fought between Sywaldus and Regnaldus in Zealand, warriors of picked valour being chosen on both sides. For three days they slaughtered one another; but so great was the bravery of both sides, that it was doubtful how the victory would go. Then Otharus [a warrior for Sywaldus], whether seized with weariness at the prolonged battle, or with desire of glory, broke, despising death, through the thickest of the foe, cut down Regnaldus among the bravest of his soldiers, and won the Danes a sudden victory. This battle was notable for the cowardice of the greatest nobles. For the whole mass fell into such a panic, that forty of the bravest of the Swedes are said to have turned and fled. The chief of these, Starcatherus, had been used to tremble at no fortune, however cruel, and no danger, however great. But some strange terror stole upon him, and he chose to follow the flight of his friends rather than to despise it. I should think that he was filled with this alarm by the power of heaven, that he might not think himself courageous beyond the measure of human valour. Thus the prosperity of mankind is wont ever to be incomplete [*insigne hoc praelium maximorum procerum ignauia fuit: adeo siquidem rei summa perhorruit, ut fortissimi Sueonum quadraginta terga fugae dedisse dicantur. Quorum praecipuus Starcatherus, nulla saeuitia rerum aut periculorum magnitudine quati solitus, nescio qua nunc obrepente formidine, sociorum fugam sequi quam spernere praeoptauit. Crediderim hunc metum ei diuinis uiribus iniectum, ne supra humanam fortitudinem uirtute sibi praeditus uideretur. Adeo nihil perfecti mortalium felicitas habere consueuit*].

This piece of cowardice, the first in a long career, is also the last and does not seem to have spoiled Starcatherus' reputation or diminished the "demand" for his services. At the end of book 7 he becomes familiar with Olo Vegetus, a prince endowed with so piercing a glance that it alone can accomplish what others do with the sword: "He terrified the bravest by his stern and flashing glance" (7.11.1). In book 8 Olo is made king of Denmark by a conspiracy resulting from the fact that the Seelanders could not endure being governed by a woman, the queen Hetha.

(d) *The Third Sin* [8.6.1–4] *and the Death* [8.8]

2. But he was given to cruelty, and showed himself such an unrighteous king, that all who had found it a shameful thing to be ruled by a queen now

repented their former scorn. Twelve generals, whether moved by the disasters of their country, or hating Olo for some other reason, began to plot against his life. Among these were Lennius, Atylo, Thoccus, and Withnus, the last of whom was a Dane by birth, though he held a government among the Slavs.

3. Moreover, not trusting in their strength and their cunning to accomplish their deed, they bribed Starcatherus to join them [*ceterum ad peragendum facinus parum uiribus atque ingenio freti pecunia Starcatherum asciscunt*]. He was prevailed to do the deed with the sword; he undertook the bloody work, and resolved to attack the king while at the bath. In he went while the king was washing, but was straightway stricken by the keenness of his gaze and by the restless and quivering glare of his eyes. His limbs were palsied with sudden dread; he paused, stepped back, and stayed his hand and his purpose. Thus he who had shattered the arms of so many captains and champions could not bear the gaze of a single unarmed man. But Olo, who well knew about his own countenance, covered his face, and asked him to come closer and tell him what his message was; for old fellowship made him the last to suspect treachery. But Starcatherus drew his sword, leapt forward, thrust the king through, and struck him in the throat as he tried to rise. One hundred and twenty marks of gold were kept for his reward [*at ille, destricto mucrone prosiliens, transuerberat regem nitentisque assurgere iugulum ferit. Centum et uiginti auri librae in praemio reponebantur*].

4. Soon afterwards he was smitten with remorse and shame, and lamented his crime so bitterly, that he could not refrain from tears if it happened to be named. Thus his soul, when he came to his senses, blushed for his abominable sin. Moreover, to atone for the crime he had committed, he slew some of those who had inspired him to it, thus avenging the act to which he had lent his hand.

Having thus accomplished the three *facinora* for which Othinus has burdened him with three lives, Starcatherus has little else to do but disappear. And so he does, following a long quest for death, in a dramatic scene. He plans to devote the one hundred and twenty marks of payment for his treason to purchase his own murderer, and thus to sacrifice himself; and he is finally slain by a pure young man, though not before expounding his teachings for the last time.

No commentary is needed to appreciate the meaning of this narrative: though the "three lives" are not clearly separated in Saxo's account, Othinus' prediction still compels us to distribute the three crimes between them, each "life" containing only one, and to consider these crimes, at least the last two, as the essential moments, the raison d'être, of the additional lives accorded to the hero. And these crimes—criminal sacrifice, shameful flight on the battlefield, and venal assassination—accord well, in descending order, with the three functions.

The results of previous critical works can scarcely prevail against the evidence of this structure. In particular, the murders of Wicarus and Olo can no longer be regarded as doublets, and the question of which was the model for the other, can be set aside. No longer can it be said of these two narratives, as one of the most recent commentators did: "Beide können nicht derselben Erzählungsschicht angehören, und man kann nicht zweimal ganz unabhängig Strakad zum Mörder des eigenen Herrn gemacht haben."

The only difficulty that the proposed explanation might raise lies elsewhere. Although it is not the aim of the present essay to treat the figure of Starkaðr comprehensively, we must touch upon certain points that are too important to be overlooked. These concern the connections of Starkaðr with the gods Óðinn and þórr.

In Saxo's account, these connections are simple and satisfactory: Starcatherus, who is so different in comportment from such "heroes of Óðinn" as Sigurðr or Helgi, does not in fact owe the essence of his constitution to Othinus. While Othinus has granted him his remarkable and ambiguous gifts, it is nonetheless Thor who first relieved him of the monstrous form in which he was born, by a surgical operation as crude as it was benevolent, and made him into a man of extraordinary strength, but still a man. His character and the kind of deeds he accomplishes both conform to this origin: his great bursts of anger and acts of violence, his vagabond humor, and the predilection with which he seeks out those among men who most resemble giants (the terrible "gladiator" Wisinnus in Russia, the "gigas" Tanna in Byzantium, the "athleta" Wasce in Poland, the Saxon Hama "qui gymnicis palmis clarissimus habebatur . . ."), the constancy with which he voluntarily maintains himself in a subordinate rank, a sort of *þræll* paying homage to and preaching the ethic of the *jarl*, in brief, his principal traits, with the exception of his sobriety, all seem to derive from his illustrious sponsor. Even in the favor with which he regards agriculturalists, and them alone among "beings of the third function" (he detests goldsmiths, despises servants, doorkeepers, and women), we find a parallel with a well-known concern of the god of thunder. Thus Starcatherus is presented to us as an example of a scarce type in Scandinavian literature: "a hero of þórr."

The intervention of Othinus is of a different kind, as one would expect from the sovereign god: acting alone and freely, he establishes the destiny of individuals and metes out to them their natural gifts. Sly, shrewd, disturbing, even evil, he not surprisingly dilutes his generosity and concedes longevity only at the cost of crimes. Such a concoction is entirely within his range; moreover, the first crime, the sacrifice of Wicarus, is all that interests him, the only motive for his intervention and his gifts. Finally, the relations of the god and the hero are ephemeral: once the murder of Wicarus is accomplished, Starcatherus owes nothing further to Othinus.

This is a precious lesson: the two types of warrior god—represented in the pre-Vedic period, presumably, by Vāyu and Indra, combined in the *R̥gVeda* under the name of Indra, but attested as distinct in their sons, the heroes Bhīma and Arjuna, up to the time of the epic—have their counterparts, in Scandinavian mythology, in þórr and Óðinn. The structure of this latter pair results from a phenomenon especially characteristic of Germanic religions: the overlapping of the warrior function onto the sovereign level. Óðinn, the sovereign god, while keeping his traits as a sovereign—the only ones with which he enters into the career of Starcatherus—has also annexed to himself the patronage of the brilliant, chivalrous side, or aspect, of the warrior function, illustrated by the Einherjar in the other world and by heroes such as Sigurðr and Helgi in this one. Except for his role as the god of thunder and lightning, þórr owes practically nothing to this aspect, and, in contrast, develops the other, the one incarnated by Starcatherus in the epic and rendered by Tacitus in his *interpretatio* of the continental "Donner" of his time as "Hercules."

This is where the difficulty occurs. The details of Saxo's account, from Starcatherus' birth up to and including the murder of Wicarus, cannot be reconciled with the other documents, the two documents in a Scandinavian tongue which recount the same initial events—the poem entitled the *Víkarsbálkr*, "the episode of Víkarr,"[5] and the prose passage from the *Gautrekssaga*[6] which cites the poem and offers commentary. I am not speaking in a minor difference, one in which the *Gautrekssaga* certainly offers the superior version. Ill informed about pagan rituals, Saxo understands Víkarr's sacrifice poorly and represents it clumsily, while the *sagamaðr* recalls it clearly, with the double consecratory gesture—the hanging and the thrust of the lance[7]—and Starkaðr's double simulacrum, along with the double miracle of Óðinn to which it corresponds: the slipknot made of gut which hardens suddenly like metal,[8] and the shaft of reed which, as it strikes Víkarr, turns into a lance. This much changes nothing in the course of events or in the role and responsibility of Starkaðr. The essential difference, as has already been said, is in the roles of Þórr and Óðinn.

Briefly, the *Gautrekssaga* makes Starkaðr, for this episode—the only one it deals with, into an Odinic hero, and attributes the evil which the hero accomplishes and the deficiencies which befall him to the will of Þórr. It should first be noted that there are a priori reasons—and others to be discussed below—for believing that on these two complementary points the version in the saga, more like a novel in its tone, is an alteration of what we have encountered in the *Gesta Danorum*. The motives for this alteration, and the means behind it, can easily be defined: first, a concern to free the hero from too monstrous and fabulous a birth; second, the impulse to reduce a

5. Andreas Heusler and Wilhelm Ranisch, *Eddica Minora* (1903), pp. 38–43.

6. Chaps. 3–7: Wilhelm Ranisch, *Die Gautrekssaga in zwei Fassungen* = *Palaestra* 11 (1900):12–34.

7. I do not know whether anyone has already compared the Scandinavian ritual described here with the Samoyed sacrifice of a reindeer, serving to lead the dead to his last abode: (1) the animal's neck is passed into a slipknot while the end of the rope is fixed to a tree; then the animal is beaten with a stick until it has strangled from trying to escape; (2) just at this moment a wooden lance is thrust into its heart. Marie-Antoinette Czaplicka, *Aboriginal Siberia* (1914), p. 184, following G. de Dobbeler, "Die Samoyeden," *Globus* 49 (1886):215.

8. Cf. the belief reported by Ernst Meier, *Deutsche Sagen und Gebräuche aus Schwaben* (1852), p. 167 (Num. 189): "The devil favors hanging. When someone wishes to hang himself and does not have a rope, he may simply take a piece of straw; the devil will help him pass a wire through the piece of straw to harden it. The children of Wurmlingen once tested this on one of their comrades and hung him from a ladder by a piece of straw. The straw did not break and the boy was already sticking out his tongue. . . . one of them quickly cut the straw with a curved knife, which was not easy."

rare type (a "hero of Þórr") to a common type in the sagas (the "Odinic hero"); and finally, the utilization, the borrowing, or a folkloric motif that is well known but scarcely Germanic in spirit, in which the hero's lot is cast by the precious gifts he receives from one or more "good fairies" (here Óðinn), counterbalanced by the restrictions set by a "bad fairy" (here Þórr). The following is a summary of events.

An original Starkaðr, the hero's grandfather, was an eight-armed giant who lived in Norway. He abducted a young maiden, whose father entreated the god Þórr to deliver her. Þórr then killed the giant and led the girl back to her father.[9] She was pregnant, and gave birth to a beautiful, black-haired boy, the strongest of men and a great Viking. This son, Stórvirkr, married a princess from Hálogaland and became the father of a second Starkaðr, our hero.

As a result of the misfortunes of their two families, Starkaðr grows up beside a dispossessed prince, Víkarr, whom he later joins in many exploits and helps to regain his kingdom. But very soon an old man named Hrosshársgrani, "Grani of the horsehair," enters into Starkaðr's life, protecting and counseling him, who is none other than Óðinn, disguised and biding his time. His hour arrives in chapter 7, when, in the course of a campaign, Víkarr's fleet is immobilized for some time by adverse winds near a small island. A magical consultation reveals that Óðinn desires a human sacrifice by hanging, and, as in Saxo, the drawing of lots designates Víkarr. It is here that the great divergence begins.

In the middle of the night, Hrosshársgrani awakens Starkaðr, rows away with him, lands on the island, and leads him through the forest to a clearing, where they find a Þing, a throng of men assembled around twelve seats. Eleven are already occupied by the gods. Hrosshársgrani, revealing himself as Óðinn, ascends to the twelfth and announces that the time has come to determine Starkaðr's destiny. Immediately taking the cue, Þórr recalls his grievances against Starkaðr's grandparents—a giant, and a maiden who had preferred the giant to himself, him, the Þórr of the Æsir!—and pronounces an initial verdict of destiny, a sorrowful one: Starkaðr will have no chil-

9. *Saga Heiðreks konungs ins vitra*, ed. Christopher Tolkien (1960), pp. 66–67.

dren. Óðinn retorts: He will have three human lives. Counters Þórr: While committing a *níðingsverk*, a villainy, in each one. Then Óðinn takes the initiative: He will always have the best weapons and the best garments. Þórr: He will never feel he has enough. Óðinn: He will have success and victory in every battle. Þórr: He will receive a grave wound in every battle. Óðinn: He will have the gift of poetry and improvisation. Þórr: He will forget everything he composes. Óðinn: He will win approval of the noble and the great. Þórr: He will be hated by the simple folk.

At the end of this dialogue, Hrosshársgrani takes Starkaðr back on ship and demands that he "send," that is, sacrifice, the king to him. He makes arrangements with Starkaðr for the sequence of actions, including the reassuring simulation to which the king will submit and which he, Óðinn, will transform into a real murder. He hands him the reed which, at the desired moment, will turn into a lance. And events take their course.

Such a fabulous plot cannot be old: the love stories which embellish its beginning and which are supposed to justify the hostility of Þórr, the princely origin attributed to Starkaðr, as well as the doubling of the figure into a monstrous grandfather and a normal grandson, are already clear signs of retouching. But there are others that are still more serious.

In Saxo it is understood that Starcatherus has a monstrous birth, a surplus of arms: this is the condition, the *materia prima* for the service Þórr renders him. In contrast, while the saga still presents the first Starkaðr, the hero's grandfather, as having eight arms, the trait hangs in mid-air, with neither explanation nor application, since Þórr neither fashions this monster nor mutilates him, but kills him like any other giant. These eight arms, which the retoucher has left awkwardly dangling, thus appear as testimony to the earlier rendition. It is easy to see how a *sagamaðr* could substitute the simple murder of a giant for the fashioning of a giant into a human by Þórr; it is not so easy to understand the inverse substitution: Saxo's account is the *lectio difficilior*.

In the scene of the allotment of destinies, Þórr's intervention arouses suspicion from the very start: theologically, it is not his role to fix destinies, but uniquely that of the magical sovereign Óðinn, whom none may thwart. It will prove difficult to find another example, whether in Snorri's Edda or in the epic, of this usurpation of functions.

By the same token, Óðinn's role, thus limited and amputated, falls into such evident incoherence that even the critics least disposed to favor Saxo have had to acknowledge the fault. At all times, or at least from the very beginning of chapter 7, if Óðinn takes an interest in Starkaðr it is only to make him into his instrument, his accomplice in this *níðingsverk*. Thus, to the extent that it is logical, following Saxo's account, for Othinus to set himself the accomplishment of the three crimes—the first of which is immediately necessary to him—as a condition of the gift of the three lives, it is surprising, in the *Gautrekssaga*, to see these two destinies separated, the three lives given by Óðinn, but the three crimes imposed by Þórr, Óðinn always requiring the first crime and, as in Saxo, being its beneficiary. The allusion of one verse of the *Víkarsbálkr*, also attributing responsibility to Þórr for the murder of Víkarr, or at least for Starkaðr's part in it, does not suffice to establish a preference for such an unsatisfactory version. It should not be forgotten that if the poem as a whole is anterior to this late saga (fourteenth century), we know the former, which has certainly received some retouches and interpolations,[10] only through the latter.

These few observations, which will not be augmented at this point, suffice to establish the superiority, the anteriority, of the variant conserved by Saxo, or of one very similar to it. It can merely be added in passing that, if this variant locates Starkaðr with precision in relation to Óðinn and Þórr, it defines him no less clearly in connection with the third functional god, Freyr. When we look to Saxo, we know that "Frø" and his sons appear only as the debauched, sensuous rulers of Uppsala—probably a memory of the idol of Freyr *ingenti priapo*, which Adam of Bremen still identified with it, and of the festivals which, every ninth year, gave rise to such lewd scenes that the same traveler believed it his duty to refrain from describing them. Now, shortly after the murder of Wicarus, Starcatherus makes his way to Uppsala:

... he lived at leisure for seven years' space with the sons of Frø. At last he left them and betook himself to Hacon, the tyrant of Denmark, because when

10. See especially Gustav Neckel, *Beiträge sur Eddaforschung* (1908), pp. 351–58: "Víkarsbálkr"; and the note "verdebt?" in *Eddica Minora*, p. 42, to the beginning of strophe 18.

stationed at Uppsala, at the time of the sacrifices, he was disgusted by the effeminate gestures and the clapping of the mimes on the stage, and by the unmanly clatter of the bells. Hence it is clear how far he kept his soul from lasciviousness, not even enduring to look upon it. [6.5.10]

Adeo virtus luxui resistit, the sententious author concludes, setting the principles of the second and third functions in clear opposition.[11]

11. In the first part of *ME* 2 I shall take up in its entirety the legend of Starkaðr in which the "three sins" are only one element. His birth as a monster, his reduction to human form, his relations with two antagonistic gods, his theory of royalty, and generally his conduct toward the kings will receive a harmonious explanation, and the variant of the *Gautrekssaga* will receive more consideration than it did here. Nothing will change concerning the "three sins," which, in this larger perspective, will only take on a more profound significance.

5

THE THREE SINS OF HERACLES

Dare one hope that the foregoing considerations will encourage Hellenists to revise—paying attention not only to particular episodes but also to the general structures—the distressing treatment that the story of Heracles has been receiving for several generations?

This hero, the only pan-Hellenic hero, must certainly, in many Greek regions, have given rise to diverse traditions, new episodes, or variants of traditional episodes. But when his career finds him in Argolis, in Thebes, back in Argolis, then in many provinces of Greece, not to mention Lydia and the rest of the world, let us not jump so readily to the conclusion that we have before us Argive legends, Theban legends, etc., arranged artificially, belatedly set end to end, and that the first task of criticism is to disperse them again. It is to be expected that a hero of Heracles' type should be itinerant, that he should carry out many deeds in many places.

When Homer or Pindar make use of only one episode, or a fragment of an episode, and when, in this very fragment, they fail to transcribe some detail that other versions have led us to expect, let us not immediately conclude that they were unaware of all the other legends about Heracles or even of the particular detail itself. The poet may deliberately have said only what was useful to characterize, to evoke in passing, a personage from ancient times. And when so troublesome a matter as the hero's madness was in question, the poet may have refrained from saying anything.

Finally, let us rid ourselves of philological ingenuity. One of the most intelligent studies of these legends, still useful after three-quarters of a century, is, in my opinion, the *Vorwort* that Ulrich von Wilamowitz-Moellendorff devoted to the "Raging Heracles." After scoffing at the comparative mythology of his time, which he found too facile—twenty years later he would also be able to dismiss the disappointing work of Leopold von Schröder on Heracles and Indra—he gave several detailed examples of the critical method. What confidence and what illusions! For example, with respect to the murder of the children: "Auch hier ist eine mühsame Voruntersuchung nötig, um auf dem zerstreuten Materiale die älteste Gestalt der Geschichte zu gewinnen, die dem Urteil über ihre Bedeutung allein zu Grunde gelegt werden darf" (1.81). *Eine mühsame Voruntersuchung*, "a toilsome preliminary investigation": yes, let us free ourselves from these laborious preparations, which sometimes lack clarity (p. 87), and which are too often designed to give a scientific veneer to a preformed conviction.

With the fear and trembling that accompany such an indiscretion, I will insist only that the most general framework of the legends of Heracles, in its two most systematic presentations (Diodorus of Sicily and the pseudo-Apollodorus of Athens), is clarified and gains plausibility by comparison with that of the legends of Starkaðr the sinner, of Indra the chastised sinner, and generally by reference to the epic theme that we have delineated. The career of Heracles is in fact divided into three and only three parts, each ended by a serious sin which demands an expiation. And following the first two sins is a set of adventures that is presented as its consequence. The aftereffects of these sins bear heavily upon the hero, the first one in his mental health, the second in his physical health, and the third in his life itself. Finally, these sins correspond to the three functions, following the descending hierarchical order, since they involve, in turn, a hesitation before an order of Zeus, the cowardly murder of a surprised enemy, and a guilty amorous passion. Let us follow the account of Diodorus in his fourth book.[1]

(A) *The Origin and Functional Value of Heracles* [9]

Even before his birth, Heracles—who will not have three lives, but whose conception took three nights to prepare—is officially classified as a hero of the second function. Just before Alcmene's

1. Citations from Diodorus are from the translation by C. H. Oldfather, Loeb Classical Library (1935).

parturition, Zeus, who has sired him at Tiryns, announces in the presence of the gods that the first child about to be born will be king of the Argives. As a result, Hera checks the birth-pains of Alcmene and has Eurystheus born before he is due. Now Alcmene's child will not be king. In compensation, Zeus promises that after having served Eurystheus by performing twelve labors, Heracles will attain immortality. In the scene which follows the birth, the protection which the infant receives from Athena and the hostility he arouses from Hera—Hera the queen, Athena the warrior: let us recall the "trifunctional problem" posed by Hera, Athena, and Aphrodite to the unfortunate Paris[2]—confirm the "second function" character of his destiny.

(B) *The First Sin* [10.6–11.1]

Heracles is in Thebes. The tremendous services he has rendered have led the king to give him his daughter Megara in marriage.

... but Eurystheus, who was ruler of Argolis, viewing with suspicion the growing power of Heracles, summoned him to his side and commanded him to perform Labours. And when Heracles ignored the summons Zeus despatched word to him to enter the service of Eurystheus; whereupon Heracles journeyed to Delphi, and on inquiring of the god regarding the matter he received a reply which stated that the gods had decided that he should perform twelve Labours at the command of Eurystheus and that upon their conclusion he should receive the gift of immortality.

At such a turn of affairs Heracles fell into despondency of no ordinary kind; for he felt that servitude to an inferior was a thing which his high achievements did not deserve, and yet he saw that it would be hurtful to himself and impossible not to obey Zeus, who was his father as well. While he was thus greatly at a loss, Hera sent upon him a frenzy [λύτταν],[3] and in his vexation of soul he fell into a madness [εἰς μανίαν ἐνέπεσε].

Then follows a whole cycle: the murder of his children, whom he pierces with arrows in his delirium, the painful return to reason, the submission to the will of the gods, the twelve labors accomplished under the order of Eurystheus with many sub-labors added according

2. *ME* 1:581–86.

3. See the excellent observations on the *Λύσσα* of Euripides' *Heracles*, compared to the Alecto of the seventh book of the *Aeneid* (less delicately shaded, "das Böse an sich"), in Vinzenz Buchheit's *Vergil über die Sendung Roms* (1963), pp. 101–2.

to circumstance, and finally a long series of exploits taking him throughout the world.

(c) *The Second Sin* [31.1–4]

After Heracles had completed his Labours he gave his own wife Megara in marriage to Iolaos, being apprehensive of begetting any children by her because of the calamity which had befallen their other offspring, and sought another wife by whom he might have children without apprehension. Consequently he wooed Iole, the daughter of Eurytus who was ruler of Oechalia. But Eurytus was hesitant because of the ill fortune which had come in the case of Megara and replied that he would deliberate concerning the marriage. Since Heracles had met with a refusal to his suit, because of the dishonour which had been showered upon him he now drove off the mares of Eurytus. But Iphitus, the son of Eurytus, harboured suspicions of what had been done and came to Tiryns in search of the horses, whereupon Heracles, taking him up on a lofty tower of the castle, asked to see whether they were by chance grazing anywhere; and when Iphitus was unable to discover them, he claimed that Iphitus had falsely accused him of the theft and threw him down headlong from the tower. Because of his murder of Iphitus Heracles was attacked by disease [νοσήσας . . .].

When Neleus refuses to purify him, he has Deïphobus perform the ceremony; but the disease does not disappear. For the second time he consults the oracle of Apollo, which answers "that he could easily rid himself of the disease if he should be sold as a slave and honorably pay over the purchase price of himself to the sons of Iphitus." And thus we have the sale to Omphale, the bondage in Lydia, and a new series of exploits.

In this episode, Diodorus' account attenuates the fault of Heracles: he has indeed set a trap for Iphitus, his guest, by urging him to climb the tower from which Heracles will easily be able to hurl him; but just as Heracles is about to hurl him, he warns him, even if only by his reproaches, and the surprise is no longer total. In Sophocles' *Trachiniae*, the messenger Lichas offers a better explanation for the divine punishment:

. . . and when one day Iphitus came to the hill of Tiryns, searching for the tracks of the horses that had strayed, the moment his eyes looked one way, his mind on something else, Heracles hurled him from the top of that flat bastion.

But the King was angry with this act of his, he who is the father of all,

Zeus Olympian, and had him sold and sent out of the country, *since this was the only man [of all those killed by Heracles] he had ever killed by guile [ὅθουνεκ' αὐτὸν μοῦνον ἀνθρώπων δόλῳ / ἔκτεινεν]*. If he had taken vengeance openly [ἐμφανῶς], [evidently in connection with his adversary], Zeus surely would have pardoned his rightful victory. The gods like foul play no better than do men. [269–80][4]

Thus Heracles' fault is to have violated, contrary to his regular practice, the duty and the honor of the Strong-One by substituting the trap for the duel, by taking a man by surprise who should have been able to regard himself secure in Tiryns, his safety guaranteed by the unwritten pact of hospitality: one can sense how close we are to the episode of Namuci (or Vṛtra) in the myths of Indra.

(D) *The Third Sin and the Death* [37.4–38.2]

Heracles has finally found in Deïaneira the lawful wife he had sought and who had been refused him since his separation from Megara. But before dying, the Centaur Nessus has given Deïaneira a little of his blood which is poisoned by the arrow that has been dipped in the Hydra's venom, and has told her that if her husband should be touched by a fabric saturated with this potion, his affection, if one day it were found wanting, would be assured. Soon the hero forgets that he is married.

. . . as he was leaving the territory of Itonus and was making his way through Pelasgiotis he fell in with Ormenius the king and asked of him the hand of his daughter Astydameia. When Ormenius refused him because he already had for lawful wife Deïaneira, the daughter of Oeneus, Heracles took the field against him, captured his city, and slew the king who would not obey him, and taking captive Astydameia he lay with her and begat a son Ctesipus. After finishing this exploit he set out to Oechalia to take the field against the sons of Eurytus because he had been refused in his suit for the hand of Iole. The Arcadians again fought on his side and he captured the city and slew the sons of Eurytus, who were Toxeus, Molion, and Clytius. And taking Iole captive he departed from Euboea to the promontory which is called Cenaeon.

At Cenaeon Heracles, wishing to perform a sacrifice, dispatched his attendant Lichas to Deïaneira his wife, commanding him to ask her for the shirt

4. Michael Jameson, trans., *The Woman of Trachis*, in David Grene and Richmond Lattimore, eds., *The Complete Greek Tragedies*, vol. 2, *Sophocles* (University of Chicago Press, 1959). Italics added.

and robe which he customarily wore in the celebration of sacrifices, But when Deïaneira learned from Lichas of the love which Heracles had for Iole, she wished him to have a greater affection for herself and so anointed the shirt with the love-charm which had been given her by the Centaur, whose intention was to bring about the death of Heracles. Lichas, then, in ignorance of these matters, brought back the garments for the sacrifice; and Heracles put on the shirt which had been anointed, and as the strength of the toxic drug began slowly to work he met with the most terrible calamity. For the arrow's barb had carried the poison of the Hydra, and when the shirt for this reason, as it became heated, attacked the flesh of the body, Heracles was seized with such anguish [. . . *τοῦ χιτῶνος διὰ τὴν θερμασίαν τὴν σάρκα τοῦ σώματος λυμαινομένου, περιαλγὴς γενόμενος ὁ Ἡρακλῆς* . . .].

Having fallen prey to such increasing and intolerable suffering (*ἀεὶ δὲ μᾶλλον τῇ νόσῳ βαρυνόμενος* [38.3]), the hero dispatches envoys to seek a third and last consultation at Delphi. Apollo responds: Let Heracles be carried onto mount Oete, with all his arms, and a huge pyre be built for him; as for the rest, it should be left to Zeus. And thus we have the pyre, the service of the young and pure Philoctetes who lights it, the bolt of Zeus, and the disappearance of every earthly trace of the man who has attained immortality.

Such is the three-act drama—three sins, three maladies, scanned by three Delphic oracles—which develops, in descending hierarchical order, in accord with the three functions. If the beginning of Heracles' epic (the role of the divinities of the first and second functions) and also its end (the death, suicidal in nature, after the third sin; the demand that a pure young man administer the killing) recall the epic Starcatherus, the details of the second (Iphitus) and the third (Iole) sins are even closer to the second (Namuci) and third (Ahalyā) sins of Indra; in particular, the sin of the third function concerns sexual concupiscence, as with Indra, not venality, as with Starcatherus.[5] Equally close to the Indian conception, in connection with Indra, is the theme of three "losses," which are the consequence of the three sins as well as their punishment: Indra's loss of *tejas* and then of *bala* (psychic force and physical force) after the sins of the first and second functions have the same quality as Heracles' loss of

5. See an analogous pair of variants in my *Tarpeia*, pp. 280–81 (Tarpeia betrays for love of gold, or for love of Tatius); cf. *ME* 1:428–30; 491 and n. 2; 560.

mental health and physical health after his sins of the same levels, with one difference: for Indra the three irreparable losses add themselves together to constitute in their progressive sum the equivalent of an annihilation, whereas for Heracles the first two sins are entirely atoned for, and it is the third, by itself, *ab integro*, which occasions his death. Let us draw no final conclusions about these partial agreements. It is still quite possible that, since the subject matter readily suggests definite oppositions and definite causal connections, one and the same epic framework could have been embroidered in convergent variations by the Indians, the Germans, and the Greeks. But first we must account for the framework, and our actual purpose is only to establish its existence in these three domains. Despite the variants, despite their multiplication in a fashion typical of Greek legends, despite, more especially, the frequent displacements of the Iphitus episode (second sin) in the course of the hero's career, perhaps Hellenists will agree to retain this new element of explanation and accept that fundamentally, at all times, before its further developments, the story of Heracles was marked out by these three ideologically interdependent episodes, either in their present form or equivalent forms.[6] In any case, it is harder to understand how these late compilers could have reinvented such a framework in a period

6. In the *Bibliotheca* of Apollodorus (2.4.8–7.7) the "scansion" of the multitude of Heracles exploits by three sins and three curses (μανῆναι, 4, 12; δεινῇ νόσῳ, 6. 2; ὁ τῆς ὕδρας ἰὸς τὸν χρῶτα ἔσηπε, 7. 7) is very similar, with several reservations of which the most important bears upon the first sin and its connection with the first malady: (1) the madness in which he kills his children is visited upon Heracles (or rather upon "Alcides," still his name) by Hera, no longer after (and under cover of the depression produced by) an initial sin, but simply κατά ζῆλον, from jealousy; no matter how involuntary, it is the murder of the children that determines the character of the sin—a sin, moreover, of the "first function" since he defies the sacred ties of blood; (2) at the same stroke, the first consultation at Delphi is displaced: it comes, as is natural, after the event that is the fault in this context, thus *after* the sacrilegious murder of the children (it no longer follows the disobedience of divine orders, given *before* the murder); the question that Alcides puts to the Pythian is "where he should dwell," and it is the priestess, in giving him the name "Heracles," who commands him to go and serve Eurystheus for twelve years and perform ten labors (which will become twelve); (3) the two other sins and the corresponding curses are presented as in Diodorus, but there is a consultation at Delphi only after the second, not after the third: it is on his own that Heracles, his flesh torn away, constructs his pyre (after having charged his legitimate son Hyllus to marry, when he came of age, Iole, Heracles' concubine, his partner in the third sin and the cause of his misfortune; all of which underlines the sexual character of this fault). It will be observed that neither in Apollodorus nor in Diodorus is any of the other acts of violence which Heracles commits in his long career, not even the odious murder of the *Κήρυκες*, the heralds of the king of the Minyans (Diod. 4.10.2; Apoll. 2.4.11)—and the heralds are from Zeus!—considered a fault, nor does any deed entail a divine punishment, sickness or otherwise.

when the memory of the ancient, prehistoric trifunctional structure was surely lost.

Among those who perform this series of significant sins, Starkaðr, Heracles, and Indra are warriors. As we have noted, only the Iranian Yima is of another rank. Having started, apparently, from the third function, to which the original meaning of his name ("the Twin") inclines him, Yima sits enthroned in the first as sovereign of the Golden Age. There he dominates the three functions equally, instituting the human support for each (the three social classes), and none of his characteristics indicate that he incarnates the warrior function in any special way. He does not, at any rate, sin in the manner of the warrior; his entire misfortune consists in a single sin of another type. This is not surprising: in Zoroastrianism, the warrior we are faced with is a purified warrior, a crusader in the service of the true religion, who, theoretically, is absolved of the risks of his vocation.

One of the concerns and one of the toughest enterprises of the Zoroastrian reform, as has been demonstrated frequently,[7] was the abolition of the warrior function as such, the elimination of the special ethic of the Indo-Iranian warrior, for the sake of the uniform and universal ethic which, purified and deepened, was itself no more than the ethic of the first function, of the "priestly level." The evil or demonic values given to certain concepts, or to such figures as the *mairya*, Aēšma, Indra, and Saurva, indicate the import of this correction and the energy that went into it.[8] Simultaneously, above the three functions and more important than they, the figure of the great unique god—without common measure with the rest of the good things of the earth, which are only his creation—has taken on a relief, a radiation, a "presence" until then unheard of: henceforth, it is toward Ahura Mazdā and his commandments that all the lines of force of the ideology converge. Now, if we consider that, according to Zoroaster, the warrior of the ancient type is totally and radically evil, and that his entire life, in its every moment and every act, is an abomination, it seems natural that a theme like that of the warrior's three sins and their consequences would have been eliminated;

7. Most recently, in "Les archanges de Zoroastre et les rois romains de Cicéron," *Journal de psychologie*, 1950, pp. 449–63; reprinted, with alterations, in *Idées romaines* (1969), pt. 2, chap. 4.

8. See S. Wikander, *Der arische Männerbund*, chaps. 3 and 4.

how could such a warrior be conceived as disfiguring or dishonoring an otherwise more or less honorable life by three exceptional sins?[9] And how could a warrior of the new type commit three such sins without becoming, at the same stroke, irremediably evil?

In the study which now draws to a close we have considered only those heroic careers where the impulse to sin is expressed within the framework of the three functions. There are enough such careers to make it certain that the theme is ancient. But let us not forget that this is but one particular case of the general theme of the "sins of the warrior." In the absence of a "sin of the third function," it is Tullus' disdain of the gods and the rites, then his harshness toward his sick soldiers, that earn him his punishment: first, being affected by the epidemic, then falling into degrading superstition, and finally dying in his palace set ablaze by Jupiter's thunderbolt (see above, p. 43). The gigantic Bhīma in the *Mahābhārata* accumulates faults without number or apparent classification, earning him the reproaches of the chivalrous Arjuna and the just Yudhiṣṭhira. In the Caucasus, in the Nart epic of the Ossets, peopled with archaic figures, the exemplary warrior Batraz, the man of steel, lives through a continuous series of excesses which even set him against God, and he ends, for the relief of his people, by dying voluntarily on a pyre more colossal than the one on mount Oete. And so it is in numerous epics, not only Indo-European ones. What is limited to the Indo-Europeans, to a few Indo-European peoples, and bound to the axis of their ideology, is the precise form of this fatality that we have now managed to identify.

9. See above, chap. 6, n. 19, and chap. 7, n. 6.

6

FATALITIES OF THE WARRIOR FUNCTION

The preceding pages, with increasing precision, have yielded an important lesson: even as a god, the warrior is exposed by his nature to sin. Through his own function, and for the general welfare, he is constrained to commit sinful acts, but soon he transgresses this limitation and sins against the ideals of each of the three functions, including his own. Our picture, however, will be complete and in proportion only if we address and resolve a classificatory problem analogous to the one from which we set out[1]: the relations of the notion of sin to each of the gods of the three functions. The warrior's originality will thereby be set off all the more clearly: Mitra and Varuṇa, by definition, do not sin at all; the Aśvin do not even think of sinning. Only in Indra do we find the temptation to perform misdeeds combined with the means to carry them out.

How could Mitra, Varuṇa, and the other Āditya sin? They form one body with the *ṛtá*, the moral as well as cosmic and ritual order which they created, which they uphold and which they enforce. Milder, more evenly shaded, more comforting in connection with Mitra, more rigorous, even terrible in connection with Varuṇa, it is always the *ṛtá* that is the principle of action for these gods and, in the case of Varuṇa, one can almost say his "passion." They are less in the *ṛtá* than the *ṛtá* is in them. Sin, however, is defined only by its connection with *ṛtá*; in fact, it is its violation, its negation (*ánṛta*).[2]

1. See above, pp. 53–61, with regard to the form taken by the idea of the "pair" on each of the three levels.

2. Cf. Sten Rodhe, *Deliver Us from Evil: Studies on the Vedic Ideas of Salvation* (1946). But human kings may sin (pride, contempt for the gods, tyranny, etc.); see above, p. 78, n. 7.

Astounding as they sometimes appear to the modern conscience, the actions of these gods do actually conform to *ṛtá*. The deeds of violence, the sudden seizures, the pitiless punishments of Varuṇa, indeed, even the things which relate him, the great asura, to the demonic host of asura—none of this has anything to do with sin.

And how could the Aśvin, at the third level, sin? Their entire function, their total nature, is to be benevolent, to be benefactors, σωτῆρες, like the Greek twins. The hymns addressed to them are no more than catalogs, series of allusions to the numerous services they have rendered. Moreover, in order to sin, one must stand in opposition to the *ṛtá*, and these ever useful gods, as the attentive Abel Bergnaigne has already remarked,[3] take little interest in the order of the world. Their concern is more modest, limited to special cases: first one, then another, and still another man falling prey to some well-defined hardship and needing their corresponding help. Neither the poet nor the reader would think of debating whether or not they operate in conformity with the *ṛtá*. Probably they do, in that they are good, but it is not a vital matter: the level of their activity, like that of the miracle-working saints of our occidental legends, is rather one of charity than of justice.

Indra and his warriors have been given a very different cosmic and social position. They cannot ignore order, since their function is to guard it against the thousand and one demonic or hostile endeavors that oppose it. But in order to assure this office they must first possess and entertain qualities of their own which bear a strong resemblance to the blemishes of their adversaries. In battle itself they must respond to boldness, surprise, pretense, and treachery with operations of the same style, only more effective, or else face sure defeat. Drunk or exalted, they must put themselves into a state of nervous tension, of muscular and mental preparedness, multiplying and amplifying their powers. And so they are transfigured, made strangers in the society they protect. And above all, dedicated to Force, they are the triumphant victims of the internal logic of Force, which proves itself only by surpassing boundaries—even its own boundaries and those of its raison d'être. The warrior is the one who finds comfort only in being strong, not only in the face

3. See his fine study on the "idea of law," in *La religion védique* 3 (1883):250.

of this or that adversary, in this or that situation, but strong absolutely, the strongest of all—a dangerous superlative for a being who occupies the second rank. The revolts of generals and the military coups d'état, the massacres and pillages by the undisciplined soldiery and by its leaders, all these are older than history. And that is why Indra, as Sten Rodhe puts it so well, is "the sinner among the gods."

There is still, however, the point, a significant one, at which the fatalities of the warrior again take on a positive aspect: when by itself the *ṛtá* is inflexible, inhuman, or when its strict application turns into the *summum ius* of the occidental maxim, to take opposition to it, to reform it, or to violate it, while surely a sin from the perspective of Varuṇa, is in the language of men a movement of progress. In a chapter of my *Mitra-Varuṇa* (6, "Nexum et mutuum") in which certain Roman juridical facts (§3) are treated somewhat too freely, but in which the rest, and the general direction, are valid, a study was made of this beneficent opposition of Indra to Varuṇa (§4), of the hero's ethic to that of the sovereign (§5), especially in the Indian traditions which attribute to Indra the service of saving human victims *in extremis*, or even of substituting the ritual in which only a horse perished for the old Varuṇian royal consecration ritual tainted by the practice or the memory of human sacrifices. "It will occasion no astonishment," I wrote thirty years ago, "that the god of men's societies, often frightful in so many respects, should appear in Indian fable, in opposition to the magical binder, as a merciful god, the god who delivers the regular victims, the human victims, of Varuṇa. The warrior and the sorcerer, or, on another level, the soldier and the policeman, work equally, when occasion demands, for the liberty and the life of their fellows; but each operates according to procedures which the other finds distasteful. Above all, it is the warrior, in placing himself on the margin of the code, or even beyond it, who appropriates the right to pardon, to break through the mechanisms of hard justice, in short, the right to introduce some flexibility into the strictly determined course of human relations: to pave the way for humanity."

THIRD PART

PROMOTIONS

Epiphanies
Dummies
Grimaces

1

THE MOMENTS OF A HEROIC CAREER

The foregoing essays have brought to light the perils of the martial exploit, the stain it sometimes produces, the excesses and sins it favors. Nevertheless, in every civilization the exploit is also an investment. Military or athletic, theatrical or sometimes even intellectual, accomplished independently or under the standard of the collectivity, even today it produces the national hero. At the very least, it results in a champion, a "star," a laureate, whose life, overnight, becomes glorious or even luxurious. The exploit is like success in competition, assuring promotion.

It was no different in ancient societies, especially those engaged in war. Well before Plutarch and his great captains, the career of a warrior consisted merely of a series of promotions based on a series of exploits, a series that was, moreover, monotonous. The very last exploit itself—death in battle, which the ancient Germans were not the only ones to exalt—did not differ essentially from the others, either in its motions or in its effects. While it only results, nowadays, in speeches prepared by hungry young secretaries and mouthed by politicians in front of mass-produced monuments, formerly it opened the way to a new life in the beyond, similar to the first, where the same contests continued but without their danger.

In Valhöll, the legendary abode of Óðinn, men who have died on the fields of battle, since the world began, live forever.[1] An immense throng, ever increasing; and it can continue to increase[2] as its sustenance is assured. Sæhrímnir the wild boar, devoured each day,

1. Gustav Neckel, *Walhall, Studien über germanischen Jenseitsglauben* (1913).

2. Karl Helm, "Die Zahl der Einherjar," *Arkiv för Nordisk Filologi* 42 (1926):314–19. The interpretation of Magnus Olsen, according to which the image of Valhöll and the

revives every evening to be placed in the cauldron Eldrímnir by the hands of Andrímnir the cook; every evening the udders of the goat Heiðrún fill a huge bowl with mead, for only Óðinn drinks wine, the luxury of luxuries in ancient Scandinavia. And the time that the elect do not devote to this prodigious menu, they give up entirely to their former passion on earth: every morning, day after day, they take up their arms, go out, and fight.[3] It was formerly thought that this blessed other world was first concerned during the Viking period, a transposition of the ideal life of the conquering band. The interpretation tallies with the fact, but not with the date. Óðinn's elect surely form a "band," a men's society, such as abounded among the Vikings; but the type was as old as the Germanic world. Proof is furnished by the very name of Óðinn's elect, the *Einherjar* (**aina-harija-*),[4] the second element of which is none other than the name of an ancient people of continental Germany, the Harii, whom Tacitus (*Germania*, 43.6) quite appropriately depicts as such a men's society, although without entirely understanding its mechanism:

> The Harii, apart from strength in which they surpass the peoples just enumerated, are fierce in nature, and trick out this natural ferocity by the help of art and season: they blacken their shields and dye their bodies; they choose pitchy nights for their battles; by sheer panic and darkness they strike terror like an army of ghosts [*feralis exercitus*]. No enemy can face this novel and, as it were, phantasmal vision [*nouum ac uelut infernam aspectum*]: in every battle after all the eye is conquered first.[5]

Mortally wounded at the end of the battle of Kurukṣetra, Duryodhana—who, although deserving his misfortunes, shows to the very

---

Einherjar were inspired by the Colosseum and the gladiators (μονο-μάχοι), is no more than an ingenious construction: "Valhall med de mange dörer," *Acta Philologica Scandinavica* 6 (1931–32):151–70 (reprinted in *Norrone Studier*, 1938); cf. Jan de Vries, *Altgermanische Religionsgeschichte*[2] 2 (1957):378–79.

3. Such is the description in Snorri's Edda, *Gylfaginning*, 38–41; another description is in the Edda in verse, *Grimnismál*, st. 8–23 (in which beer appears).

4. For *ein-*, see above, p. 60, and cf. Erik, *Ein-ríkr*, "unique potent," the name of several kings, one of whom, a legendary figure, has the honors of chapter 20 of the Ynglingasaga and of Saxo, 5.10 (cf. *Ainarich, Einrih*, etc.); see Arwid Johansson, *Arkiv för Nordisk Filologi* 49 (1933):234–37.

5. The translation of Tacitus' *Germania* is by W. Peterson (Loeb Classical Library, 1914). It has sometimes even been thought that *Harii* was not the name of a people but of a society of warriors; their name may have survived in that of the *Herilunga* or *Harlunge* of German epic; see Ludwig Weniger, "Exercitus Feralis," *Archiv für Religionswissenschaft* 9 (1906):201–47 (with Greek comparisons), and the commentary by Rudolf Much in his edition of the *Germania* (1937), pp. 382–86.

end several of the qualities of a *kṣatriya*—sees in the blow that fells him something more than a stroke of deplorable destiny:

Glory is all that one should acquire here, and it can be obtained by battle, and by no other means. The death that a *kṣatriya* meets with at home is censurable. Death on one's bed is highly sinful. The man who casts away his body in the woods [like an ascetic] or in battle after having performed sacrifices, obtains great glory. . . . Abandoning diverse objects of enjoyment, I shall now, by righteous battle, proceed to the regions of Indra, obtaining the companionship of those who have attained the highest end. Without doubt, the habitation of heroes of righteous behavior, who never retreat from battle . . . is in heaven. The diverse tribes of Apsaras, without doubt, joyfully gaze[6] at such heroes when engaged in battle. Without doubt, the Fathers behold them worshipped in the assembly of the gods and rejoicing in heaven, in the company of Apsaras. We will now ascend the path that is trod by the celestials and by heroes unreturning from battle. . . .[7]

In the fourteenth Philippic, even Cicero, already destined for another mode of death, entrusts the dead of the *legio Martia*, the heroes of a hollow victory, to the eponymous god.

In flight death is disgraceful; in victory glorious; for Mars himself is wont to claim out of the battle-line the bravest as his own. Those impious wretches then whom you have slain will even among the shades below pay the penalty of their treason; but you who have poured out your last breath in victory have won the seats and the abodes of the pious.[8]

If the concluding exploit, equal to the others but brightened with these expectations, paradoxically takes on the character of an

6. Śloka 35: *mudā nūnaṃ* prapaśyanti *yuddhe hy apsarasāṃ gaṇāḥ*; cf., at the end of the seventh book of the *Aeneid*, the young men and women "following with the eyes" the young horsewoman Camille, 813: . . . *iuuentus turbaque miratur matrum et* prospectat *euntem / attonitis inhians animis* . . .

7. 9.4.29–37, especially 30:

gr̥he yat kṣatriyasyāpi nidhanaṃ tad vigarhitam
adharmaḥ sumahān eṣa yac chayāmaraṇaṃ gr̥he.

Cf. 11.26.12–13. Edward W. Hopkins, *Epic Mythology* (1915), p. 109: "the dead in the battle of Kurukṣetra will not go to the kingdom of Yama, but directly to heaven" (9.52, rejected into a note after śl. 16 in the Poona edition: *yamasya viṣayaṃ te tu na drakṣyanti kadācana*); motive (18): raised by wind, the dust of the battlefield will purify even the most sinful among them and bring them to heaven.

8. 32: *Vos uero patriae natos iudico, quorum etiam nomen a Marte est, ut idem deus urbem hanc gentibus, uos huic urbi genuisse uideatur. In fuga foeda mors est, in uictoria gloriosa. Etenim Mars ipse ex acie fortissimum quemque pignerari solet. Illi igitur impii, quos cecidistis, etiam ad infernos poenas parricidii luent, uos uero, qui extremum spiritum in uictoria effudistis, piorum estis sedem et locum consecuti.*

initiatory test for the life beyond, the very first exploit, the one which introduces the young warrior to his earthly career, is hardly different from those he will accomplish henceforth, on to his death. The singular moment of the first exploit is, after all, original only for putting an end to a sort of minority by age, generally spent in a detailed and thorough training. This explains why the comparison of the myths and legends that illustrate the function of the warrior among diverse peoples so often brings to light homologous motifs—for example, a fight with a type of especially strong or terrifying adversary—employed with little variation, here in an "initiation" narrative for the glory of the heroic novice, there in a tale of "confirmation" or "promotion" for the glory of the hero who has already been tested. As we have seen,[9] Cúchulainn's victory over the three sons of Nechta is the very model of the initiatory combat, one of the *macgnímratha* that the child accomplishes, for the first time away from the supervision of his preceptors, while the conquest of the three Curiaces is achieved by a victor who is chosen with his two brothers for the decisive encounter just because of his known experience: Rome does not entrust her fate to newly enlisted men. The two scenes are nonetheless neighboring renditions of a common theme, simply allocated to two different moments on the ascent to glory. The exegete must not forget this elementary fact, and must refrain from generalizing the notions of "Jünglings-" or of "Kriegerweihe."

It will now be shown that several of the exploits of Indra in the mythology of the hymns and the *Brāhmaṇa*, and still more in the mythology of the epics which so often extend para-Vedic material that is as old as or older than that of the *R̥g Veda*, are clarified by being compared with scenes—whether of initiation or promotion—occurring in the myths or legends of other peoples of the family.

9. See above, p. 10, and below, pp. 133–37.

2

Vr̥trahán, Vərəθrağna, Vahagn

The first problem to be faced in dealing with our present subject is that of the relation of the Vedic Indra Vr̥trahán to the Iranian god Vərəθrağna. Emile Benveniste and the late Louis Renou devoted an important book to that problem a third of a century ago,[1] and the test of time has confirmed their linguistic and philological analyses. Time has also shown that an understanding of the religious realities underlying and sustaining the texts will require further observations and approaches, in addition to those set by the authors to define the limits of their study.

One of the most significant results of the 1934 book was to establish the secondary character of the demon Vr̥tra: the Vedic hymns present him in vague terms, while in Iran he does not even exist as a demon, either in the Avesta or in the lateral traditions. What is consistent and "living" is his adversary, either the "slayer (or destroyer) of *vr̥trá*," the *vr̥trahán*, the *vərəθragan*,[2] or "the destruction of the *vərəθra*," that is, the neuter *vərəθrağna*, secondarily personified as masculine in the god of the same name. Moreover, in conformity with the etymology, the neuter *vr̥trá*, which only India has explicitly made into a demon, is properly "resistance," the imposing but passive mass, object of the assailant's blows and opposed to his offensive force, *áma*, the quality which animates him.

The personification of *vərəθrağna* as a "yazata" is surely connected with the far-reaching reform which produced the divine world of Zoroastrianism, entirely dominated by Ahura Mazdā, from Indo-Iranian polytheism, and, more precisely, with the veritable revolution

1. *Vr̥tra et Vr̥θragna* (*V. et V.*) = *Cahiers de la Société Asiatique* 3 (1934).
2. Nomin. *vərəθrajā̊*, etc.

which degraded one of the foremost gods of the conquering bands into an archdemon. In Indo-Iranian theology, the functions and the functional gods were juxtaposed, thus justifying different moral codes for the different human groups. Among these, warrior societies were, in essence, disquieting to priests and breeder-agriculturalists alike. We may apply to these *márya*, often excessive—especially in their relations with women—what has been said about the Scandinavian *berserkir*: aside from their service in battle, they were "aufdringlich und bösartig" in peacetime, and consequently hated.[3] Polytheism consecrated this natural fatality, as we have seen, in the conduct of various divine beings, the principal of whom was Indra, Indra the sinner: the violence which he controlled, and which his actions exemplified, contributed no less to the social and cosmic equilibrium than the various forms of good behavior patronized by Mitra and Varuṇa or the unfailing and unconditional readiness to serve personified by the Twins.[4] Mazdaism changed all this and replaced a harmonization of different moralities by the uniform, universal law of one great god. Theologically, and probably socially, the most vigorous and difficult attack had to be carried out against the traditional warriors, human and divine; the problem was to redeploy them in the service of the good religion, that is, to preserve their force and valor while depriving them of their autonomy.[5] Most certainly the operation could not have been performed without difficulty, and the primary victim was Indra. The purified "warrior function," the domesticated heritage of the god who was henceforth to be no more than one of the most pernicious auxiliaries of the Evil Spirit, found itself apportioned between a god of the "first function," Miθra, who, by his very nature, was able to retain his traditional name in the new system, and a personified abstraction, Vərəθrağna, the spirit of offensive victory, subordinate, in fact, to Miθra. Henceforth, it was Miθra who was to hurl the *vazra* against infidels and rebels, and Vərəθrağna who was to encounter them with another gift of the former celestial champion, his capacity for animal metamorphoses. Together they assured the community of the faithful what Indra

3. Finnur Jónsson, *Egils saga Skallagrímssonar* (1894), p. 30, note to 9.3.

4. See above, pp. 105–6.

5. "Les archanges de Zoroastre et les rois romains de Cicéron, retouches homologues à des traditions parallèles," *Journal de Psychologie*, 43 (1950): 449–65, reprinted, with modifications, in *Idées romaines* (1969), pt. 2, chap. 4.

had until then assured the tribes of the Arya: success by means of arms, conquest.

Under this name, scarcely modified by the passage to the abstract, it is certain that Vərəθrağna reappropriated one of the most popular titles of the Indo-Iranian Indra. There is no reason to think that the Vedas innovated in making *Vr̥trahán* one of the epithets, the most prestigious one, of this god.

To be sure, Indra had no monopoly on the name. It is found applied to all that is victorious by nature, or, in a particular circumstance:[6] to multivalent, or, more precisely, trivalent divinities like Soma, Agni, and Sarasvatī; to Manyu, the personification of the "furor" of the combatant; to concepts or mythical representations connected with battle such as force, intoxication, or the *vájra*, Indra's weapon. But it is also conferred upon a mere mortal, *Trasádasyu*, properly upon "him who makes the enemies (or the demons) tremble," of interest for our purposes because several texts present him as an extraordinary warrior, and also because he bears in his name one of the rare Vedic attestations of the root *tras-*, related to Latin *terrēre*, surely an important one in the ideology as well as the techniques of the Indo-European warrior.[7] *R̥gVeda* 4.38.1, for example, calls him *kṣetrāsā́m . . . urvarāsā́ṃ ghanám dásyubhyo abhíbhūtim ugrám*, "conqueror of the habitable lands, conqueror of the ploughed lands, destruction for the enemies, superior, strong." As such he is the object of the attentions of Indra (8.36.7): *prá Trasádasyum āvitha tvám éka ín nr̥sā́hya índra*, "you alone, oh Indra, have aided Trasadasyu in the battle of men." Now, as soon as he is born, this personage, in the two consecutive strophes 4.42.8 and 9, is called *índram ná vr̥tratúram ardhadevám*, "conqueror of Vr̥tra like Indra, demi-god," and then, as an equivalent, *vr̥trahánam . . . ardhadevám*, "destroyer of Vr̥tra, demi-god." The latter epithet, hapax in the *R̥gVeda*, elevates him rhetorically above the human condition, even though his mother and father, mentioned several times, are human. It is remarkable that it is found thus combined, second in importance, with the other

6. Renou, *V. et. V.*, pp. 115–16; exceptionally to the Aśvin, as in *RV* 8.8.9 and 22; on this attribution to the Aśvin, on the trifunctional character given to them by several hymns of the eighth book, see "Les trois fonctions dans le *R̥gVeda* et les dieux indiens de Mitani," *Bulletin de l'Académie Royale de Belgique, Classe des Lettres, 5e série*, 47:265–98.

7. "Ombrien Tursa," *Latomus* 20 (1961):253–57.

epithet, *vṛtrahán*, or with its synonym *vṛtratúr(a)*,[8] as if the exploit or the series of exploits signified by *vṛtrahán* had its natural outcome in an ascent in the hierarchy of beings. The use that the *Avesta* makes of the adjective *vərəθragan* is no different.[9] In bellicose contexts it is applied to the contending entities or to the Savior (Vāta, Sraoša, Saošyant), several times to Haoma as in the *ṚgVeda* to Soma, and to prayers which are the most effective weapon in the struggle of Good against Evil. It is also conferred upon heroes: "To have killed the monster Dahāka," writes Benveniste, "earns for Θraētaona the title *verəθrajå taxmō Θraētaonō* (*Yašt* 5.61)," and his weapon shares the same privilege (*Yašt* 19.92).

It remains nonetheless that, in the *ṚgVeda*, Indra is *vṛtrahán* par excellence, the model for others, and he has won this title by a victory over a demonic being whose appearance is uncertain but whose name is precise, the "serpent (or dragon) Vṛtra," Resistance personified. Several texts say quite plainly that this victory brought about a substantial promotion in the life of the god. Thus 6.20.2:

> Upon you, o Indra, the quality of *ásura*, like that of Dyaus [the typical divine *ásura*], was conferred [root *dhā-*] by the gods, when —— [obscure epithet[10]], associated with Viṣṇu, you killed the serpent Vṛtra [*vṛtrám* . . . root *han-*].

However imprecise the notion of *ásura* may be in the *ṚgVeda*, reserved to a small number among the gods, and whatever may be the allusions of the hymns to other ways in which the *asuryà* could have been conferred upon or conquered by Indra, this text establishes a link of succession and causality between the murder of a demonic being designated as Vṛtra and the presentation to the murderer of a new quality and a new power.

In 1948, in two documents, on Parsee and the other Pahlavi, based on lost parts of the Avestan compilation, Father Jean de Menasce found evidence that Vərəθrağna—Vahrām or Bahrām in this period

8. Cf. Avest. *vərəθrataurva* joined to *vərəθragan* in *Yašt* 14.57; Benveniste, *V. et. V.*, p. 20.

9. Benveniste, *V. et V.*, pp. 20–22.

10. *ṛjīṣín*, epithet of Indra, "vordringend, gerade drauf los eilend" (Grassmann), "Trinker des Trestersafts" (Geldner), "der weisse Labung habende" (Thieme). For other forms of the god's promotion connected with (before, or after) the victory over Vṛtra, see Bernfried Schlerath, *Das Königtum* (1960), pp. 56, 58–59; there is nothing systematic in the numerous representations of Indra's "preferment."

of the language—had also benefited from a promotion after having, by the most grandiose exploit imaginable, saved the good creation.[11]

The first of these documents, a Parsee fragment from the *Rivayāt* of Munich, had been published by Christian Bartholomae, but no use had been made of it by the historians of Mazdaism. Here it is in full, from Menasce's translation:

Question on the subject of the seventh Amšasfand, Bahrām Yazad[12] the victorious [*pīrūzgar*], destroyer of the adversary [*dušman zadār*]. Answer: the cursed Ahriman once made a great attack. Ormizd the creator spoke to the six Amšasfand: "Go and bring me, bound up, the impure Ahriman." All six of the Amšasfand set out and sought Ahriman for a long time, with no success in seizing him. And Bahman, Ardībehišt, Šahravīr, Asfandarmat, Xūrdād, and Amurdād went back and came to the Omniscient, saying: "We have sought Ahriman for a long time, but he has not fallen into our hands." Then the Omniscient said to Bahrām Yazad: "You whom I have created victorious from the very beginning [*az awwal*], give evidence of victory; go with the six Amšasfand and bring Ahriman to me bound." Bahrām Yazad set out with the six Amšasfand and brought the impure Ahriman, bound, before Ormizd. Ormizd said to him: "This impure one, spiritually bound, shut him away, head downwards, in hell." Then Bahrām Yazad led the impure Ahriman into hell and thrust him there, head downwards; he returned to Ormizd, saying: "I have thrust this impure one into hell." Ormizd the creator rejoiced and said: "From the beginning I have declared you victorious, now you have acquired the victory; I bestow on you the title of Amšasfand, for you have accomplished what the six Amšasfand could not accomplish." That is why they say that Bahrām Yazad is the seventh Amšasfand.

11. "La promotion de Vahrām," *Revue de l'histoire des religions* 133 (1947):5–18. One cannot give enough consideration to the final warning: "We begin to suspect the importance of the filtering process which the mobeds were able to impose on a religious tradition whose diversity and exuberance are revealed to us only by the accidents of research and discovery. But it would be mistaken to reckon without the chance losses which may have occurred, independent of any trend, before the fixing of the canon into writing [cf. Stig Wikander, *Feuerpriester in Kleinasien und Iran* (1946), pp. 170–75]. Some forgotten or eccentric traditions have been conserved, even in the orthodox milieu. In any case, it is clear how much can still be drawn from the Pahlavi manuscripts, easily accessible but which go unedited, and from others, full of promise, whose titles are only known through the catalogues of Indian libraries. One cannot help but wish that the all too meager collection of Iranian materials could be speedily enriched."

12. Avest. *yazata*, "being worthy of worship," a designation for gods subordinate to Ahura Mazdā (*daēva* having become the generic name for demons); the *yazata* are next in dignity to the Aməša Spənta, the "Efficacious (Beneficent) Immortals," in whom Zoroastrianism has sublimated the former canonical gods of the three functions and the goddess who was joined to them.

The Pahlavi text, somewhat drawn out, refers directly to a passage from the *Avesta* and presents the narrative as a response from Ohrmazd himself to two questions of Zoroaster: "Who is the seventh Amarhaspand?" and then "Why is the seventh Amarhaspand, Vahrām Yazat, more than all the other Amarhaspand, and have you made him better, greater, and more powerful than the others?" The lesson is ostensibly the same as in the *Rivayāt*, with few new details. The most important is found at the beginning, in the description of the peril which the Evil Spirit, here called Gannak Mēnōk, unleashes first of all upon spiritual creation (*mēnōk*), but also upon material creation (*gētīk*):

At the time, says Ohrmazd, when the cursed Gannak Mēnōk went about through the world, all sorts of sufferings, hardships, and adversities swept down on this one. One time when he went about through the sky, it burst into three parts,[13] whereupon this cursed malefactor became, among the Amarhaspand of the *mēnōk* who were in the *mēnōk* domain, more formidable, more noxious, and more wicked. Then the whole world of beings of the *mēnōk* came before Ohrmazd to complain: ". . . At present, the cursed Gannak Mēnōk has the power to work all sorts of malicious deeds in the world, for which no one finds a remedy. Since you are the Omniscient, you should be able to effect some means whereby the cursed Gannak Mēnōk may be made to fall, head downward, into the realm of hell."

After the exploit, the justification for Vahrām's recompense is the same as in the other document, and God's commentary upon it, intended for Zoroaster, is instructive, for it connects the scene firmly with the theology of Vərəθrağna:

That is why Ohrmazd says to him: "On the first day I created you victorious, but now you have attained victory and have assured the protection of the *mēnōk* and the *gētīk*. By reason of this deed, I now name you Amarhaspand, since this act could not be accomplished by the six Amarhaspand. . . . I name you the seventh Amarhaspand, Varhām Yazat, the destroyer of the foe, my own [foe], mine who am Ohrmazd. And it is thus that Zartušt will call you when he [—?—] the man of the *gētīk*." O Zartušt, son of Spitama, I will tell you still another thing which is said in praise of Vahrām Yazat in this same passage of the *Avesta* and of the *Zand*, namely, that the valor of Vahrām Yazat was created stronger than that of the other Yazat. This victory will

13. The Evil Spirit thus takes the form and value of the "triple adversary"; see above, pp. 16–18 and n., and below, pp. 149–54.

occur at the Resurrection and at the time of the Body-to-come when he will bind Gannak Mēnōk together with the *dēv* and the *druǰ*. Of this Vahrām Yazat whom you call victorious, in the *Avesta* and the *Zand* it is said that he goes through the *mēnōk* and the *gētīk* with greater blessing and greater glory, that is to say, that he pays attention to the two worlds and that he goes about by taking ten forms [which are enumerated; then:] And Ohrmazd says: "Oh Zartušt, by transforming himself in these ten ways among the creatures of Ohrmazd, by this act he separated and removed the curses, sufferings, and sorrows from men."

One very important difference may be observed between the Indian and Iranian conceptions of the exploit which earns the divine personage his promotion. Indra has obtained the surname Vṛtrahán, along with his higher rank, only by an exploit which consists, in effect, of destroying Vṛtra or a symbolic form of "resistance"; up to then, whatever success he may have had, his triumph in this major incident could not have been taken for granted. For Vərəθrağna, however, there could be no doubt: "he has been created victorious," *pērzōgar*—which is no more than a gloss on his name as the post-Avestan tradition understood it.[14] And so he is "from the beginning," in his very essence, and Ahura Mazdā knows it better than anyone when he addresses this specialist (for the first time, to judge from his words) after the failure of the Aməša Spənta—a failure, moreover, which is not humiliating since they have been neither defeated nor proved incapable of actual victory, but simply unable to locate the foe. If Ahura Mazdā promotes him, then, to a superior rank, it is because he has answered to the definition which his name had already anticipated. We are reminded of the Roman soldiers after a victory, when they hailed with the title of *imperator* the one who, from the point of view of the *res publica*, had been their *imperator* right from the time he took command on the Field of Mars. Of the Indian and the Mazdaean traditions in question, the latter is certainly the one which innovated. In substituting for Indra a god for whom *vərəθragna* was not a surname but the very root of the name itself, the reformed theology condemned itself to a less simple, less satisfactory articulation of concepts than that or the Vedic tradition and, most likely, that of the Indo-Iranian tradition as well.

14. Benveniste, *V. et V.*, p. 26.

In actual practice, however, this minor complication was of little consequence. The Vedic Arya who praised Indra, with or without Vṛtrahán as a qualification, counted on him for victory with the vigorous means and abundant results characteristic of victory. The *Vərəθrağna Yašt* ends with the same expectation (14.57–65): there it is said that the god inspires the incantations and rites which give victory, that he ruins and destroys the opposing army, and that he deprives those who fail Miθra of the use of their arms. In this connection, Menasce has called attention to a number of benedictions which appear in late Avestan and Pahlavi texts.[15] The *Afrīn i Paigambar Zartušt* and the *Vištāsp Yašt* reveal such formulas as these:

> May you be truly beneficent, like Mazdā!
> Victorious, like Θraētaona! . . .
> Conqueror of your enemies, like Vərəθrağna!

Finally, the Armenians, who have borrowed this god along with several others from the Parthians and have changed his name into *Vahagn*,[16] count on him for the same kind of service. In this respect we have a precious text: in the letter-edict by which Tiridate undertakes to strengthen polytheism, he desires for his subjects, by the grace of the principal gods, certain qualities or advantages each of which corresponds to the vocation of the particular god mentioned with it. Here is what we read when we come to Vahagn: "May valor fall to you, coming from the valiant Vahagn!"[17]

15. "La promotion de Vahrām," pp. 5–6. The formulas do not clearly entreat that the gods mentioned give the privileges desired; at least they make these gods the standards for the measurement of these qualities.

16. For *Vahagn* < **Varhragn* < **Varθragna*, see Benveniste, *V. et V.*, p. 82. Under this name the god is nationalized as Armenian; when it is a question of the Iranian god as such, the Armenian authors employ *Vṙam*; Wikander, *Feuerpriester*, pp. 96, 101.

17. Agathangelos, 12: *kʿaǰutʿiwn hascʿē jez i kʿaǰn Vahagnē*, ἀρετὴ ὑμῖν φθάσῃ ἀπὸ τοῦ ἐναρέτου Ἡρακλέους. The human valor requested here from Vahagn, as if from the source of all valor, joins together with the central theme of *Yašt* 14. All the more is this true since the virtue designated by the words *kʿaǰutʿiwn*, ἀρετή, is an active, offensive virtue, altogether like the complex of qualities covered by the name Vərəθrağna: cf. the cry of the warriors killing the enemies "for *kʿaǰ* Aršak" (their king imprisoned for long years in Persia) in Faustos of Byzantium, 5.5, and the truly "vərəθrağnian" formula of Moses of Chorene, *sahmankʿ kʿaǰacʿ zēnn iwreancʿ*, "the frontiers of the valiant, (these are) their weapons" (1.8; the formula is attributed to another Aršak, king of the Persians and Parthians). In pre-Christian Armenia, it seems that *kʿaǰkʿ* could have designated a sort of Männerbund. They have survived in folklore as a race of rather demonic spirits; and they have been borrowed by the Georgians (for whom they play a considerable role in the epic of Rusthaveli, *The Knight in the Tiger's Skin*), and by the Ossets. For the first (*kʿaĵi*),

Vahagn, indeed, was the celestial model for the victorious warrior. The Armenian historian Moses of Chorene (1.31) still knew of songs that presented Vahagn as having traits that are not strictly Avestan. In fact, compared to the Vərəθrağna of Yašt 14, they show Vahagn to have more in common with the Vedic Indra Vṛtrahán: what the songs described, Moses of Chorene said, were the battles (*kṙuel*) of Vahagn with the dragons (*ənd višapacᶜ*), his victories (*yałtel*), and generally such feats as were reminiscent of Heracles.[18]

The authors of the Vedic hymns left in the shadows, as was so often their wont, one aspect of Indra's victory over Vṛtra which had hardly any place among prayers or invocations of praise, but which the more narrative literatures of the *Brāhmaṇa* and above all the epic recorded and developed. Its antiquity, since it corresponds to a widespread feature of mythical or legendary combat narratives (both of the Indo-European world and beyond), is probable a priori.

As we have emphasized, a number of Indra's exploits entail stain or sin, disagreeable results which the *Ṛg Veda* also overlooked. It happens that in the epic the murder of Vṛtra falls into this category. Sometimes, however, the painful consequences of this exploit is of a different kind.

In the Middle Ages it was believed of the Scandinavian *berserkir*—the warrior elite who wrought havoc upon their enemy—that so long as their *berserks gangr*, their "berserkr furor," lasted, they were so strong that nothing could resist them, but once this crisis had passed they became weak, impotent (*ómáttugr*), to the point of having to lie down with what amounted to an illness.[19] The murder of the Serpent, of Vṛtra, also had such an effect on the conqueror. Before he could fully enjoy his new title, he underwent a terrible depression, sometimes attributed to a *post eventum* terror, sometimes considered as the shock he had to pay for the physical and moral effort he had expended. The *Ṛg Veda* alludes only once (1.32.14) to this lamentable

see Georges Charachidzé, *Le système religieux de la Géorgie païenne* (1968), sec. 7, chap. 2, "Saint Georges chez les Kadzhi," pp. 515–43; chap. 3, "Retour de Saint Georges et ses conséquences," pp. 545–57; for the second (*Kadzitæ*), see my *Livre des héros* (1965), pp. 195–96, 202–4.

18. Moses has created a prehistoric king, Tigran, of whom Vahagn is one of three sons, divinized (*astuacacᶜeal*); on this arrangement, see Heinrich Gelzer, *Die Anfänge der armenischen Kirche* (1895), p. 107.

19. *Egils saga Skallagrímssonar*, 27.13: . . . *en fyrst, er af var gengit, þá váru þeir ómátkari, en at vanða.*

condition, but with remarkable precision as to the itinerary of his flight, if not to his place of refuge:

> Whom have you seen, O Indra, as avenger of the Serpent, that fear would have entered your heart after killing him, and that, as a frightened hawk [crosses] the regions, you would have traversed the ninety-nine water-courses? . . .

It is obvious that these four verses could not have produced the exuberant later tradition of the flight of the conqueror god: rather, they constitute the surfacing, unique in the entire hymnal, of a mythical theme that was perplexing rather than useful. Among the detailed accounts that can be read in the epic, the most trustworthy variant—said to reproduce an ancient tradition, an *itihāsa*—is to be found in a celebrated episode of the fifth book of the *Mahābhārata*. There, in accord with epic mythology, Indra functions not only as the god of the thunderbolt, but as the king of the gods.[20] Having told of the murder of the demon, the poet follows the murderer first in his dethronement, and then in his glorious restoration, of benefit not only to the god but to all mankind, which permits him to avail himself, in full security, of the title he has gained.

After his triumph, Indra flees to the end of the earth, where he lives concealed in the waters, like a cringing serpent. The universe, earth and sky, men and gods, are in terrible distress. Menaced by the unreasonable demands of the "temporary king" Nahuṣa, to whom the gods have had to commit themselves, Indra's wife Śacī undertakes to find her husband and bring him back. She addresses herself to a sort of divine feminine clairvoyant, Upaśruti,[21] who guides her toward the hiding-place, leading her across mountains and forests, past the Himalayas:

> And having reached the sea, extending over many *yojanas*, she [Upaśruti] came upon a large island covered with various trees and plants. And there

20. 5.14–18. Published by Adolf Holtzmann in 1841 in *Indravidschaya, eine Episode des Mahābhārata*. See the other epic versions, some analogous to this one, others of a different type with numerous common points, in Holtzmann, "Indra nach den Vorstellungen des Mahābhārata," *Zeitschrift der deutschen morgenländischen Gesellschaft* 22 (1878):305–11, and in Edward W. Hopkins, *Epic Mythology* (1915), pp. 129–32. There are versions with many similarities in the Purāṇa: thus *BhāgavataPur*. 2.13.10–17 (Indra, "whose messenger is Agni," dwells for a thousand years in the midst of the fibres of a lotus stalk, 15).

21. Properly "Rumor"; "boon-granting-Rumor, an evil spirit in Sūtras" (Hopkins, p. 130); "Divination" (translation of Pratap Chandra Roy); "sorte d'oracle prédisant l'avenir" (Renou-Stchoupak-Nitti, *s.v.*).

she saw a beautiful lake, of heavenly appearance, covered with birds, eight hundred miles in length and as many in breadth. And upon it, O descendent of Bharata, were full-blown lotuses of heavenly appearance, of five colors, hummed round by bees, and counting by thousands. And in the middle of that lake, there was a large and beautiful assemblage of lotuses having in its midst a large white lotus standing on a lofty stalk. And penetrating into the lotus-stalk, along with Śacī, she saw Indra there who had entered into its fibres.[22] And seeing her lord lying there in a minute form, Śacī also assumed a minute form, so did the goddess of divination too.

Indra's wife then tells of all her perils and exhorts the divine slayer of demons to rediscover his true self and recover his *tejas*, his energy. But Indra answers that "this is not the time for putting forth valor," that Nahuṣa is the stronger. He counsels, in order to gain time, that she deceive Nahuṣa with a ruse. And his luckless wife then turns to the brahman-god, Br̥haspati, chaplain to the gods. The latter invokes Agni, Fire, and charges him to find Indra again—another of those inconsistencies, frequent in epic narratives, which prove that the poets sought to make use of a variant, precious from other points of view, of what they had already recited.[23] As fast as thought, "in the twinkling of an eye," Fire explores all the terrestrial and aerial regions; but no Indra. "Enter the waters," commands Br̥haspati. Fire protests: water is the only element he cannot enter; he will die. . . . Br̥haspati insists, spellbinds him with eulogies, and repeats his command. And Fire no longer hesitates: "I shall show Indra to thee (*darśayiṣyāmi te śakram*)," he says, and rushes into the waters: seas, ponds, and at last the lake where Indra is hidden:

[and there,] while searching the lotus flowers, he saw the king of the gods lying within the fibres of a lotus-stalk.[24] And soon coming back, he informed Br̥haspati how Indra had taken refuge in the fibers of a lotus-stalk, assuming a minute form.

Br̥haspati proceeds immediately to the place indicated and enchants Indra with the praises of his former exploits (*purāṇaiḥ karmabhiḥ*

22. 5.14.9: *padmasya bhittvā nālañ ca viveśa sahitā tayā / visatantupraviṣṭañ ca tatrāpaśyac chatakratum.*

23. Holtzmann, pp. 309–10, has no doubt, and he is certainly correct, that the "quest" of Fire, on the order of Br̥haspati, is the older form of the episode, and that the "quest" of Upaśruti, connected with the story of Nahuṣa, is a retouched version.

24. 5.16.11: *atha tatrāpi padmāni vicinvan bhāratarṣabha / anvapaśyat sa devendraṃ visamadhyagataṃ tadā.*

devaṃ tuṣṭāva balasūdanam), a eulogy which builds up to a crescendo (Namuci, Śambara, Bala, "all thy foes") culminating in the verse:

. . . . "It is by you that Vṛtra has been killed, O king of the gods, lord of the world!"[25]

leading to the expected conclusion:

"Protect the gods and the worlds, O great Indra, obtain strength!"

And the incantation has its desired effect:

thus glorified, Indra increased little by little (*so 'vardhata śanaiḥ śanaiḥ*)[26]; and having assumed his own form, he waxed strong. . . .

His first words are to ask: "What business of yours yet remains; the great Asura, son of Tvaṣṭṛ [= the Tricephal] has been killed; and Vṛtra also, whose form was exceedingly big and who destroyed the worlds?" Then, between Indra and the gods who hasten to aid him, or rather from Indra to the other gods, there occurs a distribution of rewards in the course of which the order of the world is established: to one goes the lordship of the waters, to another that of riches, to another that of the netherworld. Fire, which has played such an important part in the entire affair, obtains the major recompense: the institution of a type of sacrifice in which he will be inseparable from Indra himself. But at the moment when the reinvigorated god is about to depart for the destruction of the usurper Nahuṣa, the sage Agastya arrives and announces that Nahuṣa, precipitated by his own *hybris*, has been hurled from heaven. We are thus left with no more than the peaceful departure of the god, glorious nonetheless: escorted by all the other gods, "Indra, slayer of Vṛtra" (*śakro vṛtranisūdanaḥ*),[27] regains possession of the lordship of the three worlds. The poet has only to specify the advantage that this ancient tradition assures for the one who piously recites it. Indeed, it is the boon one would expect from the exemplary victor, the very one that the *Vištāsp Yašt* associated with the name Vərəθrağna and that the

25. Ibid., 16: *tvayā vṛtro hataḥ pūrvaṃ devarāja jagatpate. Pūrvam*, "formerly," is nearer in meaning here to "having just" slain.

26. Renou, *V. et V.*, p. 159, following Abel Bergaigne, on "le rôle immense" of the root *vṛdh-*, "to increase," as applied to Indra.

27. On these synonyms of *Vṛtrahán*, see Renou, *V. et V.*, p. 117.

Armenian *Tiridate* requested of Vahagn: "he ever encounters victory, never defeat.[28]

Just as it would be ridiculous to attribute all the details of this novella to the *itihāsa*, so it would be rash not to pay attention to the general course of events. The *R̥gVeda*, which makes only on allusion (but how lucid!) to Indra's disappearance,[29] says nothing of his "invention"; but the one must inevitably entail the other. The "invention," in fact, had greater importance for the future of the world, of mankind, than did the disappearance. The *itihāsa* utilized here in the *Mahābhārata* actually resolves a difficulty of the first magnitude: How has the title Vr̥trahan become glorious, of good connotation, when the exploit or exploits to which the title refers have first let the victor feel only a baneful effect? Indra's dispirited retreat into the lotus stalk in the middle of the lake, Agni's "quest," the incantatory eulogies, and the god's recovery make sure, in four steps, that the necessary restoration does occur. It might well be thought that the solution given here is entirely an Indian invention, post-Vedic Indian at that, the Indians having been sensitive to the same difficulty long before us. But a happy coincidence has preserved, among the Armenian traditions about Vahagn, an episode which guarantees that the picturesque rebirth of Indra Vr̥trahan has derived from an Indo-Iranian tradition.

Mythographers will never cease to scold Moses of Chorene for citing so little from the "songs" which were still accessible to him. What he did save deserves recognition. It deals with the appearance, the birth of Vahagn.[30]

28. 5.18.20: *sarvatra jayam āpnoti na kadācit parājayam.*

29. A very different sort of episode is involved here from that of the "fears" which seize so many gods and heroes of India (sometimes Indra himself), Iran (Ātar, Tištriya), Greece, etc., *before* the exploit (at the sight of a formidable foe) or *in the course of* the exploit (after an initial setback).

30. *erknēr erkin ew erkir,*
erknēr ew cirani cov,
erkn i covun unēr z-karmrik ełegnikn.
ənd ełegan pᶜoł cux elanēr,
ənd ełegan pᶜoł bocᶜ elanēr,
ew i bocᶜoyn patanekik vazēr.
na hur her unēr,
[*apa tᶜē:*]
bocᶜ unēr murus,
ew ačᶜkunkᶜn ēin aregakunkᶜ.

In travail were sky and earth,
in travail also purple sea,
the travail in the sea held the red reed.
Through the neck of the reed smoke arose,
through the neck of the reed flame arose,
and, from the flame, a small adolescent bounded forth.
He had hair of fire,
mustaches he had of flame,
and his little eyes were suns.

Beyond these verses, Moses cites nothing. But they are enough to authenticate the divine epiphany in the Indian *itihāsa*.[31] Through the efforts of the three worlds, a small adolescent, the future slayer of dragons, blazing with fire, preceded by smoke and flames, emerges from the hollow of a reed which is found in the sea: this is Vahagn. A former and future slayer of demons and dragons, his body reduced to an atom, is hidden in an upraised lotus stalk on the top of the lake in an island encompassed by the enormous ocean; Fire goes throughout the three worlds to look for him, finally finds him; incantations restore his initial vigor; he emerges from the stalk, awarding Fire a share in his cult, and resumes the lordship of the three worlds: this is Indra Vṛtrahan. A merely fortuitous coincidence? It is worth pointing out that neither of these accounts tells the common, banal story of vegetal birth: Vahagn emerges from the reed in a true pyrotechnic display, and Indra Vṛtrahan, hidden in the stalk, discovered there by Fire, is not one of those "Hindu and Chinese gods" who sits serenely on the lotus or is tranquilly born from it, like the

There have been frequent attempts to correct, to make further cuts in, this song in order to obtain more regular versification: especially Mkrtič Emin, *Vēpkᶜ hnoyn Hayastani* (1880), p. 26; Yervand A. Lalayean, *Azkakragan Hantēs* 1 (1895):22–23 (who underlines the method of "parallelism" in this poetic technique and compares it with the canticle of *Exodus* 15); Lukas Patrubány, *Beiträge zur armenischen Ethnologie* 1 (1897), (cf. *Hantēs Amsoreay* [1897], cols. 123–24); Louis H. Gray, *Revue des études arméniennes* 6 (1926):160, 162; Father Nerses Akinean, *Hantēs Amsoreay* (1929), cols. 320 and 698 (discussion with Father Kerovpe Sarkisean, *Pazmavēb* [1929], p. 211). It is generally admitted that the *apa tᶜē*, "then, that . . ." of the eighth line is a formula of connection introduced by the author or by a copyist (but Gray translates "vraiment"). Aram Raffi, "Armenia, Its Epics, Folk-Songs, and Medieval Poetry" (1916) (appendix to Zabel C. Boyadjian, *Armenia, Legends and Poems*), pp. 139–40, has examined diverse aspects of the fragment (the diminutives; *cirani*, which he translates "variegated").

31. What follows is, in essence, reprinted from my article "Vahagn," *Revue de l'histoire des religions* 117 (1938):152–70.

gods referred to by Father Ghevond Ališan[32] in connection with the Armenian god. Not only is there a parallel in events, but also a coincidence in name: these two scenes, so close in their overall plans, are bound up with the Armenian[33] and Indian forms of one and the same figure. The most straightforward attitude, the one most respectful of the materials, is not to assume the convergence of two late and independent fantasies; rather, it is to suppose that Iranicized Armenia has transmitted to us a form of Vərəθrağna, still closely resembling his Indo-Iranian prototype which, free of the requirements of the moralizing theology of Mazdaism, was enabled to survive for a long time in more than one part of Iran, just as the *itihāsa*, the source for the epic traditions, may have conserved the same material in India, outside the Vedic literature.

Now, having achieved its place among Indo-Iranian documents concerning the god of victory, the Armenian poem deserves to be carefully examined. Perhaps it is less removed than it seems from the Avestan tradition itself.

First of all, we notice the only word which describes the attitude, the bearing of Vahagn in his manifestation: *vaȥēr*, "he bounded, he sprang forth."[34] The ten epiphanies of Vərəθrağna—for it is really as successive epiphanies before Zoroaster that *Yašt* 14 describes the incarnations of the god, whose sixth is that of a "young man of fifteen years," a true *patanekik*—do not merely emphasize the god's physical strength. Recognizing agility no less than force as an essential advantage of the warrior and the very means to offensive victory, the myth presents the god in many forms (six out of ten) which are adapted to the race course or to lightning-like flight. Quickness is thus one of the factors common to (1) the "impetuous" Wind, (3) the Horse, (4) the Camel, depicted as the good "walker,"[35] (5) the

32. *Hin hawatk^{c} kam het^{c}anosakan krōnk^{c} Hayoc^{c}* (1895), p. 294.

33. There is, of course, nothing to retain, except perhaps a lesson, from the philological efforts of Grigor Khalatianz, *Armjanskij épos v istorii Armenii Moiseja Xorenskago, opyt kritiki istočnikov* (1895), 1:201–8; 2:51. The author thought that the passage from Moses concerning Vahagn, including the fragment of the song, was a learned puzzle composed of "formulas" taken from the Bible.

34. In modern Armenian, *vaȥel* is the ordinary word for "to run"; in the classical language, it signifies "to bound, to leap."

35. Cf. the rapid camel, incarnation of Vayu, "Wind" (*Dēnkart* 9.23), to which Benveniste, *V. et V.*, p. 35, compares the camel incarnation of Vərəθrağna.

"rapid" Boar,[36] probably to (6) the Young Man of fifteen years "with the slender heel," and definitely to (7) the bird Vārağna, the falcon,[37] "who is swiftest among the birds and flies with the greatest haste." It is probably along these lines that the connections, the confluences, between the liturgies of Vərəθrağna and Čistā—the entity in whom Benveniste has recognized the patron of roadways and of free circulation,[38]—should be interpreted, equivalent connections to those in the *R̥gVeda* which exist between Indra Vr̥trahan and Viṣṇu *urukramá*, "of the wide strides." Thus, when Vahagn "bounds forth," he does so in the best Iranian tradition. In fact, he abides by a still older tradition: the same trait, if we may judge from the Vedic formulas, actually belongs to the Indian myths; it must have been a later restaging that ended the *Mahābhārata* account with the god's ponderous processional epiphany: in the earlier version, Indra Vr̥trahan probably emerged from the stalk, behind the Fire or the god of incantations, with the same speed with which he had arrived (cf. *RV* 1.32.14).[39] Renou's analyses give full weight to this remark. The opposition of the swift, agile god to the heavy adversary-obstacle was a dramatic expression, in the ancient forms of myth, of the fundamental conceptual opposition deciphered by Benveniste: the god of the *offensive* triumphs over *resistance.*

Second, the Armenian song gives Vahagn's epiphany a cosmic character: the three parts of the universe—sky, earth, sea—are in travail, although a solitary reed is all that gives birth. It might certainly be thought that this is an epic amplification, without mythical value. But a consideration of the Indian materials, the "scale" of the events and interventions which precede and accompany the reappearance of Indra Vr̥trahan, do not recommend this interpretation. We have seen Fire, in the twinkling of an eye, explore first earth and sky, then the sea, before finding the stalk from which the god will be reborn. At the beginning of the *itihāsa*, Indra's disappearance is a veritable cosmic catastrophe: sky and earth, gods and men are

36. Cf. the boar "who surpasses his adversary," incarnation of Vərəθrağna as companion of Miθra, in *Yašt* 10. Benveniste, *V. et V.*, p. 35.

37. The meaning "falcon" is demonstrated by the related Sogdian word: Benveniste. *V. et V.*, p. 34.

38. *V. et V.*, pp. 62–63.

39. In the *Mahābhārata*, it is only Fire's explorations in the sky, on the earth, and under the waters which retain this vertiginous speed.

afraid of the very event that Vṛtra's murder had been designed to avoid—the destruction of the three worlds. At the moment of his departure from the stalk, Indra allocates the quarters of the world to his allies as Zeus does to Poseidon and Pluto before setting out for battle against Kronos. Finally, without mentioning the hymns, which can always be suspected of rhetorical embellishment, the Vedic prose texts already make Earth and Sky intervene at the time of the god's exploit. When we look to Mazdaism, we find a parallel affirmation: certain systematically constructed verses of *Yašt* 14—although they do not, of course, assure Vərəθrağna the collaboration of Sky, Earth, and Waters (which actually do not appear as a triad in the *Avesta*) for any exploits or for some restoration not described in the text—do, indeed, firmly attest his mastery in the three regions of the world. It is a peculiar, visual mastery, which he transmits to his worshiper Zoroaster, but which is no less useful for "offensive victory" than are force or speed. Strictly speaking, in fact, it is a form of speed, the very form which permits Fire, in the *itihāsa*, not only to scour the three regions in the twinkling of an eye, but to discover Indra Vṛtrahan with neither hesitation nor delay. To Zoroaster, who offers him three sacrifices, he thrice gives the same list of privileges, but each time with a nuance in the last term, the one concerning the eyes: first he gives him the sight of the Kara fish which has unlimited vision under water, then that of the stallion which sees everywhere on earth, and finally that of the vulture which sees all from the height of the sky. This is another rendition of the god's special relation to the entire cosmos, a necessary attribute for him since, on the one hand, the only truly effective victory must be a total one, and, on the other, the universe, highly interested in the assailant god's victory, must contribute to it with all its elements.

Finally, the close relationships between the fire and Vahagn, between Fire and Indra Vṛtrahan in the *itihāsa*—the latter confirmed by the *Atharva Veda* and *Brāhmaṇa* texts which Renou has mentioned, and by well-known features of the ritual—should counsel us not to assume a late or secondary development in the relationship which Mazdaean Iran also established between the Fire (Ātar), the "fire of the warriors" on the one hand, and Vərəθrağna on the other.[40]

40. Benveniste, *V. et V.*, pp. 39, 72, 84 and note 4; Wikander, *Feuerpriester*, pp. 106–11, 166–67. One cannot overestimate the importance of the Indian and Armenian theme

There is, however, an important difference between the *itihāsa* and the Armenian song.[41] The first presents Indra as an adult, giving battle as he had done many times before, passing first through a depression and only then departing from the stalk in a sort of glorious "rebirth." In contrast, the second, before every exploit, with neither fortunate nor distressing antecedents, describes the beginning, the very "birth," of Vahagn in the form of a small adolescent. This difference recapitulates the one we observed in connection with the promotions of Indra and Vahrām, and has the same explanation. The reformed god Vərəθragna which the Armenians borrowed in a form more popular—though clearly Mazdaean—than that which appeared in the *Avesta*, had no test to pass. He did not have to qualify himself in a "battle against a **vərəθra*": "from birth," as the Pahlavi text cited by Menasce puts it so emphatically, he was "created victorious." It seems that Iranian popular mythology, while conserving the equivalent of Indra's epiphany when he has "become" Vṛtrahan, has transferred it "to the beginning" of the career of Vərəθragna and, in the place of a rebirth after an annihilation, has set a birth with no unsavory preliminaries.[42] For such displacements we are

---

of "the fire in the water"; Hermann Güntert has developed it well in *Der arische Weltkönig und Heiland* (1923), p. 20, n. 1, setting the Vedic Agni's sojourn in the waters (and in the sap of the plants) alongside what the Armenian song says about the birth of Vahagn (concerning Apāṃ Napāt, the fire as it resides in the water, see my article "Le puits de Nechtan," *Celtica* 5 [1963]: 50–61). Emin already sensed the importance of these connections: that is one of the enduringly useful aspects of his work *Vahagn-Višapakʿał armjanskoj mifologii est' Indra-Vritrahan Rig-Vedy* (1873), reprinted in the collection of the *Izsledovanii i stat'i*... (1896), by the author, pp. 61–83 (Vahagn and Agni, pp. 82–83). Emin's article provoked a counterpamphlet by Kerovpe Patkanov (1873), to which Emin responded (1874); in all, Patkanov was right (Emin denied that Vahagn was borrowed from the Iranians, explained him by a compound "*veh* + a name for fire" recalling the Sanskrit *agni*, badly translated *erkn* . . . *unēr* in the second verse of the fragment, etc.).

41. This responds to the objection of Ugo Bianchi, *Zamān i Ōhrmazd* (1958), p. 36. His discussion on pp. 35–39 is valid only if it is admitted (Louis Renou, 1934, myself in 1938) that Vṛtrahán was first the name of a divine or heroic personage distinct from Indra, but not if Vṛtrahán is considered an epithet, a title, of which Indra is the exemplary beneficiary; similarly, Vərəθragna is not a title like Vṛtrahán, vərəθragan, but the name of a god imagined by the reformers to receive a part of the purified mission of Indra. As to the criticisms offered, pp. 39–40, of certain passages from *Le Festin d'immortalité* and *Le Problème des Centaures*, I accept all the more readily that which I myself, several times, and well before 1958, expressed about these books of youth.

42. It may be that there is a vestige, much elaborated, of the theme of the salt-water reed sheltering a victorious hero in the *Great Bundahišn*: ed. B. T. Arklesaria, *Zand Ākāsīh, Iranian or Great Bundahišn* (Bombay, 1956), chap. 35, §38: "It [Revelation, Scripture] says also: the *xᵛarrah* of Frētōn [= the *xᵛarənah* of Θraētaona, the conqueror of the Tricephal, see above, pp. 17–18] rests in the Fraxᵛkart sea, in the stalk of a reed." There follows a

not lacking in parallel examples, and they do not depreciate the results of the comparisons. Here I will recall only one example, related to the case in question: that concerning the "initial combat" of the Irish hero Cúchulainn and the "birth" of Batraz, hero of the Ossets.[43]

After achieving his victory at the frontier of his homeland Ulster, defeating the three sons of Nechta, the child Cúchulainn and his charioteer go back to Emain Macha, the capital, carrying the three heads. From within the town the sorceress Leborchann announces their approach with anxiety: "A warrior comes in a chariot, his approach is frightful. . . . If care is not taken against him tonight, he will kill all the warriors in Ulster." King Conchobar has more to add: "We know this traveler who comes in a chariot; it is the small boy, my sister's son. He has gone as far as the frontiers of the neighboring province, his hands are all red with blood; he is not yet sated with combat and, if care is not taken, all the warriors of Emain will perish by his doing." And so, the text continues, Conchobar takes the following steps: "Bring out the women, send them before

---

singular account: "Nōtarga, having by sorcery made a cow *pat būzdat* (that is, probably: "having transformed a cow into a wild goat" [J. de Menasce, personal communication]; cf. the wild goat as next to last incarnation of Vərəθrağna?), for a year he gave him cut reeds; having brought back the cow and having milked it, he gave its milk to his three sons . . ." (see also Harold W. Bailey, *Zoroastrian Problems in the Ninth-Century Books* [1943], p. 27, n. 2, following the manuscript first published by B. T. Anklesaria in 1908; Edward W. West, *Sacred Books of the East* 5:138). The close connection between the *x*^{v}*arənah* and Vərəθrağna is established; see Benveniste, *V. et V.*, pp. 7, 31, and especially 49–50: "The epithet *barō.x*^{v}*arəna-* . . . is not given to anyone but Vərəθrağna. . . . But *barō.x*^{v}*arəna-* is not a simple doublet of *x*^{v}*arənahvant-* . . . . The first member *barō-* must be understood in its concrete sense, just as *x*^{v}*arənah* similarly evokes the concrete image of the royal nimbus. Vərəθrağna thus appears as the 'bearer of the *x*^{v}*arənah*.' The Pahlavi translation indicates the manner in which this must be understood. . . . The *x*^{v}*arənah* was imagined as a banner carried by Vərəθrağna. A passage from the *Great Bundahišn* gives an echo of this: 'Vahrān is the standard-bearer of the celestial Īzeds; there is no one more victorious than he, always holding the standard of victory for the gods.'" In these conditions, it is remarkable that it is said of the *x*^{v}*arənah* of Θraētaona (the victorious hero, also directly protected by Vərəθrağna) that it is hidden in the stalk of a reed which is itself found in the sea. As has happened to other pre-Mazdaean myths, the theme has been transferred—without the reed—onto Zoroaster and his sons, *Great Bundahišn* (1956), chaps. 33, 35 (cf. Bailey, p. 27, n. 2): the *x*^{v}*arrah* of Zoroaster is conserved in the Kayansah sea, under the protection of the *x*^{v}*arrah* of the waters, and will serve to fecundate the mothers of the three posthumous sons of the prophet, the Saviors.

43. What follows is adapted from my *Horace et les Curiaces* (1942) (see above, pp. 8–9), pp. 37–38, 41–44, 58–59. I thank Editions Gallimard for having authorized me to use this text.

the small boy, three times fifty women, or ten in addition to seven times twenty, lewd, completely nude [literally: red-nude], with their conductress Scandlach at their head, to show him their nudity and modesty":

> The troop of young women then came out and showed him their nudity and modesty. But he hid his face, turning it against the side of his chariot, so as not to see the nudity and modesty of the women. Then he was made to come out of the chariot. To calm his anger, they brought him three vats of cold water. They put him in the first vat and he gave the water such powerful heat that it burst the staves and the rings of the vat as one cracks a nutshell. In the second vat, the water made bubbles as big as fists. In the third vat the heat was that which certain men can withstand and others cannot withstand. Then the furor [*ferg*] of the small boy diminished, and they handed him his clothes.[44]

The text then describes the celebrated monstrous "forms" (*delba*) which Cúchulainn, for the first time, assumes or submits to. The tradition has preserved several lists, generally in agreement, to which we shall return.

The meaning of this operation is clear. The first consequence of the "exemplary combat," here specified as an initiatory combat, is not, as in the case of the victory of Indra Vṛtrahan, to deflate the victor and to rob the society of his future services, but, on the contrary, to bring him to such a state of exaltation that he even places his own society, which he has served and must continue to serve, in danger. In both cases, however, the underlying motivation is fundamentally the same: the exploit has its good effect, for the concerned party and for the hero's own kind, only after a bad phase in which the power acquired by the hero appears in disordered form, either a diminution analogous to an annihilation, or an intolerable excess.

44. Such is the version of the *Book of Leinster*. That of the *Yellow Book of Lecan* and of the *Lebor na h-Uidre* is generally in agreement; the divergences are pointed out in Rudolf Thurneysen, *Die irische Helden- und Königsage* 1 (1921):125–39. For the part cited here: it is the watchman of the king who gives the alert; the young Cúchulainn, on the point of entering Emain Macha, swears "by the gods by whom the Ulates swear" that if no warrior comes forth to offer him combat he will spill the blood of everyone in the town. The king then orders the women to stand naked before the boy. They obey, led not by Scandlach, but by Conchobar's own wife, queen Mugain: "'Here,' says Mugain [variant: Férach] to the hero, showing him her breasts, 'here are the warriors who will do combat with you....'" Modest, Cúchulainn covers his face. The men of Emain take advantage of this moment to seize him and dunk him in the three vats. When he is calmed, Mugain hands him a magnificent garment and he takes his place at Conchobar's feet.

The condition that the exploit has effected in Cúchulainn, this transfiguring rage, is in itself a good thing. Produced once, it is the state, or rather the faculty of recovering the state along with certain of the "forms" in which it is expressed, that will account for the incomparable value of the hero and will permit him to conquer his enemies as he first conquered the three sons of Nechta. But this *ferg* is as troublesome as it is precious: the child is not its master; on the contrary, it possesses him. Coming back to his home town, before assuming his new role as its protector, he constitutes a public menace. His ardor must be cooled, and it is to this end that the king applies the two "medications": first, the spectacle of the nude women, which constrains him to avert his eyes,[45] and then the immersion in the vats, which finally calms him.

Strictly speaking, once the connections between the various elements have been understood, the interpretation of each leaves little latitude to the fancy of the commentator. But there is a good reason, based on comparative insights, to see in this account not a fictitious invention, but the literary transposition of an authentic initiation sequence: the ordeal of the vats takes its place beside a usage attested elsewhere, in similar circumstances and with an analogous purpose. Only one example need be cited, that of the "medication" which, among the Kwakiutl of the Vancouver region, ends the initiation of the young man admitted to the society of "Cannibals," that terrible organization which takes on the leadership of the entire tribe during the winter ceremonies.

Much subdued after contact with Europeans, and reduced to simulacra, the initiation until recently included all the ferocity that the name of the society would seem to call for. The novice first made a retreat of three or four months in the bush near the spirits, and during this time he could reappear only once in the village in order to carry off a woman from among his relatives to prepare his food. Then he made a tumultuous return, attacking everyone he met,

45. The significance of the action of the women is a matter of controversy: see *Horace et les Curiaces*, pp. 44–50, Jacques Moreau, "Les guerriers et les femmes impudiques," *Annuaire de l'Institut de Philologie et d'Histoire Orientales et Slaves* (Bruxelles) 11 (= *Mélanges Henri Grégoire* 3), (1951):283–300 (reprinted in *Scripta Minora, Annales Universitatis Saraviensis, Philos. Fak.*, 1 (1964):200–211); Françoise Le Roux, "Pectore nudo," *Ogam* 18 (1966):369–72. Concerning the "heat" of Cúchulainn, see Alwyn and Brinley Rees, *Celtic Heritage* (1961), pp. 248–49, and generally pp. 244–58 ("Youthful Exploits").

biting them in the arms and chest and devouring the pieces of their flesh. His kinsmen, the people of his village, would satisfy him as much as possible by killing slaves. Today he is furnished only with "natural cadavers," which he swallows in shreds without chewing them, aided by the old Cannibals, who gather around him nude and full of excitement, says an ethnographer, like vultures on carrion. At this point there is an intervention by the members of a special group called "Healers," *heliga*, the hereditary custodians of a critical function; each one seizes one of the Cannibals by the head, drags him toward a basin of salt water, and plunges him into it four times. At each submersion the Cannibal struggles, splashes, and menacingly cries out "Hap! Hap!" that is to say, "Eat!" But the last bath calms him and he can go back to his house where the first thing he does is make himself vomit by drinking from large vessels filled to the brim with salt water. Not only has his paroxysm of furor passed but, in the course of the dances on the following nights, he has a dejected, shamefaced air, and no longer utters a cry. It remains for him to observe, for some time, a long list of severe rules, notably, for an entire year, the interdiction against sexual relations with his wife.[46]

Thus, like Cúchulainn, the newly initiated Cannibal makes his return in a state of exaltation which serves as evidence that the initiation has not been fruitless. Cúchulainn has assumed this condition in a battle against three foes, the Cannibal in the withdrawal to the wilds and in the "nourishment" he has taken in the scenes of murder and anthropophagy that marked his return, the difference here, in both purpose and form, being that the Cannibal is not a warrior.

Again like Cúchulainn, the Cannibal is not in control of his own condition. For his village he is a scourge, a permanent danger. He is unable, he does not know how, to put an end to his crisis. A sorcerer's apprentice, with the spell which possesses him, he threatens the devastation of the human group he ought to serve. It is here that the Healers make their appearance: just as Conchobar has his nephew

46. Franz Boas, *The Social Organization and the Secret Societies of the Kwakiutl* (1897). pp. 437–46; Boas, *VIth Report on the North-Western Tribes of Canada*, in *Report of the Sixtieth Meeting of the British Association for the Advancement of Science, Leeds, 1890* (1891) pp. 63–66 (= pp. 615–18 of the whole). James G. Frazer, in *Totemism and Exogamy* 3 (1910): 521–26, has given a good résumé and several extracts from the documentation.

plunged into three successive vats, the first bursting, the second still raising large bubbles, and only the third growing cool, so the Cannibal, by the four successive submersions imposed on him by the Healers, again becomes tractable, inoffensive, and, very literally, cooled off. The equivalence we see here between heat and furor should occasion no surprise: the Indian *tapas*, many metaphors in our own languages, even the opinion of the medical profession support the insights of the barbarous liturgists. Our present interest, however, is in the certification of authenticity which the Kwakiutl ritual furnishes for the "medication" of the Ulates: the Irish bards have only translated an actual custom into the form of a novella.

Now—and this is our reason for dwelling at such length upon this Irish legend—the theme of the three vats is found again in a comparable form in another part of the Indo-European world, among the Ossets, in connection with Batraz. This hero of the Nart legends, if one may rely on certain strong indications, has taken upon himself and thereby conserved a part of the mythology of the "Scythian Ares," the latter, in the last analysis, an heir of the Indo-Iranian *Indra.[47] Batraz has a miraculous birth. One day, while his mother is carrying him in her womb, she considers herself offended. Before leaving the country of the Narts forever and retiring to the home of her parents, she spits onto the back of her husband Xæmyts and thus transfers the embryo into an abscess which takes form between his shoulders. Satana, the sage mistress of the house of the Narts and in addition the sister of the hapless father, watches over the growth of the abscess and counts the days. When the time comes, she takes a steel cutlass and leads Xæmyts to the top of a seven-storied tower at the foot of which she has had seven cauldrons placed, each one full of water. Then she opens the abcess. Like a spout filling everything with flame, the child—a child of blazing steel—drops headlong to the seven cauldrons below; but they are unable to cool him. "Water, water," he cries, "so my steel may be tempered!" His aunt Satana runs off with six pitchers to draw water from a spring, but she is late in returning because the devil consents to let her take the water only if she yields to him, which takes a long time. Finally she returns and douses the child, at which point the Nart Syrdon can then give

47. Concerning Batraz, see my *Légendes sur les Nartes* (1930), pp. 50–74, 179–89; *Le livre des héros*, pp. 173–235; *ME* 1:460–62, 485–96, 570–75.

him a name: Batraz. The child will henceforth live in the sky, from which he will descend in a burst, incandescent as at his birth, whenever some danger or scandal threatens his kin. In another account, close in many respects, the young Batraz again clamors for water, but not to temper his steel: "Faster, faster! Fetch me water! I feel a flame of fire in me, an inextinguishable conflagration which devours me. . . ." And the good Satana goes, as above, to the spring, where she must prostitute herself not to the devil but to a seven-headed dragon, who takes, in turn, the quite unappealing forms of a monkey and an old man. Batraz, once he is finally calmed, can begin his heroic career.

The important point that distinguishes these accounts from the youthful exploits of Cúchulainn can immediately be seen: the "flame of fire" which possesses and physically devours Batraz, which will provide his force in combat and give him the appearance of an incandescent mass (no less singular than the various "*delba*," especially the "form" of the purple ball, which Cúchulainn assumes); the bodily "conflagration," to which the corresponding moral condition is a permanent state of frenetic furor: all this, for Batraz, is congenital. It does not originate, is not drawn out—like the Irish boy's *ferg*—in the initiatory exploit. The ardor which consumes Batraz is not his acquisition, but his definition. It is there before he has done a thing.

The relation between the two narratives is very similar to that we encountered between the birth of Vahagn and the restoration of Indra Vṛtrahan.

3

WARRIORS AND ANIMAL FORMS

As mentioned earlier, though only incidentally, the Avestan god of offensive victory, Vərəθraγna, has the peculiarity of presenting himself in ten forms, seven of which are animals. In the order given by *Yašt* 14, the ten are: the Wind (Vāta); an ox carrying *ama*, the assailant force, on his horns; a stallion, also bearing *ama*; a camel in rut; an impetuous boar; a young man of fifteen; the bird Vāraγna, the quickest of the birds of prey; a wild ram; a wild he-goat; and a warrior armed for combat.

These metamorphoses have often been commented upon. As to their ranking, Wind's place at the head of the list extends an Indo-Iranian theologem: in the Vāyu-Indra relationship, as it appears in the *R̥gVeda* and certain rituals, Vāyu goes first; and his privilege is justified by the fact that, of all the gods, only Vāyu, confident in his rapidity, dared to act as a scout in the "Vr̥tra affair."[1] Symmetrically, the position of the adult warrior at the bottom of the list reminds us that, whatever his other forms may have been, Vərəθraγna is in practice the model for and the protector of the human warrior. Meanwhile, the position of the young man of fifteen almost half-way down the list, in the sixth position, may also permit us to understand the second to the ninth items as a sort of preparation for the tenth—a preparation which does not, of course, exclude the return to the forms already assumed. We know, for instance, that the *Miθra Yašt* (10.70) presents Vərəθraγna as a boar: he goes before Miθra, the great god, "under the form of a boar ready for combat, with piercing defenses, of a boar who kills at one blow, unapproachable when irritated, with

1. *ŚatapathaBrāhmaṇa* 4.1.3.1–4.

a spotted snout, valiant, with feet of iron, legs of iron, muscles of iron, a tail of iron, jaws of iron; who surpasses his adversary, animated with furor; who, with virile valor, annihilates whoever fights him (he does not think he has struck him, it does not seem to him that he has delivered a blow, as long as he has not broken his vertebrae, the column of life, the vertebrae, source of power); who breaks all in pieces and spreads pell-mell over the ground the bones, hair, brain, and blood of those who betray Miθra."[2]

Is the number *ten* an original datum or the result of a posterior systematization? Are the ten incarnations of the Indian Viṣṇu, among which the boar figures, a parallel utilization of the same theme? Has Viṣṇu, in this aptitude for changing forms, taken the place of Indra, who, in the *R̥g Veda*, not only finds himself associated with the Wind god, in the conditions just recalled, but also takes the form of the bull and the ram? Today, at the present point in these debates, the "ayes" face arguments and objections.[3] But the most important matter is not in doubt: among the Iranian gods, Vərəθrağna is distinguished by this abundance, as also by the serialization, of metamorphoses the presentation of which occupies more than a third of his *Yašt*. This characteristic is not adequately explained by "a general theory, specifically Iranian, of creation," by the faculty proper to every spiritual being "of passing into a corporeal form," even if one adds the remark that "whereas terrestrial beings manifest themselves in the aspect which conforms to their nature, celestial beings appear in the forms of various and multiple species." If every god can, indeed, assume surprising shapes when occasion demands, Vərəθrağna is the only one, except for the Wind and the two human forms, who takes on a number of animal forms for his very office, in serial fashion, each of which corresponds in one or several features to specific aspects and conditions of victory.

It is probable that this theologem, like so many others, derives from an ancient conception, conserved and attested in the mythologies of the Germans and the Celts: due either to a gift of metamorphosis,

2. Benveniste, *V. et V.*, p. 35; his translation is here rendered into English.

3. See the state of the question (since Jarl T. Charpentier, *Kleine Beiträge zur indogermanischen Mythologie* [1911] pp. 25–68, chap. 2: "Die Inkarnationen des Vərəθrağna") in Benveniste, *V. et V.*, pp. 32, 194–95.

or to a monstrous heredity, the eminent warrior possesses a veritable animal nature.[4]

The Scandinavian *berserkir*, whose name signifies "having a bear envelope" (*serkr*), provide the classic example. Being the terrestrial counterparts of the *einherjar* who surround Óðinn in the other world, they follow the example of their ancestors, the first mythical *berserkir*, who already served Óðinn when he governed the Swedish Upland. In the sixth chapter of the *Ynglingasaga*, they are described as follows:

> As to his men, they went without cuirass, wild like dogs and wolves. They bit their bucklers and were as strong as bears and bulls. They massacred men and neither iron nor steel could prevail against them. This was called "berserkr furor."

Hermann Güntert[5] and the great interpreter of Danish legends Axel Olrik[6] have made excellent analyses of the numerous traditions about this branch of the old Nordic societies, and Lily Weiser[7] and Otto Höfler[8] have placed it, and hence to a large degree explained it, in its relation to the numerous "men's societies" observed among semicivilized peoples throughout the world. The *Ynglingasaga* text above says much, but not enough: the connection that Óðinn's *berserkir* had with wolves, bears, etc., was not only a resemblance in matters of force and ferocity; in a certain sense they were these animals themselves. Their furor exteriorized a second being which lived within them. The artifices of costume (cf. the *tincta corpora* of the Harii), the disguises to which the name *berserkir* and its parallel *úlfhednar* ("men with wolf's skin")[9] seem to allude, serve only to aid, to affirm this metamorphosis, to impress it upon friends and frightened enemies (again, cf. Tacitus, *Germania*, 38.4, in connection with the efforts of the Suebi to inspire *terror*).

Like many peoples, the ancient Germans apparently saw no difficulty in attributing various "souls" to one man. It also appears that

4. For broader comparisons, see Geo Widengren, *Der Feudalismus im alten Iran*, pp. 150–51. We are reminded here also of five banners bearing animal emblems in the Roman army before Marius, most of which can again be found among the incarnations of Vərəθragna.

5. *Über altisländische Berserkergeschichten, Program des heidelbergischen Gymnasiums* (1912).

6. *Danmarks Heltedigtning* I (1903), chap. 2.

7. *Altgermanische Jünglingsweihe und Männerbünde* (1927), pp. 43–82.

8. *Kultische Geheimbünde der Germanen* I (1934).

9. Concerning Heðinn, see Höfler, pp. 167–68.

the "exterior form" was considered the most distinct feature of the personality. One Nordic word—with equivalents in Old English and Old German—immediately introduces the essential in these representations: *hamr* designates (1) a garment; (2) the "exterior form"; (3) (more often the derivative *hamingja*) "a spirit attached to an individual" (actually one of his souls; cf. *hamingja*, "chance"). There are some men, with little going for them, who are declared to be *einhamr*: they have only a single *hamr*; then some, aside from their *heim-hamr* ("own, fundamental exterior"), can take on other *hamr* through an action designated by the reflexive verb *hama-sk*; they are able to go about transformed (*ham-hleypa*). Now, the *berserkr* is the exemplary *eigi einhamr*, "the man who is not of a single *hamr*." There are numerous passages from the sagas of all classifications where the *hamingja* of a warrior, or his *fylgja* (an almost synonymous notion) suddenly appears—in a dream, a vision, or in reality—in animal form. With time, the word *berserkir* came to designate only those warriors who were exceptionally powerful. Yet the belief subsisted that neither iron nor fire could wound them, and their access to "animal furor" continued to be well known.

Animal furor occurred most often in the evening. *Egils saga Skallagrímssonar* 1.2–8, for example, describes the life of a "retired" berserkr, Úlfr: after many glorious campaigns he married, enhanced his welfare, kept himself busy with his fields, his animals, his workshops, and won wide esteem for the good counsel that he distributed so liberally. "But sometimes when evening fell, he became umbrageous (*styggr*) and few men could converse with him then; he dozed through the evening (*var hann kveldsvaefr*); the rumor spread that he was *hamrammr* (that is, that he was metamorphosed and going about in the night); he received the name Kveldúlfr, Wolf of the Evening." Thus also were the terrifying Harii, their bodies dyed, the warriors of the pitchy night. . . .

As to the somnolent Úlfr's method of metamorphosis, it is the very one which the *Ynglingasaga* attributes to the master of the original *berserkir*, Óðinn. The god had the power to change appearance and form at will (chap. 6): his body remained stretched out, as if asleep or dead, while he himself was a bird or wild animal, a fish or serpent (chap. 7). Although the *berserkir*—their competence being more limited than the god's[10] and restricted especially to the actions of combat—appear only in the form of wild quadrupeds, they possess the same kind of power and technique.

Úlfr is a wolf in name only. For other legendary warriors, however, the animal nature has still deeper roots. One of the most famous is Böðvar Bjarki, paragon of all the champions of king Hrólfr Kraki, the Charlemagne of the North.[11] He too undergoes metamorphoses: in the next to last chapter of the *Hrólfs saga Kraka* we see him, in what will be his last effort, engage in a battle, before his master, in the form of an enormous bear while his body sleeps somewhere behind. In so doing, he only returns to his true nature. He was born from a certain Björn ("Bear") whom a wicked queen had effectively metamorphosed into a part-time bear, animal by day, man by night. His mother was a woman, but her name was Bera (female "Bear"). When Björn was killed in his bear aspect, the wicked queen forced Bera to eat a whole piece of his flesh and a small part of a second piece. In consequence, of the three sons she brought into the world, the eldest, Elgr (the elk), was a sort of Nordic centaur, elk from the waist down; the second had the feet of a dog; and only the third, Böðvar, was a perfect human specimen. His brothers follow diverse paths, one as a mighty brigand, the other as an often victorious king; but, despite his purely human form, it is Böðvar who becomes the most powerful, the true champion, as if his two elders were no more than rough prefigurations. We can recognize here the theme of the "third brother," studied above in the Indian traditions about Trita, the Iranian ones about Θraētaona, and the Roman ones about the conqueror of the Curiaces; but we can also recognize a sequence in the three terms, "animal, animal, man of war," which calls to mind the ten-term formula for the Avestan Vərəθrağna, "successive animals leading up to the warrior in arms," to the warrior who, in

10. Naturally, the warriors are not the only ones to metamorphose themselves: the sorcerers, their gods, and those who resemble them (in the North, Oðinn, Loki, etc.) take all sorts of forms. Those which the warriors assume—the case of the *berserkir* is like that of Vərəθragna—are oriented more strictly by their function. See Jan de Vries, *Altgermanische Religionsgeschichte*², 1 (1956):454, 492–96; 2 (1957):95–99.

11. On these matters, see Lucien Gerschel, "Un épisode trifonctionnel dans la saga de Hrólfr Kraki," *Collection Latomus* 45 (= *Hommages à Georges Dumézil*) (1960):104–16. Chapters 17–29 of the saga are concerned. The author has also recognized, among the tastes and vocations of the three brothers, another classification according to the three functions (brigand avid for riches, king, and pure warrior).

addition to his human qualities, possesses those of the quadrupeds and the bird which preceded him.

The Celts also were familiar with traditions like these. The *Mabinogi* of Math, son of Mathonwy,[12] gives a variant that is all the more interesting for being an element in a wider structure. The principal heroes, derived from mythical figures, belong to the group designated by the collective name "Children of Don." Their distribution among the three Indo-European functions is more complete than that of the chiefs of the Irish "Tribes of the goddess Dana," to whom they correspond. The males are Gwydion, Eveidd, Gilvathwy, Govannon, and Amaethon, and they are joined by a single sister, Aranrhod, herself the mother of the illustrious Lleu—the Irish Lug and the Lugus of the Gauls. The "functions" of the first and the two last of the five brothers are clear: in every circumstance, in *Mabinogi* and elsewhere, Gwydion is a great sorcerer, while Govannon and Amaethon, in conformity with their names,[13] are the Blacksmith and the Plowman, that is, craftsman and agriculturalist. Of Eveidd only one thing is said: in the company of Gilvathwy, it is he who takes the place of king Math in making the visits which are a part of the royal function throughout the countryside. This activity gives these two personages—between the sorcerer on the one hand, the artisan and the agriculturalist on the other—a noble role, the nearest to the king in his temporal duties. Of Gilvathwy, we know more. Except in times of war, king Math always had his feet placed in the lap of a young maiden. One day Gilvathwy fell madly in love with the girl who was performing the service. His brother Gwydion, the sorcerer, seeing him pining away, brought on, as an effect of his magical trick, a cruel war with a neighboring country. Leaving the maiden in his palace, the king set off with his army, and Gilvathwy was able to

12. Concerning this *Mabinogi*, there exists a very learned book, which assembles a great quantity of material (folkloric, philological, comparative, etc.), but which uses a fundamentally erroneous method: William John Gruffydd, *Math vab Mathonwy* (1928). Despite this author and several others, there is no reason to attribute the material of this account to Ireland.

13. *Amaeth*, "plowman"; *gov* (plur. *govaint*), "blacksmith" (*govaniaeth*, "trade, art of the blacksmith"); still in modern Welsh (*gof*, etc.). The names of the other Children of Don have uncertain etymologies. Gilvathwy (var. Gilvaethwy and Cilv-) perhaps contains an initial term related to Irish *gilla*, "boy, knight": Gruffydd, p. 205. There exist other lists, of later date and visibly altered, of the Children of Don. For more on this group, see Alwyn and Brinley Rees, *Celtic Heritage* (1961), pp. 50–53.

satisfy his passion before rejoining him. Informed of this outrage upon his return, king Math, himself a sorcerer, imposed a significant punishment on the two culprits: with two strokes of his magic wand (*hudlath*), he transformed Gilvathwy into a doe, Gwydion into a hart, and condemned them to live together as a couple in the woods for one year. At the end of this period, the two animals came back to the court accompanied by a vigorous fawn. Two new strokes of the wand transformed the doe into a boar, the hart into a wild sow, while Math gave human form to the fawn and had him baptized under the name Hyddwn (derived from *hydd*, "hart"). At the end of the year, the pair reappeared with a young wild boar, which the king made into a boy, naming him Hychtwn (derived from *hwch*, "pig"); the boar was changed into a she-wolf, the sow into a wolf. After another year of wildness, the two animals returned with a handsome wolf-cub. This time not only was the offspring made into a man under the name Bleiddwn (derived from *blaidd*, "wolf"), but his father and mother, "sufficiently punished, according to the king, by the great shame of having had children together," again found themselves to be Gwydion and Gilvathwy as they were three years before. A tercet inserted in the *Mabinogi* reveals the finality of this triple birth:

> Three sons of the perverse Gilvaethwy:
> three true eminent warriors,
> Bleiddwn, Hyddwn, Hychtwn the long.[14]

14. *Tri meib Gilvaethwy en(n)wir*
tri chenrysseddad kywir,
Bleiddwn, Hyddwn, Hychtwn hir.

The hapax *cenrysseddad* (*cynrhysseddad*) is traditionally translated "combatants" (Lady Guest), "champions" (Ellis-Lloyd), "guerriers éminents" (Loth), "Krieger" (Buber, Mülhausen), and, although the etymology is obscure, there is no reason to take exception to this meaning.[15] From this, we can see that in the group of the Children

15. Gruffydd, on p. 320, sought, without much likelihood of success, to find in *cen-* (*cyn-*) the word for dog, and has translated this as "wolf-men." The element *-dwn* of the three proper names is not clearer. With respect to the metamorphoses, Gruffydd writes on p. 315: "The three sons of Gilvaethwy, born as animals from human parents in animal form, and afterwards transformed into human shape, have analogies, as we have seen, in other lands. In other instances, these human animals remain in their animal forms, and become famous in legend as the best animals of their species [for example, the dog Guinaloc, the

of Don it is Gilvathwy who assures the existence of the warrior function (for it is he, and not Gwydion, who is initially responsible for the misdemeanor, and in the tercet it is he who is said to have had the sons Bleiddwn, Hyddwn, and Hychtwn) by siring these three vigorous young men whose animal affinities are not metaphorical but congenital. It should be noted that two of the types of quadruped that appear in this adventure resemble several of the incarnations of Vərəθrağna, especially the most famous (boar; wild he-goat and ram), and that the third evokes the name of the Scandinavian *úlfheðnar*, "men with the wolf's skin."

One may also suspect, in the repeated pairings-off that are so unusual in the legends,[16] a memory of such homosexual relationships as are often found in warrior societies. Let us recall not only the Dorian, Cretan educational practices, but also, in the Germanic world, what Ammianus Marcellinus, 31.9.5, has to say about the Taifali—with an indignation that probably keeps him from understanding the true value of the practice he is speaking of. Among this warrior people, it is the custom for pubescent youths to serve the pleasure of the warriors, apparently with no other limit than the duration of their charms—*aetatis uiriditatem in eorum pollutis usibus consumpturi*—"except for the one who, all alone, captures a boar or slays an enormous bear and who thus finds himself freed of this pollution," *conluuione liberatur*. Ammianus interprets the facts with the moral perspective of the virtuous hypocrites of his time, but one can gather from the generality of the practice and the test which brought it to an end that, from these male unions, the younger would

boar Tortain, the horse Loriagor, in "Caradoc et le serpent," published by Gaston Paris, *Romania* 28 (1899):214–31, material that is surely Welsh]. I know of no story in which these human animals are transformed into human shape." Gruffydd, pp. 276–77, cites the birth of the "Half-Slim Champion": a man is transformed into a wolf by his wife and pursued by a pack of hounds which she unleashes against him; he escapes and takes refuge on an island in the middle of a lake. Aside from himself, there is on this island only a she-wolf, actually a woman who, years earlier, had been transformed into a she-wolf a week before she was to give birth to a hero—and her son could only be born if she returned to human form. One day, starving, exhausted, and half asleep, he dreamed there was a kid near him; he seized it, awoke, and saw that he had opened up the she-wolf's flank. Before him was an infant, who, in a moment, attained a man's stature: he was the Half-Slim Champion.

16. Gruffydd, p. 290, n. 27: "It must be remembered that the transformation of a pair—a man and a woman—into animals is common in folklore, and the transformation of two men into animals of different sexes (as far as I am aware) unknown."

salvage in protection and training whatever he gave in pleasure, and that the elder, taking full responsibility, would prepare his young partner to face the *aprum* or *ursum immanem* with courage. The Germanic and Celtic men's societies must sometimes have included an element of sexuality that propriety would not have allowed Christian authors to describe.

On a number of occasions, the Indian epic has made use of the theologem that invites the warrior to draw upon one or several animal species for the qualities—force and speed especially—that his constituents expect from him, A most striking expression is found in one of the innumerable narratives in the third book of the *Mahābhārata.*[17] In order to get the better of the ten-headed Rāvaṇa, part man, part demon, Brahmā sends Viṣṇu to incarnate himself in Rāma; then he invites Indra and all the other gods to incarnate themselves as well, not to fight but to engender combatants. Their directions, however, have nothing to do with women: "Be thou, with all the celestials, born on earth! And beget ye on monkeys and bears, heroic sons possessed of great strength and capable of assuming any form at will as allies of Viṣṇu!" With Indra taking the lead, the gods execute the order, taking advantage of "the wives of the foremost of monkeys and bears" (variant: the wives of bears and monkeys). And the offspring correspond to the supreme god's plan: the youths have an unheard-of strength, permitting them to cleave the tops of mountains; their bodies are compact like the diamond; expert in battle, they can muster up as much force as they desire; they have the strength of the elephant and the speed of the wind; some live where they will (variant: fly like the birds), others are the denizens of the forest (variant: of the sky).

17. 3.260.7–13, especially: 7, *viṣṇoḥ sahāyān ṛkṣīṣu vānarīṣu ca sarvaśaḥ / janayadhvaṃ sutān vīrān kāmarūpabalānvitān.* 11, . . . *śakraprabhṛtayaś caiva sarve te surasattamāḥ / vānararkṣavarastrīṣu janayām āsur ātmajān.*

4

SCENARIOS AND ACCESSORIES

Earlier I called attention to the probability, as it appears from the research of Benveniste and Renou, that, in connection with the surname of the god of victory (Vedic *Vṛtra-hán-*, Avestan *Vərəθra-ǵn-a-*), the object killed or destroyed (Vedic *han-*) was originally of neuter gender, the "Resistance," rather than masculine. In our texts, this Resistance either remains an abstract concept (Iran), or, secondarily assuming the masculine gender, comes to be a sort of mass, vaguely animated, basically passive, and scarcely armed (*Ṛg Veda*), such that the allusions in the hymns do not even afford a concrete representation of the encounter. This exploit, laden with consequences, which earns the victor such renown and power, does not even seem to have been difficult: there is nothing to indicate a duel with equal risks. Indra struck Vṛtra, and that was it. He struck him with his thunderbolt as one strikes a tree (2.14.2), as the axe (hits) the trees (10.89.7; cf. 10.28.7–8). The verbal root which usually characterizes Vṛtra's position, whether before the combat or after his death, is *śī-*, the same as the Greek κεῖσθαι, "to be lying." In short, this great inert mass threatened the life of the world economically rather than militarily: he had "barred the waters" (*apó vavrivā́ṃsam vṛtrám*, 2.14.2, or the equivalent), "the rivers had been devoured by the serpent" (*síndhūṃr áhinā jagrasānā́n*, 4.17.1).[1]

These judicious remarks take on their full value if set alongside the particulars given in the *Brāhmaṇa* and the epic: the three-headed

1. Renou, *V. et V.*, pp. 118–20 (the preverb *ví*, implying a breach by a separation into two parts, is characteristic of the manner in which Indra slays Vṛtra); p. 127 (in the *Ṛg Veda* he is presented in only one passage as the provoker, in only one is it said that he hurls himself); pp. 130–33 (Vṛtra is without arms).

monster, and Vṛtra after him, are the sons, but still more the "products," of Tvaṣṭṛ, the craftsman-god and carpenter. This personage is not easily distinguished from another celestial artificer, Viśvakarman, "the maker of all things"; the purpose of each is "to make" the accessories, the various beings—whether animate or not—which the gods, and occasionally their enemies, the demons, require. We thus find their trademarks on palaces, chariots, talismans, weapons (including the most prestigious: Indra's thunderbolt, Śiva's sword, Viṣṇu's discus), but also on Tilottamā, the Pandora of Indian fable, and Sitā, another strange and supernatural woman. The great adversaries of Indra, even if the epic Vṛtra is sometimes more active and generally more destructive than his Vedic counterpart, also have their place on this list of masterpieces.

The Tricephal is particularly noteworthy. Let us go back to a passage in the fifth book (section 9.3–40), one of those in which the *Mahābhārata* describes the exploit of Indra. From hostility toward Indra (*Indradrohāt*), Tvaṣṭṛ comes to create a three-headed being, extremely strong, who immediately covets the god's place. His three faces blaze like the sun, the moon, and the fire. With one mouth he recites the Veda and drinks the soma reserved for the gods; with another he drinks *surā*, the alcoholic liquor; and he regards all the directions of the world, the *diśaḥ*, with an expression of such avidity that he seems ready to drink them too with his third mouth.

Indra is disturbed. His first recourse is to a device that the gods often employ to get the best of an ascetic or a being of too much strength: he instructs the Apsaras, celestial women, to seduce the monster and weaken him through pleasure. But the Apsaras soon return, crestfallen. Indra must now resign himself to taking action on his own. In a great effort, but without a reaction from his foe, Indra hurls his *vajra*. Struck by this blow, the Tricephal falls to the earth like the peak of a mountain (*parvatasyeva śikharaṃ praṇunnaṃ medinītale*). Seeing him thus, Indra is ill at ease and can find no peace, burned as he is by the splendor of the corpse, for the latter, though slain, has a blazing and effulgent aspect and appears living (*hato 'pi dīptatejāḥ sa jīvann iva ca dṛśyate*). Fortunately for Indra, a carpenter (*takṣā*) passes by, and, seeing him, the god demands that he quickly cut off the three heads (*kṣipraṃ chindhi śirāṃsy asya*). The carpenter has objections on both practical and moral grounds: the axe will not be equal to the task, to do so would be a sin. To each objection Indra has a ready answer: upon his command, the axe will become as powerful as his *vajra*, and he will take the sin upon himself. But the carpenter continues to object until the god makes him an interesting proposal: henceforth, in every sacrifice which men will offer, the head of the sacrificial animal will be the portion allotted to carpenters (*śiraḥ paśos te dāsyanti bhāgaṃ yajñeṣu mānavāḥ*). The workman immediately complies, meeting with no difficulties and no unfortunate consequences. The only strange feature is that a bird or a flock of birds flies forth from each of the severed heads: from the one which read the Veda and drank the soma come the *kapiñjala* or partridges, from the one which drank the *surā* come the *kalaviṅka* or sparrows, and from the one which threatened to swallow the four directions come the *tittira* or quails. Relieved and full of joy, Indra returns to heaven, while the carpenter goes quietly home.

Let us pause to consider: this monster—so easy to kill but who, when dead, remains *jīvann iva*, "as if living," as if the blow had done nothing to change his three blazing faces or his all-devouring mouths—gives the impression of being a dummy. That Indra, having "killed" him, should be obliged to ask a carpenter returning from work to cut off the three heads with his axe; that these heads then turn out to be hollow and release various birds into the air—these two singularities make for a good deal of precision. Everything takes place as if the Tricephal were an assemblage of wooden pieces and wooden heads, submissive to the tool of a human artisan after being "mounted" by the artificer of the gods. The literary embellishments have done nothing to change this essential feature of these two details, which the hymns, of course, ignore, but which are attested in the *Brāhmaṇa*. One of them is even illustrated in a ritual regulation:[2] as already prescribed by such texts as *MaitrāyaniSaṃhitā* 3.4.1 and

2. Pp. 123–24 of Willem Caland, "Kritisch-exegetische Bemerkungen zu den Brāhmaṇas," *Wiener Zeitschrift für die Kunde des Morgenlandes* 26 (1912):107–26. After bringing the old texts together with the *Mahābhārata*, Caland remarks: "Die Vorschrift, dass der Zimmermann, der ja beim Tieropfer zur Anfertigung des Opferpfahles beteiligt ist, den Kopf des Opfertiers erhält, ist mir aus keiner anderen Quelle bekannt." A comparable ritual motif, found in the etiological myth in which the divine artificer Tvaṣṭṛ (or his son the Tricephal) plays a role, is the prohibition against eating the brain: see, with an Iranian parallel, "Deux traits du monstre tricéphale indo-iranien," *Revue de l'histoire des religions* 120 (1939):5–20 (still valid, except pp. 17–20, for which the perspective has been modified by chap. 5 of *Naissance d'Archanges* [1945]).

Kaṭhaka 12.10, when an animal is sacrificed, the head is the portion allotted "to the carpenter";[3] and several *Brāhmaṇa* passages, especially two in the *Śatapatha* (1.6.3.1–5; 5.5.4.2–6), also say that three kinds of birds fly out of the mouth of the fallen Tricephal. Moreover, a peculiarity of each (color, cry) is explained with reference to the former specialty of the mouth which released it.

This fossil carries us far back into the past: for the myth of one of his foremost victories, Indra has taken upon himself a young warrior's initiation scenario. One would not dare to be affirmative on this point if another social group, a stranger to the Indo-European world and expert at initiations, had not carried out several of its ceremonies in connection with an analogous mythical form.

The place where the Indo-Iranian myths and legends about the Tricephal find their most illuminating parallels is, by an interesting concord, in British Columbia on the west coast of Canada. Under the name of Sīsiutl among the Kwakiutl and Bella Coola Indians, under the name of Senotlke among the people along the Thompson River, a large role is played in both myths and rites by the "three-headed monster."[4] He is an ambivalent being, sometimes the benevolent

3. What follows here is adapted from *Horace et les Curiaces* (see above, chap 13, n. 43), pp. 128–30.

4. In the literature the monster with the three heads is generally called the "double-headed snake." In the myths he is indeed bicephalic; in the rituals he is either bi- or tricephalic as a dummy, tricephalic as a mask. A beautiful Kwakiutl mask is reproduced, from Franz Boas, in Hartley B. Alexander, *North America*, vol. 10 of *The Mythology of All Races* (1916), pl. 31, 2, between pp. 246–47, with the commentary: "The face in the middle represents the 'man in the middle of the serpent,' with his two plumes; at each end are plumed serpent heads with movable tongues, which by means of strings can be pulled back and out. The two sides of the mask [= the two serpents' heads] can be folded forward and backward." Gottfried W. Locher, *The Serpent in the Kwakiutl Religion* (1932), is somewhat confused but brings together a good deal of material (bibliography, pp. 115–18). The double-headed snake is just one particular case of the mythical serpents who play such a major role in North American Indian representations, especially in the Sioux group (struggle of the Serpent and the Thunderbird, etc.). It calls to mind the (three-) plumed serpent of Mexico, the horned serpent of the Pueblo Indians, etc.—The documents utilized here are: BELLA-COOLA: Franz Boas, *The Mythology of the Bella-Coola Indians* (1900), vol. 1 of *The Jesup North Pacific Expedition*, pp. 28, 44–45. KWAKIUTL: Boas, *VIth Report on the North-Western Tribes of Canada*, in *Report of the Sixtieth Meeting of the British Association for the Advancement of Science, Leeds* 1890 (1891), pp. 67–68 (= 619–620 of the whole); idem, *Indianische Sagen von der Nord-Pacifischen Küste Americas* (1895), p. 160; idem, *The Social Organization and the Secret Societies of the Kwakiutl Indians* (1897), pp. 370–74, 482, 514, 713; idem, and G. Hunt, *Kwakiutl Texts*, I (1905), vol. 3 of *The Jesup Expedition* . . . , pp. 60–63; Boas, *Kwakiutl Texts*, II (1908), vol. 10, pt. 1 of *The Jesup Expedition* . . . , pp. 103–13, 192–207. UTAMQT, SQUAMISH, COMOX: Boas, *Indianische Sagen* . . . , pp. 56–61, 65–68; James A. Teit, *Mythology of the Thompson River* (1913), vol. 8, pt. 2 of *The Jesup Expedition* . . . , p. 269. Here are a few excerpts:

protector, more often the demonic foe. He has numerous functions and purposes, salient among which are his roles in the tricks of medicine men and in the myths of liberation of the waters. But his most important interventions are in matters of initiation, whether of the sorcerer or the chief, the hunter or the warrior. In some cases it suffices for the hero to have the chance of meeting the monster, in others he must also fight him and bring back his remains. The bond is particularly close between the monster and the warriors: among the Bella Coola, the Sīsiutl is the particular serpent of the Great Lady who bears the name "Warrior"; among the Kwakiutl, the Sīsiutl's dance is that of the warrior chief, and the ritual of Tōq'uit,

---

A general presentation of the ambivalent Sīsiutl among the Kwakiutl (Boas, *Social Organization* . . . , pp. 371–72): "Perhaps the most important among these [fabulous monsters] is the Sīsiutl, the fabulous double-headed snake, which has one head at each end, a human head in the middle, one horn on each terminal head, and two on the central human head. It has the power to assume the shape of a fish. To eat it or even to touch or to see it is sure death, as all the joints of the unfortunate one become dislocated, the head being turned backward. But to those who enjoy supernatural help it may bring power; its blood, wherever it touches the skin, makes it as hard as stone; its skin used as a belt enables the owner to perform wonderful feats; it may became a canoe which moves by the motions of the Sīsiutl fins; its eyes, when used as sling stones, kill even whales. It is essentially the helper of warriors."

A summary (given by H. B. Alexander, *North America*, p. 243) of a Squamish myth (Boas, *Indianische Sagen* . . . , pp. 58–61): "A Squamish myth tells of a young man who pursued the serpent Senotlke for four years, finally slaying it; as he did so, he himself fell dead, but he regained life and, on his return to his own people, became a great shaman, having the power to slay all who beheld him and to make them live again—a myth which seems clearly reminiscent of initiation rites."

A description of the Tōq'uit dance of the Kwakiutl (Boas, *Report* . . . , p. 619): "Tōq'uit is danced by women, the arms of the dancer being raised high upward, the palms of the hands being turned forward. The upper part of the dancer's body is naked; hemlock branches are tied around her waist. She has four attendants who always surround her. The dance is said to have originally been a war dance. The warriors, before going on an expedition, went into the woods in order to meet the double-headed snake [the double snake-heads flanking the head of a man], the Sīsiutl, which gives them great strength and power. After returning from the woods, they engage a woman to dance the Tōq'uit. Very elaborate arrangements are made for this dance. A double-headed snake, about twenty feet long, made of woods, blankets and skins, is hidden in a long ditch, which is partly covered with boards. Strings are attached to it, which pass over the beams of the house and are worked by men who hide in the bedrooms. As soon as the dancer appears, the people begin to sing and to beat time. In dancing the woman acts as though she were trying to catch something; and when she is supposed to have got it, she throws back her hands and the Sīsiutl rises from out of the ground, moving his heads. . . . Finally the snake disappears in the ditch." At another point in the ritual (pp. 619–20), a monstrous figure would appear behind the spectators: "It consists of a series of flat carved boards, which are connected on their narrow sides by plugs, which are passed through rings of cedar ropes. It has two or three points on top and is ornamented with mica. It is intended to represent the Sīsiutl."

in which the Sīsiutl, represented by a scaffolding, plays the dominant role, is explicitly connected with the preparation of the warriors for military expeditions. On the Thompson River, the Squamish and Utamqt accounts are also as clear as possible in this regard: it is by seeking, pursuing, killing, and despoiling the Senotlke that the young man becomes (1) an infallible marksman, and (2) an invincible war chief, furnished in particular with that supreme weapon which is also found at the disposal of the ancient Scandinavian *berserkir* and the Greek conqueror of Medusa: the capacity to petrify the adversary, to gain immediate victory from a distance—the secret dream of every warrior.

In the rites, especially in the initiatory dances, the monster is represented in various ways. In general, he is a man provided with a mask that flanks the human face with two serpent heads, one on the right, one on the left. The heads are fastened to the mask, but they are mobile, running over the shoulders. Sometimes, in certain Kwakiutl rituals, the representation involves a heavy structure with boards and fabrics, set so that it emerges from a thicket where it is animated by invisible stage hands. In the myths, where it is often the partner not only of the terrestrial hero but of the Thunderbird, the Sīsiutl is more freely conceived, although still in images which reflect the ritual props.

The analogy of these North American representations to those of India may enable us also to perceive the ritual origin of the Tricephal in Iran. Throughout the epic texts, this monster, who still bears the Avestan name Aži Dahāka (Aždahak, Ḍahāk, Zohak . . .)—containing the word *aẓi*, "serpent," followed by an obscure appellative—is only rarely a monster. First he was a man like others until one day a serpent's head pushed up from each of his shoulders.[5] There is nothing to make us suppose this conception to be secondary to the Avestan, itself very vague but further removed from the human sphere; nor is there any reason to place it posterior to the R̥gVedic configuration. It suffices to glance at the American Indian documentation, here barely skimmed, to ascertain that one and the same people may, with no difficulty, have several concurrent practices, sometimes very

5. The most detailed version is in Al Thaᶜālibī, *Histoire des rois de Perse*, ed. and trans. Hermann Zotenberg (1900; photographic reprint, Teheran, 1963), pp. 18–33; see "Deux traits du monstre tricéphale indo-iranien" (above, n. 2), p. 12.

different, in which the "two- or three-headed serpent" plays a major role. But Aždahak, with the serpent heads surging from his shoulders and flanking his human head, best corresponds to the most frequent ritual representation of the Sīsiutl. On the other hand, Iran seems to confirm the two features of the story of the Indian Tricephal which first oriented us toward the dummy interpretation: the connection of the monster with birds, and the intervention of a human workman in the victory. The Iranian hero who goes to kill the three-headed tyrant is actually led, exhorted, by a blacksmith, and the tyrant's palace is called "the palace of the Stork." Though the name has not been explained, it cannot be ignored.[6]

The Indo-Iranian myths of the victory over the Tricephal seem to retain definite traces of a type of ritual in which the hero's victim was an other-worldly being who was represented materially, either by a lavishly masked man or by an imposing piece of mechanical woodwork. Evidently those western traditions in which the hero triumphs over three brothers are much less ancient. Presumably they represent a free literary variation, rationalized and historicized, on the theme of the triple adversary.

But it is the Germanic peoples of the north who furnish the most direct proof that, in our ancient world, such dummy monsters were put to use on the occasion of initiation or promotion ceremonies. There are two documents to consider here: an account, which reads like a novel, of the first combat of a young warrior, and the account of the first "regulation duel" of the god Þórr.

We have already encountered Böðvar Bjarki, the champion of king Hrólfr, in connection with his strange birth as the third of three brothers and his final battle in the form of a bear. He also acts as the master of initiation in a celebrated episode.[7]

Saxo Grammaticus, 2.6.9, offers only a brief schema here. In contrast, the *Hrólfs saga Kraka*, in chapter 23, develops it at length.

6. Formerly I sought to interpret the *Tarvos Trigaranos*, the "bull with three cranes" of the Gallic monuments (Lutèce, Trèves), in an analogous manner: *Horace et les Curiaces*, p. 133. Since then other explanations have been offered, better supported by strictly Celtic facts.

7. What follows is adapted from my *Mythes et dieux des Germains* (1939), pp. 93–98. The texts are conveniently assembled and translated in Raymond W. Chambers, *Beowulf*[3] (1959), pp. 132–33 (Saxo), 138–46 (saga), 182–86 (*rímur*).

And a poem in Bjarki's honor, the *Bjarkarímur*, furnishes a third variant.

In the Danish account, the hero Biarco is present at a wedding banquet at which his neighbor Hialto is bullied by a number of rowdy warriors. He takes Hialto under his protection and kills the most insolent tormenters. Shortly afterward, Biarco kills a gigantic bear with one stroke of his sword; he makes Hialto drink the blood which flows from the wound so that he will be more vigorous: "for it was believed that a draught of this sort caused an increase in bodily strength."[8]

In the saga, Böðvar Bjarki, the itinerant champion, again takes the young Höttr under his wing. The youth is here the terrorized whipping boy of the *hirðmenn*, the "bodyguards" of king Hrólfr,[9] and it is one of the latter that Böðvar Bjarki kills. Instead of punishing him, Hrólfr—who appreciates strength—offers him the dead man's position. Böðvar accepts, but only on the condition that the unfortunate Höttr will remain beside him and be treated as his equal. Soon, however, at the approach of the midwinter festival (*jól*), everyone becomes somber. Höttr explains to his protector that, for the past two years, an enormous winged monster had appeared at *jól* and had killed the king's best champions (*kappar*). "This is not an animal," concludes Höttr, "but the biggest troll" (*þat er ekki dýr, heldr er þat hit mesta troll*). On the eve of *jól*, Hrólfr forbids his men to leave. But Böðvar departs secretly, taking the thoroughly frightened Höttr with him. Upon seeing the monster, Höttr howls, and screams that he will be devoured. His elder throws him in the mud, where he remains in terror, not daring to flee back to the royal homestead. Then Böðvar advances toward the animal, which is apparently motionless, draws his sword, and with one stroke—and no opposition—pierces its heart. The animal falls down stiff. Böðvar goes to fish

8. *Ursum quippe eximiae magnitudinis obuium sibi inter dumeta factum iaculo confecit* [*Biarco*] *comitemque suum Hialtonem, quo uiribus maior euaderet, applicato ore egestum beluae cruorem haurire iussit. Creditum namque erat, hoc potionis genere corporei roboris incrementa praestari.* The practice is attested among the *berserkir* (cf. Achilles at the home of the Centaur Chiron, the Luperci, or at least their prototype in the etiological myth): they ate raw meat and drank blood. As a literary theme, the motif is common in the traditions of northern Europe, as well as in other places: James G. Frazer, *Spirits of the Corn and of the Wild* 2 (1912; vol. 5 of *The Golden Bough*³), chap. 12, "Homeopathic magic of a flesh diet"; cf. *La saga de Hadingus* (1953), p. 44 and n. 4.

9. Axel Olrik justifiably sees here a memory, a literary rendering, of the troops of the *berserkir*.

Höttr up. He forces him to drink two great gulps of blood and to eat a piece of the heart; then, turning against him, he takes him on in a lengthy duel. Höttr has become truly strong and courageous.

But here the saga account takes up again. "Well done, comrade Höttr!" says Böðvar, "come, let us straighten out the animal and arrange him in such a way that others will believe that he is living" (*reisum upp dýrit ok búum svá um, at aðrir aetli at kvikt muni vera*). The next day the king's scouts report that the monster is still near the castle. The king approaches it with his troops, and says: "I do not see any movement in the animal; who will take it upon himself to confront it?" Böðvar proposes Höttr, and, much to the king's surprise, the latter accepts. "You have changed greatly in little time!" (*mikit hefir um þik skipaz á skammri stundu!*), says the king. Höttr, who has no weapon, asks for the king's sword Gullinhjalti ("Hilt of Gold"), with which he easily "kills" the monster's corpse. But the king is not fooled. He tells Böðvar that he suspects the truth, and adds: "It is no less a good deed for you to have made another champion of this Höttr, who did not appear destined for great things." Finally he changes Höttr's name to confirm the promotion: the new champion will bear the name Hjalti after Gullinhjalti, the king's sword.

To Axel Olrik, this theme of a dead animal rearranged to look like a dummy was merely a literary trick by the author of the saga, and he recalled several more or less analogous occurrences in the Nordic literature. It is hard to see the point of such a trick when the king is not taken in and when it adds nothing to Höttr's merit, his vigor, or his future chances. It is more likely that an ancient initiatory scenario has surfaced here, retaining that apparent naïveté—so necessary a part of any human action—which assumes it can direct invisible forces, have an effect upon the sacred. For to be surprised that a scene which deceives no one, which could not deceive anyone, whether participant or spectator, suffices to give a young Dane or a young Kwakiutl a valor or certain powers he never had before, is to question the very principle of all rituals: merely by being used in a ceremony a dummy becomes a living being, just as a mask, worn ceremonially, incarnates a new personality in the body of the dancer.

But Böðvar Bjarki's dummy can be substantiated by a more remarkable parallel from Scandinavia itself.[10]

10. What follows is adapted from *Mythes et dieux des Germains*, pp. 99–105. Two articles in the *Festschrift Felix Genzmer, Edda, Skalden, Saga* (1952), were devoted to the Hrungnir

Snorri, in the *Skáldskaparmál*, 17,[11] tells how once, while þórr was away slaying monsters, an undesirable guest, the giant Hrungnir, entered the home of the Æsir in full "giant rage" (*Hrungnir hafði svá mikinn jötunmóð* . . .). The Æsir could do nothing but invite him to their banquet, where he terrorized them, threatening to carry off Valhöll to his own country, to kill all the gods, to take the goddesses Freyja and Sif with him, and—while Freyja fills his cup—to drink all the beer of the Æsir. The Æsir then pronounced the name þórr, and immediately the god appeared in the hall, full of rage. Hrungnir, rather troubled, remarked to "Ásaþórr" that he would gain little glory by killing an unarmed foe. He proposed an encounter, one against one, at Grjótúnagarðr, "on the frontier." þórr showed all the more willingness to agree to this rendezvous as it was the first time that he was given the chance to go *til einvígis*, to a regulation duel, at a place fixed in advance, *hólmr* (*þórr vill fyrir öngan mun bila at koma til einvígis, er hónum var hólmr skoraðr, þvíat engi hafði hónum þat fyr veitt*).[12]

Here we seem to have an incoherence. Actually, it is a significant one: the giants, assessing the importance of the duel and not wishing Hrungnir to succumb, "made a man of clay at Grjótúnagarðr, nine leagues high and as big as three under the arms" (*þá gerðu jotnar man af leiri, ok var hann .ix. rasta hár, en þriggja breiðr undir hand*). They could not find a heart big enough to put in him, except for the heart of a mare; but þórr arrives too soon. We would expect that this "dummy" would be substituted for the actual Hrungnir, but, instead, the latter comes to the rendezvous and simply stations himself nearby. Indeed, he himself is a sort of statue: his heart had been made of hard stone "with three horns, of the form which then became that of the runic sign called the 'heart of Hrungnir.'[13] He also has a head

episode: Hermann Schneider, "Die Gesehichte vom Riesen Hrungnir," pp. 200–10, and Kurt Wais, "Ullikummi, Hrungnir, Armilus und Verwandte," pp. 211–61 (on which see Jan de Vries, *Altgermanische Religionsgeschichte*², 2 [1957]:136, n. 2).

11. Cf. seven strophes of the *Haustlöng* ("Pastimes of autumn [evenings]"?) by the skald þjóðólfr ór Hvíni (end of ninth century), conserved in Snorri's Edda, l.c.: Ernst A. Kock, *Den norsk-isländska skaldediktningen* 1 (1946):9–12. On the connections between these various texts, see the judicious remarks of Jan de Vries, *Altgermanische Religionsgeschichte*², 2 (1957): 134; Edward O. G. Turville Petre, *Myth and Religion in Scandinavia* (1964), pp. 76–77.

12. Jan de Vries, pp. 430–31.

13. A vertical stroke with two diagonal strokes branching upward from the middle of the vertical, each half as long as the vertical and at right angles to each other; this sign equals *hr* (van Langenhove).

of stone, a stone shield, and, for his offensive weapon, a whetstone (*hein*). The giant and the man of clay wait at the appointed spot, Hrungnir holding his shield before him, the man of clay so afraid that, it is said, he urinates at the first sight of Þórr.

The god is victorious, but in part thanks to a ruse performed by his "valet" and companion Þjálfi. The latter arrives before Þórr and, passing himself off for a traitor, warns Hrungnir that the god expects to surge up from under the ground. It is for this reason that Hrungnir places his shield beneath his feet, and does not keep it in front of his chest and head. Scarcely has he adopted this unusual posture when Þórr appears, with lightning and thunder, from the sky. His hammer breaks the whetstone (a fragment becomes lodged in the god's head) and smashes Hrungnir's skull. But in his fall, the giant drops on the victorious Þórr and pins Þórr's head under one of his feet. Meanwhile, at Þórr's side, Þjálfi attacks the man of clay "who falls with little glory." Then Þjálfi tries to disengage his master's neck, but Hrungnir's foot is too heavy. Learning that Þórr has fallen, the Æsir also attempt to free him. But it is not possible. An appeal must be made to Þórr's own son, Magni ("Force"), a three-night-old tot, who removes the foot with ease. In recompense, Þórr gives him Hrungnir's horse, thus earning a reprimand from Óðinn, according to whom Þórr should give the booty not to his son but to his father.

Many of the details of this account have caused difficulties for the commentators, who have often tried to surmount them by declaring that the whole business, including the man of clay, is no more than the literary embellishment of several old myths of the storm. In this there is little likelihood. The dummy man of clay, defeated in a subordinate duel by Þórr's "second," is probably to be interpreted at face value, offering besides, and by counterstroke, an explanation of Þórr's own conquests, the stone giant—that ponderous, immobile target "Resistance," overcome without any difficulty by the god's agility and offensive "flashes." Is Þjálfi Þórr's "student" here? Or, to put it differently, is his duel—in which his opponent is described as a dummy—simply a double for his master's engagement, as every ritual doubles the myth which justifies it? Perhaps. We would thus have a two-leveled account, the warrior "initiation" of Þjálfi reproducing in a realistic, terrestrial form—also a slightly ridiculous one, as with Höttr-Hjalti—the fabulous and almost cosmic martial exploit of þórr. For present purposes, it is not a major matter. What concerns us is that this fabulous exploit (the god's first "regulation duel") shows certain parallels with the exploit of the god *Vṛtrahán*, the vanquisher of the Tricephal and the conqueror of Resistance. Just as the Tricephal, with his three mouths, threatens to swallow the cardinal points and the beverages of the gods, just as the demonic Resistance threatens to destroy the world and the gods, so Hrungnir with the three-horned heart threatens to drink all the beer of the Æsir, to massacre the gods, and to transport their residence to his homeland. Just as the storm god after overthrowing Vṛtra is at first as good as annihilated, to the gods' despair, and able to regain his force and glory only through the incantations of one of them, so þórr, after slaying Hrungnir, is, materially, the captive of his exploit, immobilized through an accident which alarms the gods, and he is taken care of only by one of their own.

Finally, like the three-headed Triśiras, Hrungnir is a triple being, having a three-horned heart. The triplicity of the monster adversary of the new Victor-type champion is such a general feature in the Indo-European world that one is tempted to see it as an inherited detail from the common prehistory. There are different ways this triplicity has been expressed. We have met the principal ones at several points in this book: sometimes it is a three-headed or three-bodied being (the Vedic and Iranian Tricephal, the Greek Geryon), sometimes triplet brothers (the three sons of Nechta, scourges of the Ulates and adversaries of the young Cúchulainn on the day of his first exploit; the three Curiaces, etc.), sometimes, finally, a being whose heart, a particularly dangerous organ, is triple in some way. In Ireland for instance, such is the case with the adversary of a certain Mac Cecht, who is probably the celebrated champion of Conaire. The *Dindšenchas of Rennes*, 13,[14] writes summarily but clearly: "Meche, son of Morrígan (one of the goddesses of war), in him were three hearts until Mac Cecht killed him on the plain of Meche, which, up to then, had been named the Plain of Fertaig. Thus were those hearts, with the shapes of three serpents through them (*amlaidh badar na*

14. *Revue celtique* 15 (1894): 304. Cormac translates Cecht as "power"; the word is found again in the name of Dian Cecht, the physician of the Tuatha Dé Danann. In a note to a paragraph from the *Dindšenchas*, the editor, Whitley Stokes, writes: "Mac Cecht, one of the Tuatha Dé Danann, or, more probably, Conaire's champion."

cride sin, co ndelbaid tri nathrach treithib). Now, if death had not befallen Meche, the serpents in him would have grown, and what they left alive in Ireland would have been destroyed" (*meni torsed dano bas do Mechi arforbertais na nathracha ind ocus focnafed ana faigbet béo i nHérinn*).[15]

At the end of Snorri's account, þórr incurs Óðinn's disapprobation because he has lacked regard for his father, gratifying the "young" instead of the "old." There is no reason to consider this trait a late addition, for such an opposition between age classes is fully at home in a myth of the warrior function.

Once it is set alongside the *human* episode of Höttr-Hjalti and the analogous scenes from other Indo-European mythologies, the duel between þórr and Hrungnir, doubled by the duel between þjálfi and the man of clay, may now be interpreted literally, point for point, as a memory of much older rituals and myths of initiation or military promotion.[16] This does not, of course, prevent the myths from having also been—and even congenitally—myths of the storm. It is the destiny of the warrior gods, patrons of the terrestrial warriors, to be storm gods as well, or to have a tendency to become confused with them. þórr, the "thunder," with his hammer, like Indra with his thunderbolt, has obvious nature-god significance, and the story of Hrungnir, in both þjóðólfr and Snorri, is one of those where he is at his most "superhuman": he appears instantaneously in the hall of the Æsir; he no less suddenly assails the giant from amidst the flashes and rumblings of the sky.

15. After the death of Meche, Mac Cecht burns the hearts and casts their ashes in the stream, which then begins to boil so that the fish all perish. Thus both the plain and the river receive new names.

16. An indication of such a view is already given by Christianus C. Uhlenbeck, *Acta Philologica Scandinavica* 1 (1926):209 (discussing G. Schütte, *Dänisches Heidentum*, p. 134): "Die Geschichte des artifiziellen Riesen Mökkurkálfi beruht vielleicht auf wirklich geübten Zauberbrauch. Die Herstellung artifizieller Tiere um Feinde zu töten findet sich bei den grönländischen Eskimo (s. Heinrich Johannes Rink, *Tales and Traditions of the Eskimo*, pp. 53, 151 f., 201 f., 414 ff., 457 f.)."

5

SIGNS UPON THE HERO

One feature of the myth of Hrungnir confirms the "initiatory" or "promotional" value of this famous duel: since that time, it is said, þórr bears in his head, as a bothersome certificate of victory, a piece of the whetstone (*hein*)—the giant's weapon—that became lodged there.[1] We are dealing here with an authentic popular tradition, one borrowed also by the Lapps. It is now three centuries since Scheffer, in his book *Laponia*, described the idol of the Lappish god Hora galles, the "goodman þórr": *in capite infigunt clauum ferreum, cum silicis particulis, ut si uideatur ignem Thor excutiat.* The explanation may be a secondary one, but the fact is there: the idol of the Lappish þórr had a piece of flint fixed in its head by a nail.[2]

This sign, a consequence of the god's victory in his first *einvígr*, recalls one of the signs—numerous, excessive, often monstrous—which appear upon the young Cúchulainn after his first combat. Some of these immediately become stable features, others reappear only in the hero's attacks of martial furor.[3] The sign that is similar to þórr's is mentioned in the episode in the *Macgnímrada* of the Táin Bó Cuailnge, "rising from the summit of his skull." In the *In carpat serda* episode, however, it is described with much greater precision:

1. Cf. my article "Horwendillus et Aurvandill," *Mélanges Claude Lévi-Strauss* (1970).

2. Jan de Vries, *Altgermanische Religionsgeschichte*², 2 (1957):389; the author also draws the nails (*reginnaglar*) of "the post of the seat of honor" (*öndvegissúlnа*) into the comparison.

3. These signs have been studied by comparing them with the figures on Gallic coins: Marie-Louise Sjoestedt-Jonval, "Légendes épiques irlandaises et monnaies gauloises, recherches sur la constitution de la légende de Cúchulainn," *Etudes celtiques* 1 (1936):1–77 (with plate, pp. 42–43). The thesis is surely false: the peculiarities of the Irish Cúchulainn were certainly not produced by the ingenious interpretations of figures clumsily traced by the continental Celts; but the idea of bringing the two sets of data together is a good one and the documentation is valuable; the "moon of the hero" is treated on pp. 11–12, 14–16.

"The moon of the hero protruded from his forehead, as long, as thick, as the whetstone of a warrior, as long as the nose." Some of the figures represented on certain Gallic coins also have an emanation protruding from the forehead, sometimes in the form of a round-headed nail. It is likely that they attest to an appreciation by the continental Celts of the same stigmata of valor.

Among the "forms" which appear on the victorious Cúchulainn, the greatest number, I repeat, are fantastic. There are some, however, which may be no more than exaggerations of a heroic grimace. A remarkable example is to be found in the *Macgnímrada* episode: "He closed one of his eyes to the point where it was no larger than the eye of a needle, and he opened the other wide to the point where it was as big as the top of a cup of mead"; and in *In carpat serda*: "He swallowed one of his eyes in his head, to the point where a wild heron would have had trouble managing to bring it from the bottom of his skull to the surface of his cheek, while the other jutted out and sat on his cheek, on the outside."[4] Without permitting themselves such distortions, the Viking adventurers, when it came to solemn circumstances, assumed attitudes and made grimaces of their own which established their rank and dignity, and backed up their demands. Behind such countenances there was probably an older tradition. Received and fully banqueted by king Aðalsteinn, from whom he has the right to expect a large remuneration, Egill, the warrior scald, sits down on the far side of the hall, on the seat of honor, facing the king.[5] He keeps his helmet on his head, puts his shield at his feet and his sword on his knees, alternately drawing the sword halfway out and putting it back in its scabbard. He holds himself stiff and straight, and refuses all drink. In addition, again alternately, he makes one of his eyebrows drop down to his chin while lifting the other to his hairline. The effect must have been impressive, for he had contiguous eyebrows above his black eyes.[6] The king then

4. In connection with the Gallic coins, cf. M.-L. Sjoestedt-Jonval, p. 19: "The monstrous expansion of the eye, which is displaced downward to the point of finding itself toward the middle of the cheek, at the level of the wing of the nose, is one of the most striking characteristics of various series of Armorican pieces of late style, attributed to the Curiosilities [references], as on the coins of Anglo-Norman islands. It even happens that the opposite eye may be indicated by a point ("as small as the eye of a needle"!), the profile then appearing as turned slightly toward the three-quarter position [references]."

5. *Egils saga Skallagrímssonar*, 45.6–11.

6. §9: *þá hleypði hann annarri brúninni ofan á kinnina, en annarri upp í harrœtr. Egill var svarteygr ok skolbrúnn*. The meaning of this last word has been discussed; see the note by

gets up, puts a highly precious ring on the tip of his bare sword, walks toward the Viking and offers him his present over the hearth. The Viking gets up in turn, sword bared, approaches the hearth from the other side, and receives the ring on the tip of his sword. Both sit down again. Egill puts the ring on his finger. And only then do his eyebrows return to their normal position.[7] He lays down his sword and shield and accepts the cup, which until then has been offered in vain.

Indian mythology has not ignored such corporeal, often monstrous signs. In fact, it has worked out a theory, several theories, about them, although in doing so it has moved in a different direction. The Indian *lakṣana* are congenital and permanent signs which designate a boy for a glorious future: *mahāpuruṣa*, "great man," *cakravartin*, "he who turns the cosmic wheel," that is to say, the hero, the one who—depending on the period and the milieu—bears the marks of either an exceptional sage or a king. A brief allusion from the *Mahābhārata*, however, may prove to upset our files.

Arjuna, as we know, represents the warrior ideal. The son or partial incarnation of Indra, he has all this god's qualities and in addition a certain refinement, and sometimes a self-control, which are sadly lacking in his model. Not only have the masters of human weaponry prepared him for his inimitable career, but the gods themselves, when they have upon occasion been visited by the hero in the other world, have taken care to provide him with the most marvelous of arms. The price for this honor is a life without respite, lived in constant danger and fatigue. Even after the harsh and taxing battle of Kurukṣetra, he knows no repose. His older brother, Yudhiṣṭhira the king, decides to celebrate the *aśvamedha*, "horse sacrifice," the imperial sacrifice *par excellence*; and it is Arjuna who must escort the future victim in its free course through the kingdoms of India for an entire year, giving one battle after another to defend it, according to the rule recorded in the liturgical books. Then, at the

---

Finnur Jónsson in his edition (1894), p. 160; Jónsson sides with the interpretation "cui supercilia contigua sunt" (against "with brown eyebrows" and against "with slanting eyebrows").

7. §11: *En er Egill settiz niðr, dró hann hringinn á hönd sér; ok þá fóru brýnn hans í lag.* On the "attitudes of parade" of the Vikings, see Paul Hermann, *Die Heldensagen des Saxo Grammaticus*, pt. 2., *Kommentar: Erläuterungen zu den ersten neun Büchern der Dänischen Geschichte* (1922), p. 126 and n. 2.

end of this grueling mission, a curious dialogue takes place between Yudhiṣṭhira and the omniscient Kṛṣṇa.[8]

Kṛṣṇa notifies the king that he has learned from his informers that the horse and its escort are approaching; it is time to prepare the sacrifice. Arjuna, he adds, returns greatly emaciated, worn out from so many battles. These words stir an anxiety which the eldest Pāṇḍava has long kept in his heart: Why, he asks, has his younger brother always been deprived of rest and comfort? Is his destiny not lamentable? What sign could there be upon him to require such miseries and discomforts, to exact this "exceedingly large share of unhappiness?" Kṛṣṇa responds:

> I do not see any censurable feature in this prince, except that the cheekbones of this lion among men are a little too high. It is in consequence of this that that foremost of men has always to be on the march. For I do not see anything else in consequence of which he could be made so unhappy."[9]

This physical disgrace, these cheekbones that are a little too high, thus condemn Arjuna to agitation, expeditions, fatigue (for it is indeed a question of this, and this alone: *adhvasu . . . vartate* clarifies and sets the limits to *duḥkham*), in brief, to the career of a warrior. On his countenance, they are the sign of his vocation. I do not know if the literature of India mentions such a connection anywhere else. But could it not be simply the stylization into *lakṣaṇa*, into a congenital sign, of a "form," a *delb* in the Irish manner, appearing on the tested warrior and distinguishing his appearance from that of the ordinary man, a "form" which, in its origin, is probably derived from a traditional heroic contortion?

8. 14.89.2–8. On the distribution of the tasks among the five Pāṇḍava, following their "functional nature," during the preparation for the horse sacrifice (Wikander), see *ME* 1:101–2.

9. *na hy asya nṛpate kiñcid aniṣṭam upalakṣaye*
ṛte puruṣasiṃhasya piṇḍike 'syādhike yataḥ.
tābhyāṃ sa puruṣavyāghro nityam adhvasu vartate,
na hy anyad anupaśyāmi yenāsau duḥkhabhājanam. [Śl. 7–8]

Numerous variants; for *aniṣṭam* ("undesirable," Poona): *saṃśliṣṭam, saṃkliṣṭam, saṃhṛṣṭam,* etc.; for *piṇḍike 'syādhike yataḥ: p. 'syātikāyataḥ* (Poona), *-kāyake, -kāyike* ("excessively developed"); for *duḥkhabhājanam* ("receptacle of misery"): *duḥkhabhāgjayaḥ* (Poona) or *bhavet* ("he must be"). *Piṇḍikā*, which designates "a globular swelling or protuberance," here certainly has the meaning "cheekbone." Draupadī, the common wife of the five Pāṇḍava, who has a preference for Arjuna (cf. 17.2.6, *pakṣāpata*), takes strong exception to a challenge of this kind to the hero's perfect beauty; she throws an angry glance at Kṛṣṇa, who, in his own affection for Arjuna, enjoys her feminine reaction.

INDEX